HILLARY'S AMERICA

HILLARY'S AMERICA

THE SECRET HISTORY OF THE DEMOCRATIC PARTY

DINESH D'SOUZA

REGNERY
PUBLISHING
A Division of Salem Media Group

Regnery® is a registered trademark of Salem Communications Holding Corporation

Cataloging-in-Publication data on file with the Library of Congress

ISBN 978-1-62157-347-0

Published in the United States by
Regnery Publishing
A Division of Salem Media Group
300 New Jersey Ave NW
Washington, DC 20001
www.Regnery.com

Manufactured in the United States of America

10 9 8 7 6 5 4 3

Books are available in quantity for promotional or premium use. For information on discounts and terms, please visit our website: www.Regnery.com.

Distributed to the trade by
Perseus Distribution
250 West 57th Street
New York, NY 10107

For my brother Shashi and my sister Nandini

CONTENTS

The mass of mankind has not been born with saddles on their backs, nor a favored few booted and spurred, ready to ride them legitimately, by the grace of God.

—Thomas Jefferson

CHAPTER 1

THE HILLARY ENIGMA

SECRETS OF
THE DEMOCRATIC PARTY

To vice industrious, but to nobler deeds timorous and slothful.[1]
—John Milton on the devil Belial, *Paradise Lost*

To understand Hillary, we must solve the Hillary enigma. The Hillary enigma is why anyone—any American, any Democrat, even Bill—would consider voting for her. Yes, I know she wants to be the first woman president. But women across the country, in high positions and in low, are doing things, accomplishing things. This woman has been in public life for decades, and yet she has accomplished nothing.

In a classic case of nepotism, Hillary was appointed to head the Task Force on National Health Care Reform during Clinton's first term. The plan was so half-baked, and presented so poorly, that even Democrats shunned it, and the whole scheme collapsed and had to be withdrawn.

Hillary served as a U.S. senator from New York but did not propose a single important piece of legislation; her record is literally a blank slate. Liberal blogger Markos Moulitsas admits that she "doesn't have a single memorable policy or legislative accomplishment to her name."[2] Despite traveling millions of miles as secretary of state, Hillary negotiated no treaties, secured no agreements, prevented no conflicts—in short, she accomplished nothing.

Lack of accomplishment is one thing; deceit is quite another. Everyone who has followed her career knows that Hillary is dishonest to the core, a "congenital liar" as columnist William Safire once put it. The writer Christopher Hitchens titled his book about the Clintons *No One Left to Lie To*. Even Hollywood mogul David Geffen, an avid progressive, said a few years ago of the Clintons, "Everybody in politics lies but they do it with such ease, it's troubling."[3]

She said her mother named her after the famed climber Sir Edmund Hillary, until someone pointed out that Hillary was born in 1947 and her "namesake" only became famous in 1953. On the campaign trail in 2008, Hillary said she had attempted as a young woman to have applied to join the Marines but they wouldn't take her because she was a woman and wore glasses. In fact, Hillary at this stage of life detested the Marines and would never have wanted to join.

She also said a senior professor at Harvard Law School discouraged her from going there by saying, "We don't need any more women."[4] If this incident actually occurred one might expect Hillary to have identified the professor. Certainly it would be interesting to get his side of the story. But she never has, suggesting it's another made-up episode.

As first lady, she claimed to know nothing about the Travelgate firings when the evidence showed she ordered them herself. Later, on the 2008 campaign trail, she repeatedly told a story about how she had been under sniper fire and ran for cover when her plane landed in Tuzla, Bosnia. Video footage, however, showed there was no sniper fire and in fact Hillary was greeted on the tarmac by a child who read her a poem. She blamed the Benghazi attacks on an Internet video when she knew that was a fable. This is a highly abbreviated list.

She is more than just a liar; she and her husband Bill are corrupt and known to be corrupt, going back to their Arkansas days. Just prior to leaving the White House, the Clintons pardoned a notorious fugitive who had fled the country to escape prosecution on racketeering and tax fraud.

Pardons don't come free—the man's family and friends poured millions of dollars into the Clinton coffers in exchange.

This was too much even for Hamilton Jordan—Jimmy Carter's chief of staff. Jordan said the Clintons "are not a couple but a business partnership." Every move they make is "part of their grand scheme to claw their way to the very top." Jordan dubbed the Clintons "the first grifters…a term used in the Great Depression to describe fast-talking con artists who roamed the countryside, always one step ahead of the law, moving on before they were held accountable for their schemes and half-truths."[5]

The *Wall Street Journal* reports that during Hillary's tenure as secretary of state, some sixty companies that lobbied the State Department donated more than $26 million to the Clinton Foundation. "At least 44 of those 60 companies also participated in philanthropic projects valued at $3.2 billion that were set up through a wing of the foundation called the Clinton Global Initiative."

In some cases, the *Journal* reports, "donations came after Mrs. Clinton took action that helped a company. In other cases, the donation came first. In some instances, donations came before and after." In 2012, for example, Hillary lobbied the Algerian government to let GE build power plants in that country. A month later, GE gave between $500,000 and $1 million to the Foundation. The following September, GE got the contract.[6]

This is how Hillary conducts government policy.

She is ruthless, she is grasping, she appears to have little empathy or concern for people. She is old, and mean, and even her laugh is a witch's cackle. There is almost nothing appealing about her. How, then, could she be the first choice of progressive Democrats and the apparent front-runner for winning the presidency in November 2016?

The Hillary enigma is very different than the Obama enigma. The enigma of Obama was: Who is this guy? In 2008, Obama came out of nowhere. Very little was known about his past. What little was known was mostly camouflage. So there was an understandable appetite to learn about him. Moreover, Obama was intriguing; his story generated obvious interest.

As an immigrant, I was fascinated by Obama's background, his charisma, his objectives. I wrote two books, *The Roots of Obama's Rage* and *Obama's America*, trying to explain Obama and predict what he would do. I predicted he was an anti-colonialist, in his father's image, and that he would seek to "remake America" by reducing its wealth and power. Many people, even many conservatives, were initially baffled by my interpretation of this strange man. Only now—eight years later—do most people see that I was largely correct.

With Hillary, however, there is no guesswork about her background, her personality, or her ideology. We all know who this broad is. She has been part of our public life for a generation now. Not only are we all too familiar with her, we are sick of her. Even Democrats seem mildly nauseated; why else would so many of them turn to the Rip Van Winkle candidacy of Bernie Sanders?

Normally an out-of-it socialist who just woke up from a twenty-year nap would not be a serious contender in the Democratic Party. Just yesterday Bernie was sleeping on his neighbor's couch, unable to pay his own rent. But just as Democrats in 2008 turned to Obama because they wanted anyone-but-another-Clinton, this year many have turned to Bernie because they want anyone-but-Hillary.

Yet enough Democrats voted for Hillary, and she received sufficiently robust backing from the Democratic and progressive establishment, that the success of her candidacy was never really in doubt. Even when Bernie got the votes, Hillary got the delegates. From the beginning, Bernie seemed to be running a "show" candidacy designed to fade at the appropriate moment and become part of the Hillary coronation pageant.

Hillary marched inexorably toward the nomination even while shunting aside the risks of an FBI investigation. While some Republicans have long suspected the FBI would recommend an indictment that would end her candidacy, Hillary has operated on the premise that the Obama Justice Department won't indict her—the Democratic Party's front-runner, and Obama's presumptive successor. So far, she's proven right.

Even in the unlikely event she is indicted, I expect her to slog on, with her trademark tenacity, hoping to deal with the problem after she wins the presidency.

Yet when is the last time a major political party nominated someone who has been investigated for corruption so many times, and with an ongoing FBI inquiry? Nixon of course was impeached and resigned in disgrace, but there was no investigation and no impeachment prior to his 1972 reelection. Nixon up to that point had a spotless record, while Hillary's record could only be described as very, very spotty. Yet she has a whole team rooting for her.

THE MOVEMENT BEHIND HILLARY

So the Hillary enigma is actually the enigma of her supporters—the Democratic Party and the progressive movement. That's why this book isn't just about Hillary; it is also about the party and ideological movement that propel her forward. I wrote about Obama as an individual because that is the best way to understand him; I'm writing about Hillary as the head of a movement or gang because that is the best way to understand her and what she represents.

I call this book about Hillary Clinton and the Democratic Party the "secret history" because the story I tell is true and yet will come as a surprise. Did you know about the Democratic president who is the founder of modern progressivism—and also responsible for the revival of the Ku Klux Klan? What about the most popular Democratic president of the twentieth century—who blocked anti-lynching laws and for more than a decade cut deals with racists to exclude blacks from government programs? Then there is the president who is the hero of the Civil Rights laws—the same fellow that called blacks "niggers" and said he wanted to keep them confined to the Democratic plantation.

Hillary places herself in this progressive tradition, and in a sense she belongs there. She's just as bad—actually worse—than her shameful predecessors. It's an eye-opening story. The facts told here, both about history and about Hillary's story, are indisputable and yet they are scarcely known to most people. Until I researched this book, I didn't know them all myself. That's because I'm a victim, as you are, of a progressive cover-up.

The cover-up is the work of progressives in education and the media. The progressives are part of the Democratic team; they are, in fact, the ideologues of the party. They have been given a very specific assignment: to bury the truth and spin a lie to sell their team's political merchandise. This they have assiduously and effectively carried out. Progressives can be counted on to respond with outrage to this book, not because what I say is false, but rather because it is true.

For years, I bought into the lie, as have most conservatives and Republicans. If you ask most people on the Right, they will say: The Democratic Party used to be a good party, made up of good people. The leaders of the Democratic Party were stalwarts like FDR, Harry Truman, and John F. Kennedy. This party was patriotic and principled, and the disagreements of American politics were not disagreements of goals, but of means.

Unfortunately, of late—so the right-wing narrative continues—the Democrats have changed. At some point, whether it be Jimmy Carter in 1980 or Obama in 2008, the Democratic Party lost its moorings and became radicalized. It became the party that we know today. Basically the story of the Democrats is a story of how a basically good bunch of people went astray.

The Democrats, of course, tell a different story. This story has two separate versions, both of which I deal with in this book. The first version is that the Democrats have always been the good guys. This story is the equivalent of the defense lawyer who says, "My client is not guilty and has always been, as he is now, an upstanding citizen."

This is the portrait of the Democratic Party that will be on full display at the Democratic National Convention in Philadelphia. In a sense, this entire book is a refutation of what will be presented there that week. There we'll hear about how the Democrats are the party of racial equality, social justice, and economic opportunity. This is the moral basis for the party's claim to rule.

Democrats—the mantra goes—are the party of the common man, the ordinary person. For two hundred years, Democrats have been looking out for the little guy, including historically marginalized groups like women, blacks, Hispanics, and other minorities. Where would these people be without the Democratic Party to protect them and secure their basic rights? Democrats are the party of equal rights, civil rights, and human dignity.

Democrats—the mantra continues—support not only racial and social justice but also economic justice, in other words widely shared prosperity and Obama's "fair share." Economic justice is the centerpiece of Hillary's 2016 campaign. Why, she asks, should the fat cats—the top 1 percent—take the lion's share of the profits that accrue from American productivity? Why should they be permitted to cause so much inequality? In Hillary's view, government is the instrument that takes from those at the very top and redistributes to the rest of us.

Interestingly Democrats say they are not merely the party that did great things in the past; they are also the party of the future. That's why most Democrats like to be called "progressives"; the term links them with progress. At one time Democrats called themselves "liberals," until the term fell into disrepute. Progressive is now the preferred label. Voting for progressive Democrats, we will hear, assures that America's future will be better than America's past.

By contrast, Democrats insist, the Republican Party is the party of racism and reaction. The Democrats' prime exhibit is the GOP presidential candidate Donald Trump. We hear that Trump is completely beyond the pale because he is a racist and a fascist. He represents the rotten core of the Republican Party, the crazy bigoted uncle who has come out of the basement and taken over the party, embarrassing the hosts who had attempted to keep him hidden away from sight.

Listen to progressive darling, Senator Elizabeth Warren, who tweeted recently that Trump "incites supporters to violence" and "built his campaign on racism, sexism and xenophobia." Warren added, "There's more enthusiasm for @realdonaldtrump among leaders of the KKK than leaders of the political party he now controls." Robert Reich, labor secretary under Bill Clinton, writes, "Viewing Donald Trump in light of the fascists of the first half of the twentieth century...helps explain what he is doing and how he is succeeding."[7]

While Warren and Reich both suggest that Republicans are uncomfortable with their association with Trump, the broader Democratic indictment goes beyond Trump and extends to the GOP as a whole. Recently the Democratic National Committee sent out a fundraising email which branded Trump supporters as bigots and Confederate sympathizers and insisted that "these are the values of the GOP."[8]

In this view, Republicans represent rich white guys, in opposition to women, minorities, and everyone else. Those guys typically run big corporations, so the GOP is the party of corporate America. When wealth is created in America, the corporations and rich guys swoop in and steal it, depriving workers and the community of their fair share. Republicans are the bad guys who have to be brought to heel.

Progressives say that, of course, Republicans like to be called "conservative": that term, in this lexicon, means conserving bigotry and white privilege. Republicans today are in the tradition of their ancestors who stole the land from the Indians, enslaved and oppressed blacks, and blocked immigrants from coming to this country. No wonder the GOP is so strong in the South. That's the ancestral home of racism, and that's where most racists live today.

EXPOSING THE LIE

In this book I expose this progressive narrative as a lie. In reality the Democratic Party is now what it has been from the beginning—the party of subjugation, oppression, exploitation, and theft. The Democrats are not the party of justice or equality, but rather, of systematic injustice and inequality. Far from championing the cause of women, blacks, and other minorities, Democrats have historically brutalized, segregated, exploited, and murdered the most vulnerable members of our society.

During all this time, the main opposition to these horrors on the part of the Democratic Party came from Republicans. This book makes an astonishing claim: of all Americans, Republicans are the ones who have the least reason to feel guilty about slavery or racism. This claim comes as a surprise because Republicans are the ones who are regularly chastised by progressives for their alleged bigotry. Let's see who the real bigots are.

From the beginning, Republicans have been the good guys, fighting to stop Democratic schemes of exploitation, murder, and plunder. Republicans fought a great war, and hundreds of thousands of them died, to thwart the nefarious practices of the Democrats. Even after slavery, Republicans fought vigorously though not always successfully to defeat Democratic schemes of segregation and racial terrorism.

The bad guys—the Democrats—put up a great fight but the Republicans won in the end. It was Republicans who made possible the Civil Rights laws that finally and belatedly secured equal rights for blacks and other minorities. Democrats are the ones who bitterly resisted the Civil Rights Movement, and had the Democrats been the only party in America at the time, none of these laws, from the Civil Rights Act to the Voting Rights Act to the Fair Housing Bill, would have passed.

As I will show, American history is really the story of Democratic malefactors and Republican heroes. I begin with Andrew Jackson. He—not Thomas Jefferson or FDR—is the true founder of the modern Democratic Party.

Progressives today are divided about Jackson. Some, like Walter Russell Mead, admire Jackson as a "man of the people" but trace the Jacksonian legacy today not to the Democratic Party but to Donald Trump.[9] Most progressives are simply uncomfortable with Jackson. Some now want to remove him from the $20 bill and erase him from our collective memory. He was, in this view, a very bad American.

I support the debunking of Jackson, but not because he was a bad American—rather, because he was a typical, crooked Democrat. Jackson established the Democratic Party as the party of theft. He mastered the art of stealing land from the Indians and then selling it at giveaway prices to white settlers. Jackson's expectation was that those people would support him politically, as indeed they did. Jackson was indeed a "man of the people," but his popularity was that of a gang leader who distributes his spoils in exchange for loyalty on the part of those who benefit from his crimes.

Jackson also figured out how to benefit personally from his land-stealing. Like Hillary Clinton, he started out broke and then became one of the richest people in the country. How? Jackson and his partners and cronies made early bids on Indian land, sometimes even before the Indians had been evacuated from that land. They acquired the land for little or nothing and later sold it for a handsome profit. Remarkably, the roots of the Clinton Foundation can be found in the land-stealing policies of America's first Democratic president.

I show in a subsequent chapter how the Democrats were the party of slavery, and how the slave-owner mentality continues to shape the policies of Democratic leaders today. The point isn't that the Democrats invented slavery, which is an ancient institution that far predates America. Rather, Democrats like Senator John C. Calhoun invented a new justification for slavery, slavery as a "positive good." For the first time in history, Democrats insisted that slavery wasn't just beneficial for masters; they said it was also good for the slaves.

Today progressive pundits attempt to conceal Democratic complicity in slavery by blaming slavery on the "South." These people have spun a whole history that portrays the slavery battle as one between the anti-slavery North and the pro-slavery South. This of course benefits Democrats today, because today the Democratic Party's main strength is in the North and the Republican Party's main strength is in the South.

But I blow the Democrats' cover by showing that the slavery debate was not mainly a North-South issue. It was actually a contest between the pro-slavery Democrats and the anti-slavery Republicans. How can I make such an outrageous statement? Let's begin by recalling that northern Democrats like Stephen Douglas protected slavery, while most southerners didn't own slaves. (Three fourths of those who fought in the Civil War on the Confederate side had no slaves and weren't fighting to protect slavery.)

Republicans, meanwhile, to one degree or another, all opposed slavery. The party itself was founded to stop slavery. Of course there were a range of views among Republicans, from abolitionists who sought to end slavery immediately to mainstream Republicans like Abraham Lincoln who recognized that this was both constitutionally and politically impossible and focused on arresting slavery's extension into the new territories. This was the platform on which Lincoln won the 1860 election.

The real clash was between the Democrats, northern and southern, who supported slavery and the Republicans across the country who opposed it. As Lincoln summarized it in his First Inaugural Address, one side believes slavery is right and ought to be extended, and the other believes it is wrong and ought to be restricted. "This," Lincoln said, "is the only substantial dispute."[10] And this, ultimately, was what the Civil War was all about.

In the end, of course, Republicans ended slavery and permanently outlawed it through the Thirteenth Amendment. Democrats responded by opposing the amendment and a group of them assassinated the man they held responsible for emancipation, Abraham Lincoln. Over the Democrats' opposition, Republicans passed the Fourteenth Amendment securing for blacks equal rights under the law, and the Fifteenth Amendment giving blacks the right to vote.

DEFENDING THE CRIMINALS

Confronted with these facts, progressives act like the lawyer who is presented with the murder weapon belonging to his client. Darn, he says to himself, I better think fast. "Yes," he now admits, "my client did murder the clerk and rob the store. But he didn't kill all those other people who were also found dead at the scene."

In other words, progressives who are forced to acknowledge the Democratic Party's pro-slavery history promptly respond, "We admit to being the party of slavery, and we did uphold the institution for more than a century, but slavery ended in 1865, so all of this was such a long time ago. You can't blame us now for the antebellum crimes of the Democratic Party."

Yes, but what about the postbellum crimes of the Democratic Party? My slavery chapter is followed by a chapter on segregation and the Ku Klux Klan. Democrats in the 1880s invented segregation and Jim Crow laws that lasted through the 1960s. Democrats also came up with the "separate but equal" rationale that justified segregation and pretended that it was for the benefit of African Americans.

The Ku Klux Klan was founded in 1866 in Pulaski, Tennessee, by a group of former Confederate soldiers; its first grand wizard was a Confederate general who was also a delegate to the Democratic National Convention. The Klan soon spread beyond the South to the Midwest and the West and became, in the words of historian Eric Foner, "the domestic terrorist arm of the Democratic Party."

The main point of the Klan's orgy of violence was to prevent blacks from voting—voting, that is, for Republicans. Leading Democrats, including at least one president, two Supreme Court justices, and innumerable senators and congressmen, were Klan members. The last one, Robert Byrd, died in 2010 and was eulogized by President Obama and former President Bill Clinton. Hillary Clinton called him her "mentor."

The sordid history of the Democratic Party in the early twentieth century is also married to the sordid history of the progressive movement during the same period. Progressives like Margaret Sanger—founder of Planned Parenthood and a role model for Hillary Clinton—supported such causes as eugenics and social Darwinism. While abortion was not an issue in Sanger's day, she backed forced sterilization for "unfit" people, notably minorities. Sanger's Negro Project was specifically focused on reducing the black population.

Progressives also led the campaign to stop poor immigrants from coming to this country. They championed laws in the 1920s that brought the massive flows of immigration to this country to a virtual halt. The motives of the progressives were openly racist, and in the way the immigration restrictions were framed, progressives succeeded in broadening the Democratic Party's target list of minority groups.

While the Democratic Party previously singled out blacks and native Indians, progressives showed Democrats how to suppress all minorities.

Included in the new list were Hispanics from Central and South America as well as Eastern and Southern Europeans. Many of these people were clearly white but progressives did not consider them white enough. Like blacks, they were considered "unfit" on the basis of their complexion.

During the 1920s, progressives developed a fascination with and admiration for Italian and German fascism, and the fascists, for their part, praised American progressives. These were likeminded people who spoke the same language, and progressives and fascists worked together to implement programs to sterilize so-called mental defectives and "unfit" people, resulting subsequently in tens of thousands of forced sterilizations in America and hundreds of thousands in Nazi Germany.

During the 1930s, President Franklin D. Roosevelt sent members of his brain trust to Europe to study fascist economic programs, which he considered more advanced than anything his New Deal had implemented to date. FDR was enamored with Mussolini, whom he called the "admirable Italian gentleman." Some Democrats even had a soft spot for Hitler: young JFK went to Germany before World War II and praised Hitler as a "legend" and blamed hostility to the Nazis as jealousy resulting from how much the Nazis had accomplished.

Yes, I know. Very little of this is understood by people today because progressives have done such a good job of sweeping it all under the rug. This material is simply left out of the textbooks even though it is right there in the historical record. Some progressive pundits know about it, but they don't want to talk about it. Such talk, they figure, can only hurt today's Democrats who, after all, can hardly bear responsibility for what JFK said or what FDR and Woodrow Wilson did.

But don't we have some responsibility to the truth? Shouldn't we lay out the facts of history and let people make up their own minds? The progressive answer to this question is no. Progressives detest the facts not because they are untrue but because they don't fit in with progressive political interests. Facts constitute, as Al Gore might say, an inconvenient truth.

So progressives have been working hard to come up with lies that can be passed off as facts. Progressives have a whole cultural contingent—Hollywood, the mainline media, the elite universities, even professional comedians—to peddle their propaganda. From the television show *Madame Secretary* to the front page of the *New York Times* to nightly quips by Stephen Colbert, the progressive bilge comes at us continually and relentlessly.

In this bogus narrative, Republicans are the bad guys because Republicans opposed the Civil Rights Movement of the 1950s and 1960s. For progressive Democrats, the Civil Rights Movement is the canonical event of American history. It is even more important than the American Revolution. Progressive reasoning is: We did this, so it must be the greatest thing that was ever done in America. Republicans opposed it, which makes them the bad guys.

The only problem is that Republicans were instrumental—actually indispensable—in getting the Civil Rights laws passed. While Lyndon Johnson pushed the Civil Rights Act of 1964 with the backing of some northern Democrats, Republicans voted in far higher percentages for the bill than Democrats did. This was also true of the Voting Rights Act of 1965. Neither would have passed with just Democratic votes. Indeed, the main opposition to both bills came from Democrats.

Most people know the Nineteenth Amendment granting women's suffrage was passed in 1919 and ratified by the states the following year. What few people know is there was a forty-year struggle over that amendment, with Republicans pushing for it and Democrats opposing it, until the Republicans finally had the votes to get it through.

Republicans proposed women's suffrage as early as 1878, but it was voted down by a Democrat-controlled Congress. Republicans re-introduced the issue each year, but for many years the Democrats tied it up in committees. It only got to the floor in 1887 when the Democrats again defeated it.

Frustrated, the suffragettes—who were mostly Republican—took the issue to the states. By 1900 several Republican-dominated states granted women the right to vote. In 1916, Montana Republican Jeannette Rankin became the first woman elected to Congress.

Congress, however, only took up the issue again in 1914, when it was again rejected by Senate Democrats. Only when the GOP won landslide majorities in both houses in 1918 did the Nineteenth Amendment finally have the necessary two-thirds majority to pass.

President Woodrow Wilson, who had led his party's opposition to women's suffrage, gave in when he saw its inevitability. The Democrats, however, took their opposition to the states, and eight of the nine "no" votes on the Nineteenth Amendment came from Democrat-controlled state legislatures. So the GOP is responsible for women having the right to vote.[11]

The inclusion of women in the 1964 Civil Rights Act was, oddly enough, the work of a group of racist, chauvinist Democrats. Led by Democratic Congressman Howard Smith of Virginia, this group was looking to defeat the Civil Rights Act. Smith proposed to amend the legislation and add "sex" to "race" as a category protected against discrimination.

Smith's Democratic buddies roared with laughter when he offered his one-word amendment. They thought it would make the whole civil rights thing so ridiculous that no sane person would go along with it. One scholar noted that Smith's amendment "stimulated several hours of humorous debate" among racist, chauvinist Democrats. But to their amazement, the amended version of the bill passed.[12] It bears repeating that Republicans provided the margin of victory that extended civil rights protection both to minorities and to women.

A LARGER DECEPTION

The canard about the Civil Rights Movement is embedded within a larger deception that progressives uniformly put forward. This deception is intended to defuse the sordid history of the Democratic Party's two-century involvement in a parade of evils from slavery to segregation to lynching to forced sterilization to support for fascism to the internment of Japanese Americans during World War II. All these horrors are the work of the Democratic Party.

Progressive Democrats seek to escape responsibility for all this with their tale of the Big Switch. Initially devised by progressives like Dan

Carter and Earl and Merle Black, the Big Switch can be understood as a last-ditch attempt to rescue progressive and Democratic Party history. This progressive defense is akin to the lawyer who says, "Yes, my client shot the clerk and killed all those people, but since then he has completely reformed and now lives a blameless life. Meanwhile, his accusers have all become criminals."

Actually, even if that were true, the man should still be held to account for what he did. He should be expected to make a confession of his crimes and make some reparation to his victims and to society. Progressives, of course, have no intention of doing any of this. Neither do Democrats. Whenever these people talk about reparations they want "America" to pay. But "America" didn't commit these crimes; they did. They're the ones who should be held accountable.

Back to the Big Switch: the basic idea is that starting with the Civil Rights Movement, Democrats saw the light and became the good guys, while Republicans became the bad guys. What happened to all the racist southern Democrats? Look, say the progressives, they all became Republicans! That's why the South today is largely Republican.[13] This would seem to support the progressive story line.

The narrative of the Big Switch has one more thing going for it: blacks, who once voted overwhelmingly Republican, now vote overwhelmingly Democratic. This is a switch, and it would seem to go along with the idea that Republicans used to be friendly to black interests but now Democrats are. Why else would 90 percent of blacks today support the Democratic Party?

This book takes on the narrative of the Big Switch, and debunks it as the final—and most ingenious—installment of the progressive lie. In reality there was no switch. For the film that accompanies this book, I made a list of 1,500 racist Democrats—a list that includes members of Congress, governors, appellate and Supreme Court justices, and all the notorious figures who opposed the Civil Rights Movement. Of this group, I count exactly fourteen—less than 1 percent—who switched to the Republican Party. So the idea that racist Democrats became Republicans is a myth.

Of course many southern whites did switch from voting Democrat to voting Republican, helping the GOP become the majority party in the South, as the Democrats once were. But remember that racism declined sharply in the South during the second half of the twentieth century. There is quite literally a mountain of scholarly data that documents this. And this was the very period of GOP ascendancy. So as the South became less racist, it became more Republican.

I provide evidence in this book to show that southern whites became Republican not for racist motives but for economic ones. The most racist poor whites never left the Democratic Party; they remained loyal to the party of racism until they died. In this sense, the data show that racism slowed the movement of whites toward the Republicans.

But many southern whites were not under the racist hold of the Democrats. As they became more prosperous, these whites came to see the GOP reflect their beliefs in economic opportunity and upward mobility. They also found Republicans more in tune with their patriotism as well as their socially conservative views. Quite naturally, they moved over to a party that better reflected their interests and aspirations.

Remarkably, southern whites made the journey from Democratic to Republican for the same reason that southern blacks switched parties from Republican to Democratic. In both cases, the switch occurred for economic—not racial—reasons. The black switch occurred first, in the 1930s, while the white switch occurred much later, in the 1960s and 1970s. In both cases, the timing is significant.

Blacks clearly didn't switch for reasons of race because the Democratic Party was, in the 1930s, the undisputed home of racism. It remained so until at least the early 1960s. (I say "at least" because I believe that modern progressive Democratic ideology remains infused with racism, although this racism manifests itself in a new way.) So many blacks switched reluctantly, because they knew they were leaving the party of Lincoln for the party of segregation, lynching, and the Ku Klux Klan.

Why did they do it? They did it because the Democrats promised them economic benefits. These benefits meant a great deal to blacks then living through the hardships of segregation and the Great Depression. Democrats offered blacks some of the same security that blacks had during slavery—in which the basic needs of blacks were met on the plantation—and blacks, during a desperate time, went for it.

This was one of the most significant political transformations in American history. Long-term, it has proven to be a terrible bargain for blacks. They have remained the worst-off group in America, surpassed even by poverty-stricken immigrants who came to this country much later with nothing. The inner city remains a kind of Third World enclave in America, and whether or not blacks realize it, the Democrats intend to keep it that way.

Yet counterproductive though the black shift of political allegiance has proven over the past seventy-five years, I cannot entirely blame black Americans for making it. They were under extreme economic stress. And they were conned by the artful pitch men of the Democratic Party. These pitch men said to blacks: you have had it hard enough in the past; now you deserve to be taken care of by the federal government. And many blacks figured: after all we've been through, this is our due.

But if the Democrats were such racists, why did they offer to uplift blacks in this way? Here we find the true switch, which was a switch of tactics by progressive Democrats. Democrats had already tried various exploitation schemes after slavery, from segregation to lynching to white supremacy. Yet from the 1860s through the 1920s, the Democrats remained the minority party nationwide.

A NEW SCAM

So progressive Democrats realized they needed a new and bigger scam. For two centuries they had oppressed and stolen from blacks and other minorities; now they had an idea for how to do it to the country as a whole. The new Democratic scam was progressivism, not the old progressivism of forced sterilization and support for fascism, but a new progressivism that turned blacks and other minorities into pawns in a grand larceny scheme.

The scheme works like this. Progressives supply the basic needs of poor blacks, creating for them a new plantation called the inner city. There blacks are provided with food, subsidized housing, medical care, and so on. In this regard, the new plantation functions pretty much like the old one, with a few modifications. Under slavery, this was rural paternalism; now it is urban paternalism. The slave master is replaced by the government; i.e. the Big House of slavery is now replaced by the White House.

In both cases, it's a meager living. But there is an important difference. Under slavery, blacks had to work; today's blacks don't have to work to inhabit the progressive plantation. In fact, they must not work, because if they become self-reliant, then the progressives have no future use for them. Consequently, many young blacks have productivity, creativity, even human dignity sapped out of them. This is the core of today's progressive racism.

Progressive racism is dedicated to uplifting poor blacks to a certain point and then keeping them there. The proof is that poor blacks today are about as poorly off as they were a half-century ago, when the progressive schemes of black uplift went into place. Every other ethnic group in America has dramatically improved its life except this one. Blacks have delivered for progressives, but they haven't progressed very much themselves. This, I suggest, is by design.

Several years ago the black pastor and activist Eugene Rivers made the startling statement that today's young black males in the inner city are "ill-equipped to secure gainful employment even as productive slaves." Rivers's point was that at least slaves had skills like masonry, carpentry, and agricultural skills that made them useful; today's inner-city black males don't have any skills at all. They have truly become useless people.[14]

Actually the Democrats have made them that way. That's because these inner-city blacks, though useless in the traditional sense, are useful to the Democratic Party—first, as voters, and second, as public exhibitions of the need for progressive redistribution programs. Under Democratic supervision, blacks in the inner city must *remain poor*, because their poverty is required to support and justify the progressive scheme. In this sense the 'hood is an invention of the Democratic Party.

Progressive Democrats are fiercely protective of these dilapidated, crime-ridden neighborhoods. That's why they mount fierce opposition whenever some reformer proposes to give poor black parents a choice of sending their children to private or public schools. Here the fear is that poor black children may actually get a good education, and that would liberate them from dependency on the Democratic Party.

Progressive Democrats also fought welfare reform every step of the way. They were outraged at the idea that single mothers with illegitimate children should be required to work. The progressive scheme is to increase their benefits every time they produce a new child. That child, to Democrats, represents a future Democratic voter. Progressives do not want to change this system of intergenerational dependency that has been working for them politically.

Finally, progressives scream every time entrepreneurs attempt gentrification projects in cities like Baltimore, Detroit, and St. Louis. No matter that gentrification would bring new money, new jobs, and new people into the inner city. Crime would go down, and people could move up. Here progressive opposition is most revealing of all. A transformation of the inner city is precisely what progressives do *not* want to happen.

So progressives talk incessantly about black uplift but no uplift actually occurs, even though black neighborhoods are all run by Democratic officials, from mayors to school superintendents. In fact, the Democratic establishment works to assure that no one gets off the plantation.

Now, Democrats are working overtime to create new Hispanic plantations called barrios. Long-term, they would like to have some Asian American ghettos also. Democrats have created a plantation model for blacks that they hope can be applied to other minority groups as well. In that case, black suffering would extend more broadly to minority suffering, a real political success from the Democrats' perspective.

Why? Because minority suffering is the basic moral justification for the progressive Democratic rip-off. If there were no minority suffering, then where is the need for all the social welfare programs? The suffering of blacks and other minorities has actually been caused by the Democrats themselves, but in a crafty rhetorical move, this suffering is now blamed on "America."

And here we get to the central thrust of progressive education, which is to fault America with the crimes of the Democratic Party. Here's a choice example from Michael Omi and Howard Winant: "The broad sweep of U.S. history is characterized not by racial democracy but by racial despotism, not by trajectories of reform but by implacable denial of political rights, dehumanization, extreme exploitation, and policies of minority extirpation."[15]

Well, who exactly did these things? Omi and Winant refuse to point the finger at the real culprits. From their point of view, "America" did this to the blacks and other minorities, and in recompense, America owes them. For Hispanics, this means a right of free entry and a right of amnesty for illegals; for blacks, it means that government owes you a living into the indefinite future.

So Democrats propose greater government—which is to say, Democratic—control over private industry and over the private wealth of this country, all in the name of advancing racial unification and social justice. Democrats justify their programs as the *sine qua non* of fighting racism and advancing civil rights, and define any opposition to those programs as opposition to civil rights itself and resurgent racism.

We should take a moment to appreciate the political feat the Democrats have pulled off. Through a fantastic political and rhetorical legerdemain, they have turned the tables on their opponents. In a sense, they have done a new type of switch—they have switched *the blame.*

Incredibly Republicans—who are the party of emancipation and equal rights and civil rights—are now portrayed as the enemies of blacks and other minorities, while Democrats with a straight face present themselves as the party of anti-racism. The people who have been fighting bigotry for two centuries have somehow become the new bigots. Meanwhile—and this mirrors what recently happened in Flint, Michigan—the very people who had long poisoned the wells then showed up claiming to be the Committee for Clean Drinking Water.

Poor blacks, we will see, have become the pawns and suckers of this scheme. And subsequently progressives have attempted, with mixed success, to draw in Hispanics and other ethnic minorities as well. Their larger plan is to enslave the whole country. It's the greatest rip-off in American history. If this scheme is successful, future historians may describe the history of the Democratic Party as a movement from slavery to enslavement.

Slavery and enslavement are two distinct, though related, things. Slavery represents a specific condition: the slave is quite literally owned by his master. Enslavement is a process: people are enslaved to the degree that they are deprived of their rights and the fruit of their labor. The ultimate endpoint of enslavement is slavery, but there are many points of serfdom and servitude in between.

In this book I will show how Democrats went from slavery for blacks to enslavement for the whole population. Even those who benefit from the progressive state become dependent on it and remain captive to their progressive benefactors. Meanwhile, the rest of us are forced, intimidated, and terrorized into forking over our earnings and possessions so that progressives can dispose of them as they see fit. In sum, progressive Democrats have gone from exploiting blacks to exploiting everyone. This is their actual Big Switch.

Enslaving the population is what Obama and Hillary mean by the "remaking" of America. They want to remake America into a society in which progressive Democrats control the entire wealth of the country, and citizens become serfs of the progressive Democratic state. In such a society all our major decisions are regulated and controlled by the progressives. Their goal is to own us—our property, our lives, even our dreams—and to a considerable degree, they already do.

But how to pull off such a scam? In order to carry out their heist, progressives require the consent of a majority of Americans. This, after all, is democratic theft—theft that is ratified through the democratic process. So how to obtain that consent? Progressives need a pitch, and the best pitch is the idea of social justice.

I should take a moment to explain what I mean by a pitch. A pitch is the line that criminals use when they require the consent of their victims. Imagine a gang that wants to rob an old lady and take her stuff. They could kick down the door, but it would be much easier for them if they could somehow convince the old lady to lift the latch. In that case they would only have to push their way in. So the pitch is the sweet talk the gang members use to convince the old lady to lift the latch.

I learned about the pitch in a federal confinement center where I spent eight months in overnight captivity for my sins against the Obama administration. My crime was exceeding the campaign finance laws by giving $20,000 over the campaign finance limit to a college pal of mine who was running for the U.S. Senate. I didn't do it to get anything in return; I did it simply to help an old friend. For this, I found myself at the receiving end of the full force of the U.S. government.

But since no one in American history has been prosecuted—let alone incarcerated—for doing what I did, I should be allowed to suspect that my real crime was in exposing President Obama in my film *2016: Obama's America* and my books *The Roots of Obama's Rage* and *Obama's America*. Obama hated my film, vituperatively attacking it on his website barackobama.com, and a few months later, the FBI was knocking on my door.

During my eight-month confinement, I got to know attempted murderers, drug smugglers, coyotes, armed robbers—the whole gamut of the criminal underclass. Here I learned how criminals think, how they organize themselves into gangs, how they recruit allies, how they come up with their pitches, and how they cover up their misdeeds. I realized there is a close similarity between these criminal operations and the longstanding practices of modern progressivism and the Democratic Party.

A GANGSTER *PAR EXCELLENCE*

All this talk of criminals brings me to the main subject of this book, which is Hillary Clinton. So far it may seem like this has been all about progressivism and the Democratic Party, but Hillary is there from the beginning, she is present in every chapter, her spirit haunts the history of her party because all the evil schemes of her party have, in a sense, become consolidated into her own career and life. Hillary is, in this respect, the dark id of the Democratic Party.

Her husband Bill is as crooked as they come, but his venality is circumscribed by his ambitions, which are mostly personal: to be lionized, attended to, and have his private parts regularly serviced. Obama too is lawless, but his is a lawlessness of means rather than ends. Obama will bend the law when it suits his purposes, but his purposes are mainly ideological, to reduce America's wealth and power.

These two are small-time hoods in comparison to Hillary. Obama is capable of gangsterism but it doesn't define him; neither does it define Bill; but it does define Hillary. For Hillary, gangsterism is not merely a matter of means; it is also her end. Hillary wants to be the crime boss of America. That is the only way to satisfy her unquenchable desire for money, power, and social control.

As we will see in this book, Hillary is a criminal who found the criminal practices of Saul Alinsky to be too weak-kneed for her taste, and Alinsky was a gangster who found the criminal practices of the Al Capone gang to be a tad sentimental. In short, Hillary is the true Democrat, the gangster *par excellence*.

I suspect this is why the Democratic establishment lined up so quickly behind her. While the Republicans had a real primary, hotly contested, the Democrats had a primary in which Bernie seemed to win again and again but never seemed to make a dent in Hillary's lead. That's because the Democratic super-delegates were uniformly in her camp, even though there was throughout the campaign the risk that she would be indicted.

Why? Because the Democratic establishment recognizes that they need a thuggish enforcer, and Hillary fits the profile. Hillary is, in this respect, more promising than Obama. One of the progressive Democrats' main complaints is that Obama has not been a sufficiently skilled looter. He did pull off one big job, Obamacare, but other than that he's been mainly talk, talk, talk. Democrats are hoping that Hillary will be less talk and all action. I suspect they are right.

One of the original contributions of this book is to offer a new interpretation of that bizarre arrangement called the Clinton marriage. This marriage seems to be held together by a single cord: larceny. The Clintons have been on the make since their Arkansas days. They continued their vile operations through Bill's presidency, which culminated in the pardoning of criminals who donated lavishly to the Clintons and the Democratic Party.

The Clinton marriage seems to affirm the Bonnie and Clyde principle that the couple that steals together, stays together. The famous criminal duo Bonnie and Clyde too had a complicated romantic relationship, perhaps just as twisted and bizarre as that of the Clintons. We may never know what the glue was that kept Bonnie and Clyde together, but what about the Clintons? What unites them and how did their partnership come about?

Here there are a couple of theories, both in my view mistaken. The first—occasionally whispered on the Right—is that Hillary is a lesbian. This would explain her apparent indifference to Bill's carrying-on. Strangely the best source to confirm this suspicion is Bill himself. Two of Clinton's former mistresses—former Miss Arkansas Sally Miller and Gennifer Flowers—have quoted Bill as saying that Hillary likes girls. Flowers somewhat colorfully cites Bill to the effect that Hillary "has probably eaten more p*ssy than I have."[16]

I have to confess that I cannot refute this theory, but I believe it is unsubstantiated. No woman has ever come forward saying she was even propositioned by Hillary, let alone had a relationship with her. Sometimes the absence of evidence is evidence of absence.

The second theory is probably the most widely held view, certainly among Democrats but even among many Republicans. This is the view that Bill is the predator and Hillary is the long-suffering wife. Democratic Senator Claire McCaskill spoke for many when she praised Hillary but said of Bill, "I don't want my daughter near him."[17] This view holds that Bill is the Big Creep—this is the term Monica Lewinsky used for him—and Hillary is the woman who sticks by the creep since she is married to him.

This second view is not entirely favorable to Hillary. At its worst, it depicts her as a kind of Camille Cosby, turning a blind eye to her husband's atrocious predatory behavior toward other women. But even in this analysis the main blame falls on the husband. The two Bills are the ones who did it; the wives are merely guilty of putting up with all this bad behavior.

In reality, I show that the Cosby and Clinton situations are quite different. Bill may be a big creep but Hillary is creepier than he is. She is much worse than Camille Cosby. That's because Camille, as far as we know, had no role in orchestrating her husband's drugging of unsuspecting women. Camille is, at best, a passive enabler.

Hillary's role can be understood when we realize that she is both aware of and involved in Bill's crimes. She facilitates them because she benefits from them. How does she benefit? Hillary didn't necessarily want a husband, but she needed a lifelong "pitch man" for her political schemes. Goofy, likeable, gregarious Bill was the perfect find. But why would someone like Bill want someone like Hillary? Not for sex. She couldn't do it for him in the bedroom. Hillary knew that. If she wanted him, she had to make herself useful to him in other ways

Hillary saw early on that Bill was a sex addict who could easily cross the line into sex abuse. In fact, there was already one incident at Oxford that suggested he had crossed that line. At first Hillary was appalled, but then she saw that in Bill's addiction there was, for her, an opportunity.

So she became the active enabler of his sex crimes. She showed him she could cover up for him, and clean up his messes. She took on the task of prosecuting, discrediting, and destroying the women that spoke out against him. When necessary, she played the role of the supportive wife. She protected Bill from the consequence of his actions.

The arrangement has proven successful in that both Bill and Hillary have gotten out of it what they wanted. Bill found his co-conspirator who somehow managed to get him off every time, and Hillary got an addict who became dependent on her for life. Of course she never considered divorcing him because she needed him. Without her Slick Willie, she knew she had no hope of carrying out her nefarious ambitions. With him, she now has a chance to live out her demented aspirations with all of us as her victims.

What are those aspirations? To a degree that Bill would hardly dream and that is unmatched by Obama, Hillary seeks to establish full government—which is to say progressive—control over the lives of Americans. She seeks, in her own words, the "remaking of the American way of politics, government, indeed life."[18] Obama wanted to remake America; this woman wants to remake your life.

She intends, in other words, to relocate you to the progressive plantation. There is only one way to do this: convert all of America into a plantation. This means reducing the whole country to the miserable condition that we now see only in inner cities and on native Indian reservations. For Hillary, this would represent the summit of her achievement, because it would give her what she seeks: full power and full control.

Of course it's not just about the power; it is also about the money. Here Hillary has already shown her talents. Her achievement as secretary of state has been to carry the corrupt operations of the Democratic Party to a new level. Hillary herself described what she did as "commercial diplomacy." It certainly has worked out commercially for her and Bill. In the words of Peter Schweizer, author of *Clinton Cash*, "No one has even come close in recent years to enriching themselves on the scale of the Clintons while they or a spouse continued to serve in public office."[19]

By contrast with the Clintons, earlier Democratic scam operations seem like petty thievery. Previously Democrats specialized in big city machines *a la* Tammany Hall in New York and the Daley machine in Chicago. These were local rackets that looted the city treasury. The looters—such figures as William "Boss" Tweed—made off with a few hundred thousand, perhaps as much as a million. Hillary, however, figured out how to take her racket national, indeed global.

Never before has anyone figured out how to rent out American foreign policy, how to convert the position of secretary of state into a personal money machine. Hillary, with Bill's help, figured out not only how to shake down Russian oligarchs and Canadian billionaires by offering them control of America's uranium assets; she also figured out how to rob the island nation of Haiti in the wake of the 2010 earthquake. It's one thing to rip off the world's rich; it takes a special kind of chutzpah to steal from the poorest of the poor.

Imagine what Hillary would do with her power if she went from secretary of state to president of the United States! Previously she at least had to answer to Obama; now she would be a power unto herself. Hillary has already shown how indifferent she is to the interests of the United States, selling American influence to the highest bidder. I dread to think how much havoc—how many Benghazis—are in store if we elect this woman in November.

Who is going to stop Hillary, and how? Who will block the enslavement of the American people that is the political program of the Democratic Party? My last chapter addresses these questions. The situation, at first glance, seems desperate. The Republican Party seems confused, bitterly divided, unable to contest the Democratic social justice pitch and articulate a rival vision. Can we really count on the bewildered elephant to chase down and trample the Democratic donkey?

There is no one else. The GOP has, from the beginning, been the team—and the only team—that can stop and did stop the marauding Democrats. The Republicans have done it for 150 years, from slavery through the Ku Klux Klan through eugenics and forced sterilization through the Civil Rights Movement. Why don't we have slavery today? How has the Klan gone from a massive organization to a joke? Why do blacks and other minorities today have equality of rights under the law? The answer in every case is: the Republican Party.

Republicans can come together and do it again, and in the final chapter I show how. While the threat is real and this will be a tough election, there is no cause for dispiritedness. With clear thinking, political creativity, and simple hard work, we can meet the challenges that are before us, working together, as we must, because our nation's very future seems to be at stake.

This is an election about Hillary. She is the one who embodies the debased soul of the Democratic Party. And she is the corrupt, exasperating, tenacious, malign spirit looming over the United States in the fateful year of 2016. It's time—actually it's past time, but better late than never—for all good Americans to come together and perform an exorcism.

CHAPTER 2

THE LAND STEALER

HOW ANDREW JACKSON SHAPED THE MODERN DEMOCRATIC PARTY

It was dark before we finished killing them.[1]
—Andrew Jackson on his massacre at Horseshoe Bend

In January 2015 a group of Haitians surrounded the New York offices of the Clinton Foundation. They chanted slogans, accusing Bill and Hillary Clinton of having robbed them of "billions of dollars." Two months later, the Haitians were at it again, accusing the Clintons of duplicity, malfeasance, and theft. And in May 2015, they were back, this time outside New York's Cipriani, where Bill Clinton received an award and collected a $500,000 check for his foundation. "Clinton, where's the money?" the Haitian signs read. "In whose pockets?" Said Dhoud Andre of the Commission Against Dictatorship, "We are telling the world of the crimes that Bill and Hillary Clinton are responsible for in Haiti."[2]

Haitians like Andre may sound a bit strident, but he and the protesters had good reason to be disgruntled. They had suffered a heavy blow from Mother Nature, and now it appeared that they were being battered again—this time by the Clintons. Their story goes back to 2010, when a massive 7.0 earthquake devastated the island, killing more than two hundred thousand people, leveling one hundred thousand homes, and leaving 1.5 million people destitute.

The devastating effect of the earthquake on a very poor nation provoked worldwide concern and inspired an outpouring of aid money intended to rebuild Haiti. Countries around the world, as well as private and philanthropic groups like the Red Cross and the Salvation Army, provided some $10.5 billion in aid, with $3.9 billion of it coming from the United States.

Haitians like Andre, however, noticed that very little of this aid money actually got to poor people in Haiti. Some projects championed by the Clintons, like the building of industrial parks and posh hotels, cost a great deal of money and offered scarce benefits to the truly needy. Port-au-Prince was supposed to be rebuilt; it was never rebuilt. Projects aimed at creating jobs proved to be bitter disappointments. Haitian unemployment remained high, largely undented by the funds that were supposed to pour into the country. Famine and illness continued to devastate the island nation.

The Haitians were initially sympathetic to the Clintons. One may say they believed in the message of "hope and change." With his customary overstatement, Bill told the media, "Wouldn't it be great if they become the first wireless nation in the world? They could, I'm telling you, they really could."[3]

I don't blame the Haitians for falling for it; Bill is one of the world's greatest story-tellers. He has fooled people far more sophisticated than the poor Haitians. Over time, however, the Haitians wised up. Whatever their initial expectations, many saw that much of the aid money seems never to have reached its destination; rather, it disappeared along the way.

Where did it go? It did not escape the attention of the Haitians that Bill Clinton was the designated UN representative for aid to Haiti. Following the earthquake, Bill Clinton had with media fanfare established the Haiti Reconstruction Fund. Meanwhile, his wife Hillary was the United States secretary of state. She was in charge of U.S. aid allocated to Haiti. Together the Clintons were the two most powerful people who controlled the flow of funds to Haiti from around the world.

The Haitian protesters noticed an interesting pattern involving the Clintons and the designation of how aid funds were used. They observed that a number of companies that received contracts in Haiti happened to be entities that made large donations to the Clinton Foundation. The Haitian contracts appeared less tailored to the needs of Haiti than to the needs of the companies that were performing the services. In sum, Haitian deals appeared to be a quid pro quo for filling the coffers of the Clintons.

For example, the Clinton Foundation selected Clayton Homes, a construction company owned by Warren Buffett's Berkshire Hathaway, to build temporary shelters in Haiti. Buffett is an active member of the Clinton Global Initiative who has donated generously to the Clintons as well as the Clinton Foundation. The contract was supposed to be given through the normal United Nations bidding process, with the deal going to the lowest bidder who met the project's standards. UN officials said, however, that the contract was never competitively bid for.

Clayton offered to build "hurricane-proof trailers" but what they actually delivered turned out to be a disaster. The trailers were structurally unsafe, with high levels of formaldehyde and insulation coming out of the walls. There were problems with mold and fumes. The stifling heat inside made Haitians sick and many of them abandoned the trailers because they were ill-constructed and unusable.

The Clintons also funneled $10 million in federal loans to a firm called InnoVida, headed by Clinton donor Claudio Osorio. Osorio had loaded its board with Clinton cronies, including longtime Clinton ally General Wesley Clark; Hillary's 2008 finance director Jonathan Mantz; and Democratic fundraiser Chris Korge who has helped raise millions for the Clintons.

Normally the loan approval process takes months or even years. But in this case, a government official wrote, "Former President Bill Clinton is personally in contact with the company to organize its logistical and support needs. And as Secretary of State, Hillary Clinton has made available State Department resources to assist with logistical arrangements."

InnoVida had not even provided an independently audited financial report that is normally a requirement for such applications. This

requirement, however, was waived. On the basis of the Clinton connection, InnoVida's application was fast-tracked and approved in two weeks.

The company, however, defaulted on the loan and never built any
houses. An investigation revealed that Osorio had diverted company
funds to pay for his Miami Beach mansion, his Maserati, and his Colorado ski chalet. He pleaded guilty to wire fraud and money laundering
in 2013, and is currently serving a twelve-year prison term on fraud
charges related to the loan.[4]

Several Clinton cronies showed up with Bill to a 2011 Housing Expo
that cost more than $2 million to stage. Bill Clinton said it would be a
model for the construction of thousands of homes in Haiti. In reality, no
homes have been built. A few dozen model units were constructed but
even they have not been sold. Rather, they are now abandoned and have
been taken over by squatters.

THE SCHOOLS THEY NEVER BUILT

The Clintons claim to have built schools in Haiti. But the *New York
Times* discovered that when it comes to the Clintons, "built" is a term
with a very loose interpretation. For example, the newspaper located a
school featured in the Clinton Foundation annual report as "built
through a Clinton Global Initiative Commitment to Action." In reality,
"The Clinton Foundation's sole direct contribution to the school was a
grant for an Earth Day celebration and tree-building activity."[5]

USAID contracts to remove debris in Port-au-Prince went to a Wash-
ington-based company named CHF International. The company's CEO
David Weiss, a campaign contributor to Hillary in 2008, was deputy
U.S. trade representative for North American Affairs during the Clinton
administration. The corporate secretary of the board, Lauri Fitz-Pegado,
served in a number of posts in the Clinton administration, including
assistant secretary of commerce.

USAID contracts also went to consulting firms like New York–based
Dalberg Global Development Advisors, which received a $1.5 million
contract to identify relocation sites for Haitians. This company is an

active participant and financial supporter of the Clinton Global Initiative. A later review by USAID's inspector general found that Dalberg did a terrible job, naming uninhabitable mountains with steep ravines as possible sites for Haitian rebuilding.

Foreign governments and foreign companies got Haitian deals in exchange for bankrolling the Clinton Foundation. The Clinton Foundation lists the Brazilian construction firm OAS and the InterAmerican Development Bank (IDB) as donors that have given it between $1 billion and $5 billion.

The IDB receives funding from the State Department, and some of this funding was diverted to OAS for Haitian road-building contracts. Yet an IDB auditor, Mariela Antiga, complained that the contracts were padded with "excessive costs" to build roads "no one needed." Antiga also alleged that IDB funds were going to a construction project on private land owned by former Haitian president Rene Preval—a Clinton buddy—and several of his cronies. For her efforts to expose corruption, Antiga was promptly instructed by the IDB to pack her bags and leave Haiti.[6]

In 2011, the Clinton Foundation brokered a deal with Digicel, a cell phone service provider seeking to gain access to the Haitian market. The Clintons arranged to have Digicel receive millions in U.S. taxpayer money to provide mobile phones. The USAID Food for Peace program, which the State Department administered through Hillary aide Cheryl Mills, distributed Digicel phones free to Haitians.

Digicel didn't just make money off the U.S. taxpayer; it also made money off the Haitians. When Haitians used the phones, either to make calls or transfer money, they paid Digicel for the service. Haitians using Digicel's phones also became automatically enrolled in Digicel's mobile program. By 2012, Digicel had taken over three-quarters of the cell phone market in Haiti.

Digicel is owned by Denis O'Brien, a close friend of the Clintons. O'Brien secured three speaking engagements in his native Ireland that paid $200,000 apiece. These engagements occurred right at the time that Digicel was making its deal with the U.S. State Department. O'Brien has also donated lavishly to the Clinton Foundation, giving between $1 million and $5 million sometime in 2010–2011.

Coincidentally the United States government paid Digicel $45 million to open a hotel in Port-au-Prince. Now perhaps it could be argued that Haitians could use a high-priced hotel to attract foreign investors and provide jobs for locals. Thus far, however, this particular hotel seems to employ only a few dozen locals, which hardly justifies the sizable investment that went into building it. Moreover, there are virtually no foreign investors; the rooms are mostly unoccupied; the ones that are taken seem mainly for the benefit of Digicel's visiting teams.[7]

In addition, the Clintons got their cronies to build Caracol Industrial Park, a six-hundred-acre garment factory that was supposed to make clothes for export to the United States and create—according to Bill Clinton—one hundred thousand new jobs in Haiti. The project was funded by the U.S. government and cost hundreds of millions in taxpayer money, the largest single allocation of U.S. relief aid.

Yet Caracol has proven a massive failure. First, the industrial park was built on farmland and the farmers had to be moved off their property. Many of them feel they were pushed out and inadequately compensated. Some of them lost their livelihoods. Second, Caracol was supposed to include twenty-five thousand homes for Haitian employees; in the end, the GAO reports that only around six thousand homes were built. Third, Caracol has created five thousand jobs, less than 10 percent of the jobs promised. Fourth, Caracol is exporting very few products and most of the facility is abandoned. People stand outside every day looking for work, but there is no work to be had, as Haiti's unemployment rate hovers around 40 percent.

The Clintons say Caracol can still be salvaged. But Former Haitian Prime Minister Jean Bellerive says, "I believe the momentum to attract people there in a massive way is past. Today, it has failed."[8] Still, Bellerive's standard of success may not be the same one used by the Clintons. After all, the companies that built Caracol with U.S. taxpayer money have done fine—even if poor Haitians have seen few of the benefits.

Then there is the strange and somehow predictable involvement of Hillary Clinton's brother Hugh Rodham. Rodham put in an application for $22 million from the Clinton Foundation to build homes on ten thousand acres of land that he said a "guy in Haiti" had "donated" to him.

"I deal through the Clinton Foundation," Rodham told the *New York Times*. "I hound my brother-in-law because it's his fund that we're going to get our money from." Rodham said he expected to net $1 million personally on the deal. Unfortunately, his application didn't go through.[9]

Rodham had better luck, however, on a second Haitian deal. He mysteriously found himself on the advisory board of a U.S. mining company called VCS. This by itself is odd because Rodham's resume lists no mining experience; rather, Rodham is a former private detective and prison guard.

The mining company, however, seems to have recognized Rodham's value. They brought him on board in October 2013 to help secure a valuable gold mining permit in Haiti. Rodham was promised a "finder's fee" if he could land the contract. Sure enough, he did. For the first time in fifty years, Haiti awarded two new gold mining permits and one of them went to the company that had hired Hillary's brother.

The deal provoked outrage in the Haitian Senate. "Neither Bill Clinton nor the brother of Hillary Clinton are individuals who share the interest of the Haitian people," said Haitian mining representative Samuel Nesner. "They are part of the elite class who are operating to exploit the Haitian people."[10]

Is this too harsh a verdict? I wouldn't go so far as to say the Clintons don't care about Haiti. Yet it seems clear that Haitian welfare is not their priority. Their priority is, well, themselves. The Clintons seem to believe in Haitian reconstruction and Haitian investment as long as these projects match their own private economic interests. They have steered the rebuilding of Haiti in a way that provides maximum benefit to themselves.

No wonder the Clintons refused to meet with the Haitian protesters. Each time the protesters showed up, the Clintons were nowhere to be seen. They have never directly addressed the Haitians' claims. Strangely enough, they have never been required to do so. The progressive media scarcely covered the Haitian protest. Somehow the idea of Haitian black people calling out the Clintons as aid money thieves did not appeal to the grand pooh-bahs at CBS News, the *New York Times*, and NPR.

For most Democrats, the topic is both touchy and distasteful. It's one thing to rob from the rich but quite another to rob from the poorest of the poor. Some of the Democratic primary support for Bernie Sanders was undoubtedly due to Democrats' distaste over the financial shenanigans of the Clintons. Probably these Democrats considered the Clintons to be unduly grasping and opportunistic, an embarrassment to the great traditions of the Democratic Party.

THE ELUSIVE FOUNDER

But what are the great traditions of the Democratic Party? Is the behavior of the Clintons unique, or is it part of a pattern that can be traced through Democratic Party history? This question cannot be answered without understanding what this party is, where it came from. Oddly enough the origins of the Democratic Party are shrouded in myth. Who is the actual founder of the party that we know today as the Democrats?

We all know that Abraham Lincoln is the founder of the Republican Party. Democrats sometimes attempt to claim Lincoln. Obama took a train journey from Illinois to Washington, D.C., to be inaugurated president in 2009, just as Lincoln had nearly a century and a half earlier. Obama took his oath of office on the Bible that Lincoln used at his first inauguration.

These symbolic appropriations of Lincoln are commonplace in politics; at the same time, they are deeply misleading. Let's just say that Obama is no Lincoln. Lincoln was a founder of the Republican Party and the first Republican president. His values and beliefs were radically opposed to Obama's. If Lincoln were alive to see today's Democrats, he would likely recognize them to be the same type of dirty rotten scoundrels that he encountered among Democrats in his own day. More about this in the next chapter.

But if Lincoln was a founder of the Republican Party, who started the Democratic Party? Here we get a range of confusing answers. According to the television network PBS, "The Democratic Party was formed in 1792, when supporters of Thomas Jefferson began using the name Republicans, or Jefferson Republicans, to emphasize its anti-aristocratic policies."[11]

Now this on its face is strange. How can the Democratic Party trace itself back to a man and his followers who called themselves Republicans? Right away we suspect that progressive PBS is pulling off a scam. Jefferson and his supporters were not the actual founders of the Democratic Party.

First, as PBS concedes, Jefferson's party—founded to challenge the Federalist Party—called itself the Republicans. Later Jefferson's party was called the Democratic Republican Party. Still, this nomenclature hardly establishes any meaningful kinship with either today's Republican or Democratic parties.

Jefferson's party stood for rural agricultural interests against urban commercial interests represented by Hamilton and the Federalists. In a sense, this was the ancient clash between the "country" and the "city." Today's Democrats don't represent rural people against city people; on the contrary, rural America heavily supports the GOP and the greatest stronghold of Democratic votes is the cities.

Jefferson's party also represented states' rights in contrast to the Federalists who represented the rights of the national government. Once again, today's Democrats have little sympathy for Jefferson on that score. If forced to choose, they would undoubtedly be on the Federalist side of that clash. Today's Democrats want a strong, centralized national government, which was anathema to Jefferson.

Now in one respect, Jefferson does harbinger a proclivity that would later come to be associated with the Democrats—especially with the

Clintons. Thomas Jefferson seems to have taken sexual liberties with a young female slave, Sally Hemings, and had several children by her. The issue, for Jefferson as for Bill Clinton, in his notorious sexual misconduct as governor of Arkansas and president of the United States, is not extramarital sex or having an affair. The issue is abuse of power.

In 1787, young Sally Hemings was dispatched from Virginia to Paris where Jefferson was serving as America's foreign minister. According to a blacksmith who worked on Jefferson's plantation, Sally was "very handsome" and "mighty near white" with "long straight hair running down her back."

While Sally's main duties involved looking after Jefferson's daughter Polly, she was, according to a later account given by her son Madison, also charged with "taking care of Mister Jefferson's chamber and wardrobe." Hemings was only fourteen when she arrived in Paris. This was when Jefferson seems to have made his first moves on her.

No, this was not a love relationship between consenting adults; it was a reprehensible abuse of position and power. The fact that it was fairly common among slave owners does not make it less reprehensible. So while there is no straight line between Jefferson's party and the Democrats, there is a tradition of sex abuse that connects Thomas Jefferson with Bill Clinton. In this respect it may be worth noting that Clinton's middle name is Jefferson.

"I did not have sexual relations with that woman." This is Bill Clinton, famously lying about what he did. He didn't get away with his lie. Jefferson maintained complete silence about his relationship with Hemings. He almost got away with it. Until the late 1990s, Jefferson's impregnation of Hemings was considered a foul rumor. It was traced to a scandal-mongering journalist named James Callendar, who in 1802 published an allegation in a Richmond newspaper that Jefferson had borne children by a slave "concubine."

Recent scholarship, however, has established to a high degree of likelihood Jefferson's paternity. In fact, DNA tests conducted in the 1990s show that Jefferson sired six children by Hemings.[12] At first the mainstream community of Jefferson biographers, as well as the foundation that runs Jefferson's family home at Monticello, resisted this evidence. The skeptics said evidence could point to any male in Jefferson's family being responsible for paternity. Accusing fingers were pointed at Jefferson's son.[13]

But in two important books, historian Annette Gordon-Reed has shown that Sally gave birth at times when only Jefferson could be the father. There is further circumstantial evidence that points to Jefferson's paternity. He named Sally's children after people important to him, like Madison. He personally ensured that Hemings received special treatment among the slaves. He freed all her children and some of them—being light-skinned—lived out their lives as white people. (The other slaves on Jefferson's plantation were auctioned off to pay off his debts.)

Today historians concede that the oral history of the Hemings family is correct: they can trace their lineage right back to Sally and Thomas Jefferson. Even Monticello, the foundation that administers Jefferson's family home, acknowledges Jefferson's paternity.[14] Whether William Jefferson Clinton sired any children with the various women he abused is not known. What is known is that in December 1997 he got Gennifer Flowers pregnant and gave her $200 in cash to have an abortion.[15]

Back to our main point: If Jefferson didn't found the Democratic Party, who did? Another common answer we hear is Franklin D. Roosevelt. Now this is a better answer because FDR was certainly a Democrat, and he inaugurated an important phase in the development of the modern Democratic Party.

Even so, was FDR the first Democrat? FDR was elected in 1932, so was there no Democratic Party in the early twentieth century, or in the nineteenth century? Of course there was. The Democratic Party actually predated the Republican Party.

THE FIRST DEMOCRAT

The real founder of the modern Democratic Party was Andrew Jackson. Jackson, an orphan from Appalachia, rose from obscurity to become America's most celebrated general and military hero after George Washington. He won the presidency by a landslide in 1828 and an even bigger one in 1832. His proteges dominated the Democratic Party for half a century, until the Civil War. During his lifetime Jackson was immensely popular with ordinary people, earning him the reputation of being the common man's president.

One might expect the Democrats—who even today purport to be the party of the common man—to embrace Jackson and acknowledge his paternity of their party. This, however, is not the case. So why do they distance themselves from Jackson? Why do progressives consider him such an embarrassment?

Not only do many on the Left refuse to acknowledge Jackson's founding role in the Democratic Party, they also want to kick him off the $20 bill where his face currently appears. Progressives want to see him replaced on the currency with the woman who ran the Underground Railroad, Harriet Tubman.

To some degree, the progressive objective seems clear. Jackson, after all, owned some three hundred slaves during his lifetime. At one time he ran a plantation that had 150 slaves. So Jackson's expulsion seems consistent with the general progressive antipathy toward slavery. The same antipathy explains the choice of Tubman, who was a female abolitionist. Moreover, Tubman was a woman. If the Democrats are going to place a woman, Hillary, on the presidential ticket, why not also have a woman, Tubman, on the currency?

Even so, the proposal is interesting because Jackson was a Democrat—the founding father of the Democratic Party—while Tubman was a Republican. Admittedly progressives have no intention of highlighting that fact about Tubman; indeed it goes virtually unmentioned in the news reports. The progressive media is not comfortable with a female black abolitionist representing the Republican Party while a white male slave owner represents the Democratic Party.

Yet Jackson was not unique in owning slaves; Jefferson did too. So what makes Jackson especially embarrassing for Democrats? Why are they so eager to disavow an individual from humble origins who rose to such fantastic heights, in the process successfully representing and delivering for the common man? Why don't Democrats cherish this aspect of their party's founder?

In this chapter, I will show that Jackson has become *persona non grata* precisely because of how he delivered for the common man. He did so by stealing land from the native Indians and then making it available for cheap purchase by white people, thus making those people beholden to Jackson and his Democratic Party.

Now it is shameful enough to use military power, political intimidation, and trickery to seize and occupy other people's land. It is even more disgraceful to do so while pretending to be the friends of those you are stealing from, giving them the impression you are helping them. Jackson mastered the art of posing as the ally of Native Americans while robbing them blind.

Today's Democrats in this sense are heirs of Jackson. They too appropriate resources from others and distribute them among Democratic constituencies, trading favors for votes. They too pose as the friends of those they are stealing from, justifying their confiscations as good for the victims and good for the country.

Jackson started this racket by seizing Indian land and then using it to make white settlers a bargain they could not refuse. He was, in a sense, a merchant trading in stolen goods. In this respect he exposes the low, disgraceful origins of Democratic success with the common man. No wonder Democrats are eager to bury this record, or at least foist it on someone else.

The second, less-known story of Andrew Jackson concerns the way he enriched himself through his land dealing and land stealing. Most historians ignore this story. Arthur Schlesinger's 1945 biography *Age of Jackson* says nothing on the subject. Neither does Sean Wilentz's 2005 biography *Andrew Jackson*. Jon Meacham's Pulitzer Prize–winning biography *American Lion*, published in 2008, continues the progressive conspiracy of silence. Shhh!

FROM JACKSON TO HILLARY

The full story, however, is told in Steve Inskeep's recent book *Jacksonland*, which I will rely on for my subsequent account. "Jackson managed national security affairs in a way that matched his interest in land development," Inskeep notes. "He shaped his real estate investments to complement his official duties, and performed his official duties in a way that benefited his real estate interests."[16]

As Inskeep shows, typically Jackson would set his eye on a large tract of Indian territory. Then, even before chasing the Indians off that territory, Jackson would send surveyors in to assess the land in terms of its real estate value. Jackson would then alert his cronies, and together they would make a bid to purchase that real estate. In this way Jackson became a Tennessee plantation magnate and one of the largest slave owners in his home state.

Jackson was a ruthless con artist who became fabulously wealthy by trading on his political office. Sound familiar? His career illustrates the familiar Democratic story of leaders making sure that when there are spoils to be distributed, the lion's share goes to them. Obviously not all Democrats use their political positions to get rich, but a number of them, from Jackson himself to Lyndon Johnson to Bill Clinton, certainly did.

Jackson's true modern counterpart—as you have probably figured out by now—is Hillary Clinton. Their stories are closely parallel. If Hillary started out "dead broke," as she claims she did, after her husband's presidency, so did Jackson begin with nothing as an orphan. Neither of them became successful through starting and running a successful business. Rather, they cashed in on their political influence. Just as Jackson made money on land deals stemming from his success as a general, Hillary too figured out ways to enrich herself through her government positions, becoming fabulously wealthy in just a few years.

It may seem that Hillary "succeeded" through foreign policy while Jackson "succeeded" through domestic policy. Actually, they both succeeded through foreign policy. Let's remember that Jackson was dealing with the Indian tribes who were, as a matter of law, separate nations. Consequently we may accurately say that the current nominee of the Democratic Party is a worthy successor of its founder. The roots of the Clinton Foundation can be found in the land-stealing policies of Andrew Jackson.

Unsurprisingly, it is whitewash time for Democratic historians and pundits. This whitewash takes several forms. First, the Democrats accuse "America," not Jackson and his successors, of abusing the Indians. Specifically, they blast the earliest Europeans to arrive on the American continent, and the Founders, for dispossessing the native Indians. The goal is to treat Jackson as simply a bad white American, instead of a bad Democrat.

Second, the Democrats pretend to have no connection with the thievery of Jackson and his fellow Democrats. They might acknowledge that Jackson cleared the Indians out of several states in order to build constituencies of grateful whites who then settled those states. Faced with facts, they may also concede that Jackson enriched himself and his cronies through his land stealing.

Even so, today's Democrats profess to be shocked, shocked to see their fellow Democrats engaged in such behavior. That was then, they suggest, and this is now. What does this have to do with us today? What does it have to do with Hillary? No resemblance to the current frontrunner of the Democratic Party is even suspected.

Yet as we saw with the Clintons in Haiti, the tradition of Jacksonian piracy is alive and well in today's Democratic Party. Bernie Sanders may have the same Jacksonian objectives as Hillary, but only Hillary seems capable of pulling them off. Part of the reason Democrats prefer Hillary over Bernie is that she is a more effective Jacksonian, which is to say, a more ruthless and successful thief.

BLAMING AMERICA

Returning to Jackson, let's examine the progressive narrative that faults the white man in general—rather than this specific one—for dispossessing and oppressing the native Indians. Democrats begin their tale of Indian tears with two calumnies, the first aimed at the first Europeans to arrive in America, the second aimed at the American Founders.

So what about the settlers? The first settlers—famously christened the "white man"—are accused by progressive Democrats of wiping out large segments of the native population, even to the point of genocide. Genocide, however, implies an intention to exterminate a population. Did Columbus or the early settlers attempt this? They did not. Certainly there were sporadic clashes between the white Europeans and the natives. But there was also a good deal of cooperation between them. The historical record is mixed.

How, then, did the natives perish in such large numbers? Reportedly the native Indian population declined by more than 50 percent in the first century of exposure to the white man. The reason, historian William McNeill shows, is because native Indians contracted from the white man diseases to which they had no immunity.

This is tragedy on a grand scale, but it's not genocide. In his book *Plagues and Peoples*, McNeill points out that just over a century earlier the white man himself contracted the bubonic plague and other diseases that wiped out a third of the population of Europe. These diseases came from Asia, and the white man had no immunity to them.[17] No one calls this genocide—because it isn't.

What about the Founders? Interestingly we see that white attitudes toward the Indian in the eighteenth century were largely sympathetic. The Founders did not consider Native Americans to be inherently inferior to the white man. Rather, they held that the primitive circumstances of the native were responsible for what was perceived to be his barbaric state. They were confident that education and civilization would raise the typical Indian to the level of the white man.

In his *Notes on the State of Virginia*, Jefferson praised the intelligence, courage, and integrity of the Indians. They are, he wrote, "formed in mind as well as in body on the same model as Homo sapiens Europaeus." Jefferson rejected proposals to dispossess the Indians of their land on the pretext that they were savages or barbarians. Rather, Jefferson urged that whites include the Indians in American civilization. He expressed the hope that the Indians, rather than clinging to their old ways, would "incorporate with us as citizens of the United States."[18]

Indeed, several leading figures of the founding period, such as Patrick Henry, John Marshall, and Thomas Jefferson, proposed intermarriage between whites and Indians as a way to integrate the natives into the American mainstream. "What they thought impossible with respect to blacks," political scientist Ralph Lerner writes, "was seen as highly desirable with respect to Indians."[19]

America's first president, George Washington, respected the Indians. As a military officer defending the Virginia frontier, he considered the Indian tribes he encountered so formidable in warfare that in his view only other Indians could defeat them. Whenever possible, he did his best to ally with Indians.

As president, Washington was not opposed to trading with Indians or the purchase of Indian land, but he wanted these acquisitions to be secured by treaty, not by conflict. He insisted that white settlements bypass Indian territories, leaving them unmolested. "It was a vision," historian Joseph Ellis writes, "in which the westward expansion of an American empire coexisted alongside the preservation of the original Americans."[20]

As president, Jefferson openly coveted Indian land for settlement by whites moving west. But Jefferson too sought to obtain this land through treaty and trade. He said, in effect, that they have land and we have merchandise and so both sides can benefit from the other. In one of his public messages, Jefferson commended "the wisdom of exchanging what they can spare and we want for what we can spare and they want." So, concluded Jefferson, let's make deals with the Indians to buy their land in exchange for food, medicine, clothing, and cash.

Jefferson knew, of course, that his administration had the power to seize the land. Treaties can be made; treaties can be broken. But Jefferson was unwilling to do that. His mindset in this respect is not pure. Jefferson in private correspondence admitted that Indians were reckless with money, and they had little estimation of the real value of their land. They were susceptible to going into debt, which might then compel them to sell land to settle their obligations. If he was unwilling to openly contravene existing treaties, Jefferson was not above obtaining land by exploiting the ignorance and profligacy of Native Americans.[21]

BARGAINER VS. THIEF

Still, Jefferson appears as an angel when we set him beside Andrew Jackson. The difference is one between a hard bargainer and an outright thief. Jefferson was a wheeler-dealer but he was not a murderer. Jackson seems to have had little aversion to killing Indians, especially when they stood in the way of his acquisitions. Finally Jefferson didn't enrich himself through his policies; Jackson used them to become one of the wealthiest men in the country.

Jackson's net worth when he died is estimated at $100 million in today's dollars. Since Jackson always stole in large quantities, it would be more fitting to have him on the $100 bill rather than the $20 bill. Jackson must be counted as one of America's richest presidents, almost as rich as the Clintons. Democrats today host an annual Jefferson-Jackson dinner, but if they were doing truth in advertising they would drop Jefferson and stick with Jackson.

In order to understand Jackson's founding shenanigans, it's best to begin with his inauguration day in March 1829. Thanks to the rhapsodic portraits of progressive historians, from Arthur Schlesinger to Sean Wilentz, this event has gone down in American history as the "people's day." For Wilentz, the symbolism of the day was Jackson's placing himself "on the side of egalitarianism and against privilege." Wilentz argues that "therein lies his claim to historical greatness."[22]

While previous inaugurations were sober, dignified affairs, this one was pure chaos. People broke down barriers and roamed the White House lawn, they swarmed into the ceremonial rooms of the White House, they soiled the couches and broke china, people were climbing in and out of windows, things got so out of hand that the newly-elected president had to leave and spend the night at the National Hotel on Pennsylvania Avenue.

This seems like pure plebian crassness, and it could never happen today. Today's Democrats may claim to be the party of the people but this does not extend to having them show up *en masse* to black-tie events. I cannot see Hillary at her inauguration putting up with random hordes swarming through the Blue Room, the Red Room, and the Oval Office. If you haven't made a big donation to the campaign, you can probably forget about getting your inaugural invitation. But in Jackson's time it was different, and some progressive historians treat his inauguration as a special democratic moment in which Jackson showed himself truly a man of the people.

But what was it about Jackson that made the people love him so much and feel comfortable enough to treat his new house as their house? Part of the answer is that Jackson was a frontiersman who had proved himself a military hero. Even though he was barely a teenager, Jackson fought with irregular troops in the Revolutionary War. Later he led an intrepid band of Tennessee militiamen, together with slaves, free blacks, pirates, and Indians, to victory over the British in the Battle of New Orleans in the War of 1812.

These exploits are somewhat ambiguous. As a brash fourteen-year-old, Jackson was captured by the British before he could do much fighting, and contracted smallpox soon afterward. Thus the notion that he was a "hardened veteran" in his early teens seems to be a product of hagiography, not history. Jackson surely deserved his reputation for toughness in triumph over the British in New Orleans; in this sense, his nickname Old Hickory seems fully justified.

Yet even this New Orleans triumph is vitiated somewhat when we recall that he was, even then, strong-arming his Indian compatriots to part with their land. In a manner that anticipates the intrigues and purges of the Clintons, Jackson seems to have been almost as dangerous to his allies as he was to his enemies.

Jackson's personal life, while unexceptional for a frontiersman, was nevertheless below the standard that Americans had previously expected from their foremost citizen. Arriving in Nashville in 1788, Jackson took up with a woman, Rachel Donelson Robards. Later it turned out that

Robards was separated from her husband but due to various complications the couple had never been legally divorced.

When Jackson ran for president in 1824 and again in 1828, his opponents accused him of wife stealing and bigamy. The accusations were unfair because Jackson did not know about Rachel's divorce complications. Eventually Rachel got a legal divorce and she and Jackson were formally married. Still, an aura of controversy surrounded this issue throughout Jackson's presidency.

Jackson was also known as a peevish, hot-tempered man who got into fights and provoked fights when there were none to be had. Fights in the Old South could easily escalate into lethal duels. Jackson almost got into a duel with Tennessee Governor John Sevier—a veteran of the American Revolution—in a squabble over who should head the state militia.

He dueled over a personal issue with another man, Charles Dickinson, and killed him. Jackson too was wounded, taking a bullet in his chest that remained lodged there for the rest of his life. Men of this rough mettle are often admired but rarely loved, so the mystery of Jackson's inaugural popularity remains to be solved.

AL CAPONE, MAN OF THE PEOPLE

I believe we can understand what was going on with Jackson and his inaugural mob if we fast forward about a century and envision a similar scene, this one involving the mafia chieftain Al Capone entering the Chicago baseball stadium. When Capone did this, the crowd would go into a frenetic roar, and people would throw their hats up and yell, "Big Al! Big Al! Big Al!"

Capone, of course, was a mobster, so why was the crowd for him? The reason is that he was *their* mobster. As many in Chicago saw it, Capone was merely feeding their insatiable appetite for liquor, gambling tables, and women. Prostitution and gambling were illegal at the time, as was alcohol. Still, there was a demand for those things and Capone provided them. Naturally, the people were appreciative. They wanted, and he delivered. He may have gone around the law to do it but was there any other way to achieve the same result? Clearly not.

The reason for Jackson's inaugural popularity was that he was a nineteenth-century Al Capone. The people celebrated in Jackson's White House because he was responsible for them obtaining the land to build their own houses. Jackson became a "man of the people" by providing them with something they wanted that they could not secure for themselves, namely, the land belonging to the Native Americans. Jackson was the consummate thief, and his people appreciated that quality in him.

In this case Jackson didn't do things exactly the Capone way. He didn't really go around the law; he made the law. He was a law unto himself. That's because he had the troops and the guns to make the Indians do his bidding. Of course Jackson wasn't getting the Indians off their land simply because he wanted to help poor whites to have their own land. What Jackson also wanted was the votes of those people. He was willing to make land available to them knowing that this would make them into his lifelong supporters and constituents.

To restate Jefferson's formulation, Jackson had something that poor whites wanted—namely land—and they had something he wanted—namely their political support. Jackson thus established the Democratic Party's vote-getting strategy for nearly two centuries right up to the present day: rob Peter to pay Paul.

In order to win the votes of poor white settlers, Jackson had to prove that he was more ruthless than they were. This was necessary because Jackson had to convince them that he could deliver something that they could not obtain for themselves, namely the possessions of some very powerful and warlike Indian nations. In the early nineteenth century, the Deep South region south of Tennessee and all the way to Florida was occupied by several tribes: the Chickasaw, the Choctaw, the Creek, the Cherokee, and the Seminole.

Of these, the Creek were known to be the most recalcitrant. Jackson proved his mettle by showing he could mow them down and massacre them into submission, earning his subsequent reputation as an "Indian killer." Today we may wince at the title, but it was considered a compliment among Jackson's Democratic supporters.

Just as much as his exploits with the British, Jackson's popularity was fired by his actions against the Creeks at Horseshoe Bend. In 1813, a militant band of Creeks called the Red Sticks attacked Fort Mims in the Mississippi Territory and slaughtered several hundred whites. Eyewitnesses who arrived on the scene days later found the victims scalped, including women and children. Today we think of native Indians as disconsolate, victimized people but we should not forget that they could be bloodthirsty warriors, and this is how Jackson and many other frontiersmen experienced them.

Jackson—by this time the general of the Tennessee militia—issued a proclamation calling for retaliation. Among those who responded were the frontiersman Davy Crockett. Jackson also recruited allies from other Indian tribes, notably the Cherokee leader John Ross, who was descended from Indian and Scots-Irish ancestry. Jackson's militia surprised the Creek attackers and routed them. In Davy Crockett's account, "We shot them like dogs, and then set the house on fire, and burned it up with the warriors in it."[23]

Jackson's troops then went on a rampage, torching Creek villages and slaughtering villagers. At Horseshoe Bend in the Mississippi Territory (now southern Alabama) they settled into a hill overlooking a Creek camp and aimed their cannon at the Creeks gathered there. While Jackson apologists would later speak of a Battle of Horseshoe Bend, in reality the Creeks there were refugees, not warriors; they were seeking shelter from the crossfire.

Jackson's force wiped them out. As he put it in a letter to his wife Rachel, "It was dark before we finished killing them." Jackson estimated that beyond the 557 corpses on land, an additional three hundred Indians were "buried in their watry grave." Jackson's men cut off the noses of dead Indians as they counted the bodies. Afterward there were few regrets, one of Jackson's soldiers chuckling that he had killed a boy "five or six years of age" for the reason that "he would have become an Indian someday."[24]

Jackson's Horseshoe Bend massacre could be considered a case of frontiersman "excess" but in this case Jackson *intended* to go too far. He wanted to terrorize the Indian tribes in the region, and he largely succeeded. After Horseshoe Bend, Jackson found the other tribes much more pliant.

Remarkably Jackson after his victory demanded land concessions not only from the Creeks but also from the Indian tribes allied with him. They had little choice but to submit. Altogether, his "prize" amounted to twenty-two million acres of saleable real estate in southern Georgia and central Alabama. Those sales, Jackson remarked to one of his cronies, John Coffee, would someday yield him a whole lot of votes.

While Jackson had few qualms about using force, he preferred, like his successor Democrats today, to rely on intimidation and deceit if he could thereby get the results he wanted. One might expect that the Choctaw would receive decent treatment from Jackson, given that they fought alongside him in the War of 1812. The Cherokee, headed by John Ross, felt sure Jackson would be their advocate, since Ross and others were part of Jackson's expeditionary campaign against the British and the Creek. Soon these tribes realized that Jackson was just as intent on stealing from them as he was from tribes that he fought against.

A PRETENDED FRIEND AND ALLY

Jackson cheated his native Indian allies by pretending to be their friend. He would often write them and refer to himself as their Father or their Great Father. Whenever he proposed a measure that harmed them, he usually insisted, doing his best to imitate Indian language, "Beyond the great river Mississippi, where a part of your nation has gone, your father has provided a country large enough for all of you, and advises you to remove to it." Or, on another occasion: "It is for your nation's good, and your father requests you to hear his counsel."[25]

Biographer Jon Meacham accepts this at face value; he speculates that Jackson saw himself in this paternal way because he was orphaned at fifteen and never knew his own father.[26] But if Jackson was acting as a parent to the Indians, he was certainly an abusive parent.

Contrary to what he said, Jackson wasn't offering any counsel to the Indians; he was offering them a *fait accompli*. The Indians could either surrender or be crushed. Inskeep wryly notes that "Jackson defined his parental duty to natives in a way that matched his desire to clear land for white settlement."[27]

John Ross, the Cherokee leader, was a shrewd politician who understood treaties and legal documents. What he could not fathom was the bottomless cunning and trickery of the man he was dealing with. Jackson read the Indian treaties in much the same way that Democrats and progressives today read the U.S. Constitution. They care little about what it says; they interpret it to mean what they want it to mean. Jackson didn't have any judicial authority but he usually didn't need it. He had troops to enforce his view of the documents and that was sufficient.

Ross did score one big, though temporary, victory over Jackson. In 1814, in the aftermath of Horseshoe Bend, Jackson imposed a treaty on the Indians—both his Creek enemies and his Chickasaw allies—which effectively turned the south bank of the Tennessee River over to the federal government. In this case Jackson intended the land to benefit someone near and dear to him, namely, himself.

Jackson had a whole system worked out for how to benefit personally from federal land acquisitions from the Indians. First, he appointed surveyors at government expense to mark the boundaries of the property, thus establishing its title and availability for sale. Jackson's favorite surveyor was his own business associate John Coffee.

Sometimes, though, he used other agents. In a typical correspondence, one agent, in a letter marked "Private," informed Jackson, "My Dear General, We have succeeded in acquiring an accurate knowledge of all the sections of good lands to be sold." He drew Jackson's attention to four sections of land that "would form a most desirable establishment for your old age."[28]

Knowing that the presence of surveyors might upset the Indians who still occupied the land, Jackson warned them that if they harmed the surveyor, the U.S. government would attack them and seize their lands. In case they didn't believe him, Jackson recruited mounted gunmen to ensure security from Indians who might attempt to protect their own property.

Then, as soon as the federal government put the land on the market, Jackson bid on it. He did exactly that with the Tennessee River Bank. Unknown to him, however, Ross and his fellow Cherokees were during this time in Washington, D.C., making their own claims before the federal government. This was hardly unusual at the time—Chickasaws, Creeks, and Cherokees often made conflicting and overlapping claims to the same land.

In 1816, Jackson was ready to take profitable possession of the south bank of the Tennessee when he received a stunning notification from Washington. Basically, the U.S. government had decided that it couldn't, after all, sell that land. It didn't belong to the Creek or the Chickasaw. Rather, it belonged to the Cherokee—John Ross's tribe. Jackson had been improperly laying claim to two million acres!

Outraged at President Madison, Jackson wrote him a fiery letter insisting the Cherokees "never had the least semblance of claim" to the land and accusing the president of "wantonly surrendering" land that was of "incalculable value" to the United States.

Remarkably Jackson was accusing Madison of ignoring national security. His argument was that it jeopardized the security interest of the United States to have hostile Indian nations within the geographical land mass of the country where whites lived. I think Jackson was sincere in his patriotism and believed this argument when he made it. Still, it is hard to escape notice that this land was also of immense financial and political value to him personally.

Jackson used his political connections to try to reverse the Madison administration's ruling. He stirred up land-seeking whites from his home county to deluge the government with protest letters. This correspondence urged the Madison administration to drive the Indians farther west so that white citizens could travel without "the risk of being murdered at every wigwam by some drunken savage."[29]

BUY LOW, SELL HIGH

Jackson was smarting from his defeat—not merely a humiliation, but a blow to his pocketbook—but the Cherokee maneuver would prove the first, and last, time he was beaten by the Indians. Soon Jackson convinced the Madison administration to give him the right to negotiate with the Cherokees to buy some of the land in question. Jackson implemented a new, and this time successful, rip-off scheme.

Jackson's first step was to bribe the Cherokee chiefs. Each of them received "presents" from Jackson that ranged from $50 to $100. Jackson also used threats and intimidation against Cherokee holdouts. He and his associate John Coffee warned Cherokee leaders that if they failed to sell their land, then white settlers would take it for nothing.

Jackson obviously had no intention of offering military protection to the Cherokee against these white intruders. Jackson's offer to the Cherokee was: take my money and leave, and then your safety will be guaranteed. Many Cherokee dejectedly agreed to depart from the lands on which they and their ancestors had lived for hundreds if not thousands of years.

As soon as this happened, Inskeep reports, "Jackson and his friends moved to take advantage. The scale of their gain has rarely, if ever, been calculated. Many real estate records from the era have been lost. But records that survive show that after 1816, the names of Andrew Jackson, his relatives, and his two closest business associates appeared on the titles to more than forty-five thousand acres of newly opened Alabama land. Most was in the Tennessee Valley."[30]

The U.S. government opened a land office in Huntsville, Alabama, to sell the newly acquired land. Jackson was ready, along with his associate John Coffee. While both were already quite wealthy, they needed more money to make the large purchases they coveted. So they went to a wealthy investor named James Jackson, a longtime friend of Coffee and Andrew Jackson, and together the three of them formed a business partnership "to purchase or enter lands in the Alabama Territory."

Jackson also teamed up separately with his brother-in-law, John Donelson, who brought a group of Philadelphia investors. While Jackson certainly intended to enrich his relatives and cronies, every one of these deals was structured to provide maximum benefit to Andrew Jackson.

Inskeep reports in *Jacksonland* that in order to camouflage the scale of his investments, Jackson put the land that he bought into other people's names. For instance, he listed three tracts of land on the south side of the river in the name of Andrew Jackson Hutchings, an orphaned relative of his wife Rachel. "More than twenty-two hundred acres were purchased under the name of William Donelson, Rachel Jackson's nephew. William Donelson was also the registered name for the purchaser of thirteen town lots in Coldwater, the former Indian village at the bottom of Muscle Shoals."

At times Jackson acted alone. When a large plot came up for auction at Muscle Shoals, Jackson leaped up and offered the minimum bid. There were many other bidders, but recognizing Jackson among their number, no one else raised his hand. Jackson was elated. "This section I bought at two dollars per acre," he later wrote, "no person bidding against me, and as soon as I bid, hailed by the unanimous shouts of a numerous & mixed multitude." Jackson declared that he found this "gratifying, as it was an approval of my official acts."[31] Old Hand Jackson knew the score: he was the one who created the whole racket, so naturally he expected others to let him have a piece of it.

In 1818, Jackson spied a real estate opportunity in Florida. The opportunity was created by marauding Indians conducting raids from Spanish Florida. The Monroe administration sent Jackson to Florida to stop the raids. Jackson declared his purpose to "chastise" the Indians, which in his parlance meant to kill them. Although he had been specifically instructed to deal with the Indians and not occupy Spanish land, Jackson entered West Florida, captured Pensacola, appointed a governor there, and started collecting taxes.

Jackson's illicit action caused a stir in Washington, but many ordinary people cheered Jackson. By now they knew the routine. Jackson takes land, chases off the Indians, and then we get to buy it at fire-sale prices. This was the American Dream, in the version created by the founder of the Democratic Party. The Monroe administration backed down, and once again Jackson found himself in a position to win the allegiance of future voters while amply lining his own pockets.

As Inskeep reports, Jackson and his associates were planning their Florida investments even *before* he invaded. Later Jackson's critics would say that he took Florida solely for the purpose of his personal real estate speculation. Inskeep argues—and I agree—that this is an exaggeration. Jackson wanted Florida for the United States. He wanted settlers to move there, settlers who may at some point in the future be beholden to him. And he wanted to make money out of the whole deal.

Jackson dispatched his brother-in-law and business partner John Donelson to Florida. Donelson went, carrying a letter of introduction from Jackson. There he found—voila!—that many doors were open for him. Jackson and his friends invested heavily in Florida real estate. Later they sold much of that land at many times the price they paid for it. In other words, they made out like bandits.

In five separate treaties between 1816 and 1820, Jackson forced the Indians to give up tens of millions of acres in what would eventually become five American states. In this respect, Jackson is the true architect of the map of the Deep South. We can respect the single-minded determination with which he created what Inskeep calls "Jacksonland" while at the same time deploring the self-serving means that were used to bring it about.

THE EVIDENCE DISAPPEARS

Jackson's real estate shenanigans became a hot topic in his 1828 presidential campaign. Even earlier, in 1824, his opponents suspected him of profiting from political office but they were unable to produce convincing evidence. By 1828, however, Jackson's critics had gotten smarter and more determined. Jackson, however, was ready for them. On December 4, 1827, a fire broke out in the building containing Jackson's financial papers. Conveniently, all the original records of his earlier land dealings were destroyed.[32]

Jackson professed his innocence, and again, no one could prove he was behind the fire. The whole situation, however, bears an uncanny resemblance to Hillary Clinton deleting her emails. Oops! They're gone! And now we will never have full information about why she set up her private email account and what she wanted to keep out of the official State Department email system. Hillary might have thought she was being original, but Jackson got there first. Just like his twenty-first-century counterpart, Jackson deleted the evidence that his critics might have used to incriminate him.

Thanks to his land-stealing schemes, Jackson went from living in a log cabin to running a huge plantation stretching over a thousand acres. In 1819, he and Rachel moved out of their log house and built a mansion that still stands today, with a spectacular white colonnade front that awed visitors then as it does now. As for the old log cabin, Jackson found another use for it. What good is a plantation if you don't have slaves? Jackson converted his former dwelling into slave quarters.

Jackson had been a slave owner since his early days as a young lawyer in Tennessee. His first slave was a woman named Nancy. The record of the sale notes that "Andrew Jackson Esquire" took ownership of "a Negro Woman about Eighteen or Twenty Years of Age."[33] Later, as Jackson grew rich and his real estate multiplied, he bought slaves to work that land. Altogether, Jackson owned some three hundred slaves over the course of his life. The most he owned at any one time was 150 slaves.

This made him a large slave owner by American standards. By contrast with the South American plantations, American plantations were typically quite small, employing fewer than twenty slaves. Jackson was also a slave trader, a practice disparaged by most slave owners. In one telling incident, Jackson purchased an ad in a local paper offering a bounty for one of his runaway slaves. Jackson offered a $50 reward for the return of the slave "and ten dollars extra for every hundred lashes any person will give him to the amount of three hundred."[34]

Eventually Jackson rode his wealth and popularity all the way to the White House. In 1824, the first time Jackson ran, all the candidates were from a single party, Thomas Jefferson's Democratic-Republican Party. There was at the time no system of primaries to determine who should get the nomination. Although Jackson won the most votes, he was

outmaneuvered by an adversary, Henry Clay, who steered the presidency
to John Quincy Adams.

An indignant Jackson and his supporters formed the Democratic
Party, while his opponents coalesced into a rival Whig Party. These were
the two parties that dominated American politics for the next few
decades, until the Whig Party collapsed and the Republican Party was
founded. The Whigs, led by the stalwart Henry Clay, provided modest
though largely ineffective resistance to Jackson. Until the founding of the
Republican Party, however, there was no party in America strong enough
to stop the thieving Democrats.

The Jackson Democrats won by an electoral landslide in 1828. A
central plank of Jackson's campaign was Indian removal. In defending
this policy, Jackson suggested his actions promoted the welfare of the
Indians. He spoke of "preserving this much-injured race" by placing
them under government protection "free from the mercenary influence
of white men." To listen to Jackson, one might think he was relocating
the Indians for their own good.

At the same time, speaking to Democratic audiences, Jackson supporters made their case for Indian removal in terms that didn't shy away
from bigotry. Jackson ally Lewis Cass, the governor of Michigan territory, said of the Indians, "To roam the forests at will, to pursue their
game, to attack their enemies, to spend the rest of their lives in listless
indolence, and to be ready at all times to die—these are the principal
occupations of an Indian."[35]

Upon taking office, Jackson instructed his allies in Congress to draw
up the Indian Removal Act. The legislation gave Jackson the power to
offer land west of the Mississippi to Indian tribes. The Indians were
expected to give up their land in the east for new land in the west, and
Congress appropriated money to pay for their moving expenses. Theo-
retically the Indians were being asked to move by choice, but in reality
they were being pushed out. Settlers stood ready to occupy Indian lands
whether the Indians voluntarily gave them up or not.

Although there was no Republican Party around at the time to stop
Jackson, there were many who opposed Jackson's Indian policy. One of

them was Jackson's former ally Davy Crockett. "Several of my colleagues got around me, and told me how well they loved me, and that I was ruining myself," Crockett confessed. Jackson's minions threatened that Crockett would suffer politically for his opposition. Even so, Crockett stood firm, condemning Jackson's Indian policy as "wicked" and "unjust" and "oppression with a vengeance."[36]

While most of the Indians got the message and started packing, the Cherokees refused to go. The Cherokee position was that it didn't matter what Congress decided. The Cherokee were a separate nation with their own written constitution. They were protected by a slew of treaties with the United States government going back generations. The Cherokees appealed their cause to the U.S. Supreme Court, and the decision was handed down by Supreme Court Chief Justice John Marshall.

Marshall conceded that European settlers had gained control of much of the United States and that the right of U.S. citizens to occupy the land of the country was "conceded by the world." Still, Marshall said, there was no evidence that the Cherokee Nation had relinquished its right to the lands it still possessed. Congress had expressly affirmed those rights through treaties dating back to 1778. Certainly the Indians, lacking power to enforce their rights, were now under the protection of the United States. Even so, Marshall concluded, with seemingly specific reference to Jackson, "Protection does not imply the destruction of the protected."[37]

LET HIM ENFORCE IT

How did Jackson respond to Marshall's ruling? He ignored it. "John Marshall has made his decision," he quipped. "Now let him enforce it." While historians debate whether Jackson said exactly these words, there is little doubt that these were his sentiments. In any case Jackson took no steps to carry out the Supreme Court's ruling. He allowed Georgia settlers to force the Cherokee to relocate. This was accomplished by stealing Indian livestock, burning Indian towns, and squatting on Indian land.

Jackson's conduct in this respect echoes the Obama administration's refusal to comply with laws and court rulings that Obama finds uncongenial. From the Defense of Marriage Act to welfare reform to Obamacare to immigration, today's progressives seem willing to bend the law to their own purposes. This tradition of Democratic lawlessness has its true forefather in Andrew Jackson.

The Cherokee continued to protest. The tribe owned a printing press which put out a newspaper, *The Cherokee Phoenix*. Acting on the advice of Jackson's former attorney general, John Berrien, Jackson's people raided the printing house and destroyed the press, shattering it to pieces and silencing the voice of the Cherokee people.

Jackson also had Cherokee leader John Ross arrested. The Jackson administration then opened up an investigation into whether Ross was a genuine Native American. Actually there was little doubt he was. While Ross had Scottish and Irish blood through his father and grandfather's line, Cherokee society was matrilineal, and Ross had Cherokee blood directly through his mother and grandmother. Ross's great-grandmother was a full-blooded Cherokee. The Cherokee recognized him not merely as one of their own but as their elected leader.

Jackson, however, considered Ross to be a fake Indian. In 1834, Jackson's men organized a plebiscite of the Cherokee and put before them the question of whether Ross was a legitimate Native American and whether he actually represented their interests. To Jackson's chagrin, Ross won 95 percent of the vote. Jackson tried again the next year, and once again the Cherokee overwhelmingly sided with Ross.[38]

By itself the Jackson ploy was transparent and got nowhere. But it's worth noting, because successive generations of Democrats have continued Jackson's practice of trying to discredit nonwhite opponents by portraying them as inauthentic. Today when Republicans who are black, Hispanic, or Native American expose Democratic chicanery, they are routinely denounced—not just by Democrats but also by their allies in the press—as sellouts and, in the case of African Americans, "Uncle Toms."

For example, political scientist Manning Marable said of conservative Supreme Court Justice Clarence Thomas, "Ethnically, Thomas has ceased to be an African American." Columnist Carl Rowan of the *Washington Post* wrote of black economist Thomas Sowell, "Vidkun Quisling in his collaboration with the Nazis surely did not do as much damage as Sowell is doing." And Spike Lee said that Michael Williams, a black appointee in the Bush administration, was such a traitor to his race that he deserved to be "dragged into an alley and beaten with a Louisville slugger."[39]

Back to our story. Eventually the Jackson Democrats found a small faction of Cherokee who were willing, in exchange for bribes, to sign a removal agreement. This was called the Treaty of New Echota. The leaders of this group were the true Uncle Toms. They were not the recognized leaders of the Cherokee, and more than fifteen thousand Cherokee—led by Ross—signed a petition of protest. Ignoring their pleas, the U.S. government gave the Cherokee two years to migrate voluntarily.

The deadline of 1838 came and went, and most Cherokee had not moved. The Democrats at this point did not hesitate to use force. Those who refused to move were compelled. "The soldiers cleared out one farm at a time, one valley at a time," Inskeep writes. "Approaching a house, the troops would surround it so that no one would escape, then order out the occupants with no more than they could carry."[40]

Native Indians unable to travel were rounded up in internment camps, a policy reminiscent of the Japanese internments that a later Democratic administration would enforce during World War II. Reports differ about how bad conditions in the camps were; what no one disputes is that around four thousand Indians died from malnourishment and disease. The Trail of Tears has gone down in American history as cruel and infamous. It certainly was, although its actual perpetrator was not "America" but rather the Jackson Democrats.

The Trail of Tears occurred after Jackson had left the presidency. He was by this time back at his plantation, the Hermitage. His handpicked successor, Martin Van Buren, was president. Yet Van Buren was only continuing the policies of his mentor. From a safe distance, Jackson approvingly watched his Democratic Party carry out his handiwork.

For Jackson, the Trail of Tears represented the culmination of his lifelong efforts. Far from being a disaster, this ugly chapter in U.S. history was one of the original "achievements" of the newly formed Democratic Party. Moreover, the way the Jackson Democrats treated the Indians was not an aberration. Rather, it was only the beginning of a long subsequent Democratic Party history of dispossession, cruelty, bigotry, and theft.

CHAPTER 3

PARTY OF SLAVERY

THE DEMOCRATS' DEFENSE OF OPPRESSION

In all ages of the world, some have labored, and others have, without labor, enjoyed a large proportion of the fruits. This is wrong, and should not continue.[1]

—Abraham Lincoln, Fragment on Labor, 1847

In November 2014 Hillary Clinton made some revealing comments about illegal immigrants while receiving a "History Maker" award from the New York Historical Society at the city's Mandarin Oriental Hotel. President Obama had just issued an executive order curbing the ability of law enforcement officials to deport illegal immigrants. Obama's action circumvented the law, provoking a firestorm of criticism from many Republicans.

Hillary rushed to Obama's defense, emphasizing why America needs illegals. "We should all remember...that this is about people's lives. This is about, I would venture to guess, the people who served us tonight, who prepared our food tonight." Hillary's Democratic sympathizers in the audience burst into spontaneous applause.[2]

Hillary indeed "made history" that evening because, without quite intending to, she revealed why she and many Democrats support illegal immigration. Quite simply, her argument is that there is dirty work to be done and someone has to do it. In Hillary's mind, hotels like the

Mandarin Oriental cannot maintain elegant rooms and serve five-star cuisine without illegals cleaning the rooms, serving the food, and cleaning up afterward. One cannot, it seems, rely on Americans to do such jobs.

The very idea that people might work for those wages, and take pride in their work, is incomprehensible to Hillary. The country no longer has slaves to do the dirty work, and so America needs illegal immigrants. The applause attending Hillary's remarks shows that she was not merely speaking for herself. Other Democratic fine-diners that evening were very much on board with Hillary's position.

Listening to Hillary that evening, I felt I was at a campaign rally for a Democratic presidential candidate in the mid-nineteenth century. The feel was the same, and most important, the argument was the same. A century and a half ago, the issue wasn't illegal immigration; it was slavery. Democrats then justified slavery on the grounds that there was dirty work to be done and someone had to do it. Some of them even insisted that slavery benefited both the master and the slave, because slavery gave full employment to people who were incapable of doing anything better than menial work. And here is Hillary Clinton making essentially the same case, not in defense of slavery, but in defense of illegal immigration.

A few days after Hillary's comments, the Mandarin Oriental hotel issued a press statement that it does not knowingly employ illegals. So Hillary was most likely wrong on the facts. But that's not what interests me about this episode. Nor am I interested in pressing a direct analogy between slavery and illegal immigration—obviously the two issues are quite different.

No, what interests me most here is the familiar attitude of superiority, condescension, and disdain. That was evident in the pro-slavery blather of the nineteenth century, and it was on full display at the Mandarin Oriental in November 2014. Democrats, it seems, never change their stripes.

Hillary's plan, I argue in this book, is the enslavement of America. Enslavement is not slavery, but it's related to slavery. Slavery is a condition while enslavement is a process. Enslavement is the process of converting free into unfree citizens, by confiscating their earnings, their resources, and their property in the form of taxes or fines. The ultimate end is the same: our lives and even our hopes and dreams are now in someone else's control. We have become serfs not of a plantation owner, but serfs of the progressive state.

In order to understand enslavement, we need to understand slavery. This chapter focuses on the Democratic Party's role as the champion and defender of slavery. Oddly enough, slavery for many centuries needed no defenders because it had no critics. It was like the family, a longstanding institution that was simply taken for granted.

But starting in the seventeenth century and continuing through the nineteenth century, slavery came under attack. The attack was two-pronged. The first prong of the attack was the American founding, which had no power to end slavery but which established a framework for reducing, corralling, and ultimately placing slavery on a path to extinction. The second force, which emerged almost a century later, was the Republican Party, a party explicitly founded to block and then eliminate slavery, healing the "crisis of the house divided" and creating a single union of free citizens.

These attacks on slavery provoked the defense of slavery that formed the cornerstone of the Democratic Party. The Democratic Party in the South invented the "positive good" school that argued slavery was good not only for the master but also for the slave. The champion of this school was the Democratic Senator John C. Calhoun. Northern Democrats, led by Senator Stephen Douglas, produced a subtler but no less invidious apologia for slavery: "popular sovereignty," a doctrine that allowed each state and territory to decide for itself whether it wanted slavery.

Democrats on the Supreme Court also forged the majority in the notorious *Dred Scott* decision that upheld slavery and insisted that blacks have no rights that a white man needs to respect. Democratic presidents after Jackson—from Polk to Buchanan—protected slavery from abolitionist, free soil, and Republican attack.

Even during the Civil War, many northern Democrats—the so-called Copperheads or Peace Democrats—took the side of the Confederacy, urging Lincoln to make a deal with the slave-owning South. They tried, unsuccessfully, to defeat Lincoln for reelection in 1864. Finally, even after Lee surrendered at Appomattox, a small group of Democrats made a last-ditch attempt to save their cherished institution by assassinating Lincoln.

WHITEWASHING HISTORY

"Whoa!" you might say. "We've never heard this story about the Democrats. Are you making this stuff up?" Actually, no. Nothing I write in this chapter is controversial in terms of whether it happened or not. I am relying on the mainstream historians of slavery: David Brion Davis, Kenneth Stampp, Eugene Genovese, Orlando Patterson. How, then, can my arguments sound so outrageous? The reason is that progressive Democrats have whitewashed the party's history. They have cleaned up the record.

How? They have done it in two ways. The first is to take the crimes of the Democratic Party and blame them on America. Progressives today are quick to fault "America" for slavery and a host of other outrages. America did this, America did that. As we will see in this book, America didn't do those things, the Democrats did. So the Democrats have cleverly foisted their sins on America, and then presented themselves as the messiahs offering redemption for those sins. It's crazy, but it's also ingenious. We have to give them credit for ingenuity.

The second whitewash is to portray the Civil War entirely in terms of the North versus the South. The North is supposedly the anti-slavery side and the South is the pro-slavery side. A recent example is Ta-Nehisi Coates's article about the Confederate battle flag in *The Atlantic*.[3] Now of course there is an element of truth in this, in that the Civil War was fought between northern states and southern states. But this neat and convenient division ignores several important details.

First, the defenders of the Confederate cause were, almost without exception, Democrats. Coates cites many malefactors from Senator Jefferson Davis to Senator James Henry Hammond to Georgia Governor

Joseph Brown. Yet while identifying these men as southerners and Confederates, Coates omits to identify them as Democrats.

Second, Coates and other progressives conveniently ignore the fact that northern Democrats were also protectors of slavery. We will see in this chapter how Stephen Douglas and other northern Democrats fought to protect slavery in the South and in the new territories. Moreover, the southerners who fought for the Confederacy cannot be said to have fought merely to protect slavery on their plantations. Indeed, fewer than one-third of white families in the South on the eve of the Civil War had slaves.

Thus the rigid North-South interpretation of the Civil War conceals—and is intended to conceal—the active complicity of Democrats across the country to save, protect, and even extend the "peculiar institution." As the *Charleston Mercury* editorialized during the secession debate, the duty of the South was to "rally under the banner of the Democratic Party which has recognized and supported...the rights of the South."[4]

The real divide was between the Democratic Party as the upholder of slavery and the Republican Party as the adversary of slavery. All the figures who upheld and defended American slavery—Senators John C. Calhoun and Stephen Douglas, President James Buchanan, Supreme Court Chief Justice Roger Taney, architect of the *Dred Scott* decision, and the main leaders of the Confederacy—were Democrats.

All the heroes of black emancipation—from the black abolitionists Sojourner Truth and Frederick Douglass, to the woman who organized the Underground Railroad, Harriet Tubman, to the leader whose actions finally destroyed American slavery, Abraham Lincoln—were Republicans. It is of the utmost importance to progressive propagandists to conceal or at least ignore this essential historical truth.

Let's begin with the progressive indictment of the American Founders. "Jefferson didn't mean it when he wrote that all men are created equal," historian John Hope Franklin wrote. "The truth is we're a bigoted people and always have been." Franklin argued that by betraying the principles of freedom and allowing slavery to continue, "the founding fathers set the stage for every succeeding generation of Americans to apologize, compromise and temporize on those principles."

In the same vein, Senator Bill Bradley articulates the progressive view that "slavery was our original sin." And former Supreme Court Justice Thurgood Marshall refused to "find the wisdom, foresight and sense of justice exhibited by the framers particularly profound. The government they devised was defective from the start." Instead of jingoistic celebration, Marshall wrote, Americans should seek an "understanding of the Constitution's defects."[5]

Notice the rhetoric here. "We're a bigoted people." This is an African American talking. Does he mean that he himself is bigoted? Of course not. "We" here means "Americans." So too with Bradley. "Our original sin" obviously doesn't refer to Bradley, who never owned slaves. Rather, it is an assumption of collective responsibility, or more accurately, an allocation of responsibility to America as a whole.

In the progressive narrative, America is to blame, and the first offenders were the Founders themselves. The progressive conclusion is that the founding was "defective," setting up the progressive agenda to replace and move away from founding principles, what Obama called the "remaking" of America.

SINS OF THE FOUNDERS?

So let's examine whether the progressives are right. Were the Founders a pro-slavery lot who enshrined slavery in the new republic and in the new constitution? Was their assertion in the Declaration of Independence that "all men are created equal" a big lie? If these charges are true, then America was indeed "defective" from the start.

But they aren't true. This is not to deny that the Founders were flawed and self-interested men, or that several of them owned slaves. Jefferson, for example, owned more than two hundred slaves and never freed them; Washington also owned slaves and freed them only upon his death.

Yet Jefferson's case is revealing: far from rationalizing plantation life by adopting the "happy slave" arguments that would later become popular among southern Democrats, Jefferson the Virginian vehemently denounced slavery as unfair and immoral. "The almighty has no attribute that can take side with us," he wrote. "I tremble for my country when I reflect that God is just; that his justice cannot sleep forever."

Moreover, Jefferson insisted that slavery was bad for slaves and bad for the masters. It was bad for the slaves because, unable to keep the fruits of their labor, they became unenterprising and slothful. Jefferson pointed out, however, that slavery had exactly the same effect on masters. Not having to do any work, masters too became unenterprising and slothful. Moreover, many masters exercised a despotic rule over their slaves, making them little tyrants in their own kingdom.[6]

These arguments may seem surprising coming from a slave owner, and they are. The remarkable thing is not that Jefferson the plantation owner had slaves, but that this slave-owning planter nevertheless declared that "all men are created equal."

Here we can instructively contrast Jefferson with the founder of the Democratic Party, Andrew Jackson. Unlike Jefferson, Jackson never expressed any doubt about the injustice of slavery. What provoked Jackson's indignation on the subject was abolitionist agitation. In his 1835 Annual Message to Congress, Jackson called for laws to "prohibit, under severe penalties, the circulation in the southern states, through the mail, of incendiary publications intended to instigate the slaves to insurrection."[7]

Jefferson, however, was typical of the Founders in that he recognized slavery was wrong and that black people had rights. Confronted by those who justified slavery with the argument that blacks were intellectually inferior to whites, Jefferson retorted, "Whatever be their talents, it is no measure of their rights."[8]

If Jefferson and the Founders knew that all men are created equal, and that black people have rights, why not outlaw slavery and establish equality of rights under the law at the outset? The simple answer is that had they done so, there would never have been a union. The Founders in Philadelphia were not choosing whether to have a union with slavery or a union without slavery. They were choosing whether to have a union that had slavery or no union at all. If the Founders decided not to have a union, then slavery would have continued in the various states. In that case, slavery may well have lasted much longer in America than it actually did.

The Founders chose a better option. They set a date a few years ahead for ending the slave trade—no more importation of slaves. They prohibited slavery in the Northwest Territory (essentially the modern upper Midwest, including Wisconsin, Michigan, Illinois, Indiana, and Ohio).

Most important, they established a union on anti-slavery principles that nevertheless temporarily tolerated the practice of slavery. Nowhere in the Constitution is the term "slavery" used. Slaves are always described as "persons," implying they have natural rights. The three-fifths clause, which some progressives have claimed shows the Founders' low estimation of the worth of black life, was actually a measure to curb the voting power of the slave-owning states—it helped eventually to swing the balance of power to the free states.

The Founders believed that these measures would over time weaken slavery and cause it to die out. In this they were mistaken, because Eli Whitney's invention of the cotton gin in 1793—which the Founders had no way to anticipate—revived the demand for slavery in the South.

Still, the Founders' efforts did weaken slavery. Before 1776, slavery was legal in every state. Yet by 1804 every state north of Maryland had abolished slavery either outright or gradually. Slavery was no longer a national but a sectional institution, and one under moral and political siege.

The Republican abolitionist Frederick Douglass, who had once denounced the founding as a hideous compromise with slavery, came to understand the accomplishment of the framers. "Abolish slavery tomorrow," he said, "and not a sentence or syllable of the Constitution needs to be altered." Slavery, he concluded, was merely "scaffolding to the magnificent structure, to be removed as soon as the building was completed."[9] Douglass knew that it would take Republican efforts to do this and finally end slavery.

Anti-slavery activism, of course, preceded the Republican Party, although it finally found its most effective expression in that party. The earliest opponents of slavery in America were Christians, mostly Quakers and evangelical Christians. They took seriously the biblical idea that we are all equal in the eyes of God, and interpreted it to mean that no person has the right to rule another person without his consent.

Remarkably, Christians discovered political equality through a theological interpretation of the Bible. For them, human equality is based not on an equality of human characteristics or achievements but on how we are equally loved by God. Moreover, the argument against slavery and the argument for democracy both rested on the same foundation, a foundation based on human equality and individual consent.

The American Anti-Slavery Society was founded in 1833. A few years later, the Liberty Party was founded to pursue emancipation. In 1848, the Liberty Party, anti-slavery Whigs, and Democrats who opposed the extension of slavery merged to form the Free Soil Party. Abolitionism, which sought the immediate end of slavery, had been present since the founding but grew in political strength during the middle part of the nineteenth century.

With the passage of the Kansas Nebraska Act—repealing the Missouri Compromise which curtailed the spread of slavery beyond the designated 36-30 latitude—Free Soilers, former Whigs, and abolitionists joined together and created the Republican Party.

JUSTIFYING SLAVERY

These anti-slavery forces produced a massive national backlash in defense of slavery, not merely in the South but also in the North. Today it is difficult to meet anyone who defends slavery, and it is virtually inconceivable to imagine how slavery might be justified.

To get a flavor of how plantation owners justified it, consider this anecdote from Mary Boykin Chesnut's diary about her husband James Chesnut, a Democratic senator from South Carolina. Asked if he ever had a problem with runaway slaves on his plantation, the doughty

Democrat quipped, "Never! It's pretty hard work to keep me from running away from them!"[10]

We can see from this witticism Senator Chesnut's assumption that he is doing the slaves a favor by housing, feeding, and taking care of them. In other words, they aren't supporting him; he's supporting them! He shouldn't be grateful to them; they should be grateful to him! This is the "happy slave" idea, and many slave owners and southern Democrats believed it, so they could never understand the Republican contention that slaves might not want to be slaves, dismissing it as a form of outside "agitation."

Historically the argument for slavery is one from necessity, and we find it in Aristotle. Aristotle insisted that some people are naturally inferior and incapable of governing themselves; such people are "natural slaves" and their enslavement is "natural slavery." Yet Aristotle also recognized that many people were enslaved because they were captives who became the spoils of war. Slavery of this sort, Aristotle wrote, is "conventional slavery," upheld not because it is right but because of custom or the way of the world.

One might expect Aristotle to say that while natural slavery may be justifiable, conventional slavery is not. Aristotle, however, defends both types of slavery. His reason is practical. In every society, he argues, there is a great deal of hard work to be done, and if there is going to be leisure and art and contemplation, then some people have to do the dirty work so that others are freed up to devote themselves to higher pursuits. Slavery is simply the price that humanity must pay in order to have civilization.

We can see that Aristotle's justification for slavery is essentially identical to Hillary's justification for illegal immigration: Who is going to serve us and do the dirty work if not "those people"? Aristotle's argument hasn't just reached Democrats today; it also inspired Democrats in the early to middle part of the nineteenth century.

Indeed, leading Democrats in the South picked up Aristotle's defense of slavery. In his celebrated King Cotton speech to the Senate in 1858, Democratic senator James Hammond argued, "In all social systems there must be a class to do the menial duties, to perform the drudgery of life.

Such a class you must have, or you would not have that other class which leads progress, civilization and refinement." So far Hammond is completely in line with his Greek predecessor. We can also trace a very interesting line that goes from Hammond to Hillary.

Hammond, however, goes much further than Aristotle when he continues that slavery "is no evil. On the contrary, I believe it to be the greatest of all blessings." Providence, he declares, has produced in the slave-owning South "the highest-toned, the purest, best organization of society that has ever existed on the face of the earth."

Hammond insists that slaves don't have it too bad in being slaves. "Our slaves are hired for life," he says, "and well compensated. There is no starvation, no begging, no want of employment." Remarkably, Hammond goes on to add that free laborers who don't have food, lodging or health care provided to them are worse off than slaves. He calls them a "hireling class," that is "hired for the day" and "not cared for," while slaves, he insists, are provided for in all their basic needs.[11]

Echoing Hammond, Democratic senator Albert Gallatin of Mississippi contended that slavery was "a great moral, social and political blessing—a blessing to the slave, and a blessing to the master." According to Gallatin, slavery freed gentlemen to cultivate literature and the arts and devote themselves to public service in contrast to "vulgar, contemptible, counter-jumping" Yankees. At the same time, Gallatin said, slavery benefited the slaves because it took African savages and made them into useful workers, while also giving them lifelong protection and provision.[12]

We hear the same tune from another southern Democrat, the writer George Fitzhugh, who argued that "slavery is the natural and normal condition of society" while free labor was "abnormal and anomalous." Fitzhugh didn't just want slavery to continue; he wanted it to expand. The South would never have independence or equality, he wrote, until "our equal right to increase, expansion, and protection, is fully admitted and acted on."

The founding doctrine of equality of rights, Fitzhugh insisted, was simply a mechanism for "giving license to the strong to oppress the

weak." While "free laborers must at all times work or starve," Fitzhugh
wrote, "slaves are supported whether they work or not." Slavery,
Fitzhugh concluded, was an early form of social insurance; it may even
be termed an embryonic form of socialism.[13]

Undoubtedly the most notorious defender of slavery was Democratic
senator John C. Calhoun from South Carolina. Calhoun was an enthusias-
tic Andrew Jackson supporter, and in 1828 he became Jackson's vice president, although the two men would subsequently have a falling out.
Progressive historians like to portray Calhoun as a quintessential southerner,
in order to italicize their North-South interpretation of the Civil War.

In reality, historian Clyde Wilson points out that Calhoun was controversial even in his home state; he was not a typical southerner. In fact,
he may have been just as popular in the North as in the South. According
to Wilson, "he had substantial support and admiration in many parts of
the North, from Boston to New York to Philadelphia to Cincinnati to
Detroit."

SLAVERY AS A "POSITIVE GOOD"

Calhoun's "positive good" defense of slavery is laid out in a series of
his speeches before the U.S. Senate. In an 1837 speech, Calhoun argued,
"There never has yet existed a wealthy and civilized society in which one
portion of the community did not, in point of fact, live on the labor of
the other." Here is Calhoun contending that slavery is simply a response,
one may say, to Aristotelian necessity.

But Calhoun went further, attacking the Declaration of Independence and thus separating himself from Jefferson. Calhoun attributed
the assault on slavery as arising out of "great and dangerous errors that
have their origin in the prevalent opinion that all men are free and equal.
Nothing can be more unfounded and false." Men are not equal, Calhoun
emphasized, and therefore some are destined for freedom and others are
marked for servitude.

Calhoun, like Hammond, contended that slaves were improved by
slavery, making them not only better off than they were before, but also

happy. "Never before has the black race of Central Africa, from the dawn of history to the present day, attained a condition so civilized and so improved, not only physically, but morally and intellectually. It came among us in a low, degraded and savage condition, and in the course of a few generations it has grown up under the fostering care of our institutions, to its present comparatively civilized condition. This, with the rapid increase of numbers, is conclusive proof of the general happiness of the race, in spite of all the exaggerated tales to the contrary."

Calhoun rhapsodized that "every plantation is a little community, with the master as its head, who concentrates in himself the united interests of capital and labor, of which he is the common representative." In this benign environment, he insisted, the slaves could really thrive. For Calhoun slavery was a veritable "school of civilization," although not a school from which the slaves were permitted to graduate.[14]

These arguments by southern Democrats appear to have vanished into the mist of history. They are rarely taught, scarcely read, and hardly remembered. Progressives don't want us to remember them. Yet they are worth remembering for three separate reasons.

First, they are unique. Historian Eugene Genovese says that nowhere in the new world, outside the Democratic South, did anyone celebrate slavery as a good thing for the slave. In Brazil, for example, there was widespread slavery and, according to Genovese, "slavery was defended as economically necessary and traditionally sanctioned, but no one argued with any discernible conviction that it was a good thing in itself or the proper condition of the laboring classes."[15]

Second, the pro-slavery philosophy of the southern Democrats shaped important events in American history. "The right of property in a slave is distinctly and expressly affirmed in the Constitution." This sentence is from the *Dred Scott* decision issued by a Supreme Court dominated by Jackson Democrats.[16] The statement is a lie. Nowhere does the Constitution distinctly and expressly affirm slavery. This can easily be verified by reading the Constitution today.

Yet the statement does reflect the perverted Democratic interpretation of the Constitution promulgated by the pro-slavery Democratic contingent. These are people who wanted to keep their slaves, and recover slaves who escaped to free states, and so they twisted the Constitution to achieve their self-serving objectives.

No wonder that President James Buchanan, a Democrat, hailed the Supreme Court's decision. "The right has been established of every citizen to take his property of any kind, including slaves, into the common territories and to have it protected there. Neither Congress nor a territorial legislature nor any human power has any authority to annul or impair this vested right."[17]

Ultimately the southern Democrats became so dug in with their "positive good" philosophy that they pressed for secession immediately upon Lincoln's election. A less recalcitrant group might have stayed in the union; in this case slavery would likely have endured longer than it did. So the "positive good" philosophy was actually instrumental in instigating the Civil War and, against the wishes of its proponents, bringing about a quicker end to slavery than would otherwise have been the case.

Third and finally, the arguments of the southern Democrats are worth recalling because we will see Democrats make very similar arguments—actually, the same ones—once again during the New Deal. Only this time the master had a new name: the federal government, administered by progressives according to progressive principles. Incredibly those "positive good" arguments would be pitched in the 1930s and subsequently not to sympathetic whites but to blacks themselves.

COMPLICITY OF THE NORTHERN DEMOCRATS

The northern Democratic defense of slavery was epitomized by Stephen Douglas, who made a new and ingenious defense of black servitude that went under the banner of "popular sovereignty." Douglas was no friend of blacks, and routinely referred to them as "niggers." In his second debate with Lincoln in the Illinois Senate race, for instance, Douglas said, "Those of you who believe that the nigger is your equal and ought to be on an equality with you socially, politically and legally, have a right to entertain those opinions and of course will vote for Mr. Lincoln."

In the third debate, Douglas bluntly asserted, "I hold that a Negro is not and never ought to be a citizen of the United States. I hold that this government was made on the white basis, made by white men, for the benefit of white men and their posterity forever, and should be administered by white men and none others." Indeed Douglas went on to suggest that since many of the Founders had slaves, clearly they couldn't have meant what they said that all men are created equal.[18]

Interestingly, Democrats today make the same point about the Founders, not to defend white supremacy but to suggest that the Founders are hypocrites whose ideals as set forth in the Constitution should give way to progressive alternatives. The resemblance between today's Democrats and the Democrat Douglas goes even further. Douglas's argument for popular sovereignty regarding slavery is identical in substance, and very nearly in form, to the Democratic Party's position on abortion today.

Let's follow the argument more closely. Douglas professed to be indifferent himself to whether slavery was voted up or down. To the degree he confessed to an opinion, he implied he was "personally opposed" to slavery and would not have slaves himself—as indeed he couldn't, since he lived in the free state of Illinois. Even so, Douglas contended that popular sovereignty was a democratic solution to an otherwise insoluble problem that threatened to divide the country and plunge it into chaos.

The solution, Douglas said, is for Americans to agree to disagree. Specifically, each state and territory should decide for itself whether to have slavery. Douglas staked his position not on the right or wrong of slavery, but firmly on the "right to choose." For Douglas, the moral dignity of slavery came not from its own merits but from its affirmation through the democratic process. Douglas sought to resolve the contradiction of the American founding—to eliminate its hypocrisy, if you will, on the slavery issue—by placing slavery itself on a democratic foundation.

Here we see the resemblance to the Democrats' contemporary prochoice position on abortion. Both are efforts to take something that destroys the life and liberty of another, and make it into a political good. Both embrace the high ground of freedom or "choice" in order to cancel out the choices of others. Both use the language of democracy to deny the fundamental equality of others who are somehow placed outside the orbit of humanity.

In one case it is the planter who makes the choice; in another, it is the pregnant woman. In one case the choice involves owning and enslaving a black person; in the other it involves destroying an emerging life in the womb. Still, one can hardly deny the similarities; this method of reasoning seems to be part of the Democrats' political DNA, from their pro-choice arguments about slavery to their pro-choice arguments about abortion.

Douglas's popular sovereignty doctrine was reflected in the Kansas Nebraska Act, which Douglas maneuvered through the Congress. It was a legislative victory for Douglas, yet the Act also precipitated vehement opposition, leading to the rise of Abraham Lincoln and the founding of the Republican Party. Speaking on behalf of the emerging Republican coalition, Lincoln's arguments against Douglas expose the façade of the pro-choice position, revealing it as facially neutral but actually a form of oppression. Lincoln's logic, we will see, applies equally against slavery then as it does against abortion now.

Lincoln destroyed popular sovereignty by exposing the contradiction at the core of the doctrine. Yes, Lincoln said, democracy involves the right to choose, but the right to choose cannot be defended without considering what is being chosen. Pro-choice, in other words, depends for its validity on the content of the choice. How, Lincoln asked, can Douglas Democrats invoke "choice" to deprive black people of their right to choose? Can popular consent legitimately take away other people's right to consent? Lincoln insisted that it could not.[19]

With equal acumen, Lincoln destroyed the "positive good" defense of slavery. He compared the position of the Calhoun Democrats to a pack of wolves devouring lambs, while pretending that this was good for the lambs! Lincoln said he was weary of hearing Democrats preach about how good slavery was for the slaves. If slavery was so good, he suggested, why don't Democrats try it on themselves by becoming slaves?

For Lincoln, slavery was a form of theft. The core of it was summarized in the phrase, "You work, I eat." The slave owner, in other words, was a thief, stealing not only the labor but also the life of the slave. Democratic apologists for slavery were no better than facilitators and sustainers of this system of theft. Lincoln pointed out that even popular sovereignty—the supposedly moderate position of the northern Democrats—represented not just theft but perpetual theft. Lincoln accused Douglas of placing slavery "where he openly confesses he has no desire there shall ever be an end of it."

Lincoln found this position abhorrent because he, together with his fellow Republicans, believed that slavery was morally wrong. This belief, of course, did not by itself settle the issue. Lincoln knew that the Founders had allowed slavery in the southern states in order to have a union. He believed that no matter how much he abhorred slavery, it was not within his power or the power of Congress to nullify that original pact. In other words, the federal government was constitutionally prohibited from regulating slavery in the southern states.

The Constitution, however, said nothing about new territories that were coming into the union. Lincoln argued that therefore Congress had every right, and full power, to keep slavery out of these new territories. Lincoln's position was that, within the parameters established by the Constitution, the evil of slavery should be restricted and contained. His opponents, on the other hand, wanted slavery to continue and expand. As Lincoln neatly summarized the difference, one side believes slavery is right and ought to be extended, while the other believes it is wrong and ought to be restricted.

FRUITS OF ONE'S LABOR

By contrast with the Democrats, Lincoln defended the free labor system. Such a system, he contended, not only protected liberty, it was also just. People have a right to the fruits of their labor. Once again, Lincoln spoke in simple terms that everyone could understand. "I always thought the man who made the corn should eat the corn." The hand that produces bread, Lincoln said, has the right to put that bread into its own mouth. No other man has a claim on that bread, and no other man can justly take away the fruits of another man's labor.

Lincoln combined his condemnation of slavery with a defense of free labor and earned achievement. He articulated, for his time and ours, the core principle of the Republican Party. Republicans, Lincoln said, were the party of entrepreneurship. Lincoln understood that nothing has raised the American standard of living more than new inventions and innovations. When we contemplate how people's lives have been improved from a slew of new inventions, from the steam engine to the iPhone, I don't see how anyone can disagree with Lincoln about this.

In a speech on patents and copyrights, Lincoln defended the patent laws as adding the fuel of interest to the fire of innovation. In other words, people are more likely to build new things that benefit others and raise the overall standard of society when they get to own and benefit from their creations. Lincoln celebrated the American system of "discoveries, inventions and improvements." Minerals, he pointed out, have long subsisted under the earth's surface. They lay idle, however, until someone figured out how to get them out and harness them to productive use.

Republicans, according to Lincoln, are not just the party of entrepreneurship and invention; they are also the party of the little guy making his way up the ladder. Sure, that guy may have to start out working for another. But, Lincoln insisted, he must do so as a free man, on terms to which he gave consent. In time, Lincoln hoped, men could free themselves from dependence and work for themselves. And if they were successful, perhaps they would be able to hire others to work for them. This, Lincoln said, is the free labor system, offering what Lincoln termed equal chances in the race of life.

Lincoln never defended rich people. His Republican Party was not the party of the 1 percent. Rather, Lincoln defended upward mobility—the right to try one's chances at moving up the ladder, at getting rich.

Lincoln's Republican Party sought to remove government obstacles to that process. In his time the main such obstacle was slavery. Slavery, Lincoln knew, hurt the value of people's work because it placed them in competition with slaves who worked for nothing.

Today's Republicans make a similar point about illegal immigrant labor. Illegal immigrants don't have to pay taxes. For this and other reasons, they can price their labor markedly below that of citizens. Consequently, illegal immigration harms the upward mobility of American workers.

Today's Democrats howl that such rhetoric is racist, but since there is no implication of racial inferiority, the charge is baseless. Democrats make it only because they derive political benefits from illegal immigration. In reality, the GOP is right that illegal immigration has held back the standard of living of many American workers, making it difficult for them to achieve the upward mobility that Lincoln knew epitomized the American dream.

For Democrats—then as now—these concepts of upward mobility and getting rich through one's own efforts were anathema! The Democratic Party, then as now, is all about confiscating the fruits of other people's labor. Consequently, Democrats in the North and the South attacked Lincoln with all the political weapons they could muster.

These Democrats, led by Douglas, accused Lincoln of seeking to destroy slavery in the South and of being a covert believer in equal rights for blacks, the black right to vote, and also miscegenation or the right of blacks to intermarry with whites. These—especially the miscegenation accusation—were incendiary charges in the mid-nineteenth century.

Interestingly, while Democrats in 1860 said Lincoln wanted to free all their slaves, today's progressive Democrats today make exactly the opposite accusation charge—they claim Lincoln did not really care about slavery and fought the Civil War for reasons other than emancipation. They point to a famous letter to Horace Greeley in which Lincoln said his overriding goal was to save the union, not end slavery, and if he could save the union without freeing a single slave he would do it.

ARTFUL EVASIONS

So who is right, the old Democrats or the new ones? Actually, the Democrats of 1860 were closer to the mark than the Democrats of today. Lincoln did in fact believe not merely in ending slavery but also in extending the vote and equal rights to blacks. He also seems to have had no objection whatever to racial intermarriage.

Still, Lincoln realized that he could not admit to holding these positions in public. For Lincoln to make the election of 1860 about issues like the black vote or miscegenation—opposed by wide majorities of Americans of all political stripes—would be to assure his political defeat. If the Democrats defeated the Republicans in 1860, the South would not have seceded and American slavery would have continued.

Thus we have from Lincoln artfully evasive statements like, "I do not understand that because I do not want a Negro woman for a slave I must necessarily want her for a wife." Also, in response to Democratic proclamations of the inferiority of the black man, "If God gave him but little, that little let him enjoy."

Lincoln is nowhere saying that blacks are inferior. He is not saying he rejects the idea of blacks marrying whites. He is simply refusing to go there. He is keeping the debate where it ought to be, on the simple question of whether people should be permitted to steal other people's life and labor by enslaving them. Of the black woman he says, "In her natural right to eat the bread she earns with her own hands without asking leave of anyone else, she is my equal and the equal of all others."[20]

So today's Democrats who fault Lincoln for his unenlightened views about blacks are being disingenuous. Lincoln's views were not unenlightened. Rather, in statesmanlike fashion, Lincoln was simply refusing to admit his desire to do things that *he could not in any case do*. He was also refusing to let Democrats like Douglas change the subject from the extension of slavery—the main divide between the parties—to other peripheral subjects.

Similarly, when Lincoln insisted the Civil War was about the union, not about slavery, this is understood by competent historians to reflect Lincoln's determination to keep border states—Maryland, Delaware,

Kentucky, and Missouri—within the union. These states had slavery, and if Lincoln framed the war as one to end slavery, the border states would have seceded. If they seceded, Lincoln believed the union cause was lost. Once again, Lincoln acted in statesmanlike fashion to hold the border states, and he was successful in doing so, thus shortening the war and ending slavery more quickly.

The Democrats of the mid-nineteenth century didn't just castigate the Republicans; at times, they physically assaulted them. A dramatic example occurred in 1856 when Republican senator Charles Sumner gave an especially stern denunciation of slavery on the floor of the U.S. Senate. In response, Democratic congressman Preston Brooks walked up to Sumner and struck him repeatedly with his cane.

Sumner was seriously injured and his health suffered for the rest of his life. This Democratic outrage helped persuade many Americans that there was no way to rationally resolve the slavery issue with pro-slavery Democrats.[21]

Democrats despised abolitionists like Sumner and John Brown, but most of all they hated the Republican Party. That's because the Republican Party, unlike the abolitionists, was actually capable of winning a national election and preventing slavery from going into the new territories. Many Democrats feared that if slavery were not permitted to expand, it would inevitably decline. The relative power of free states would continually increase, and slavery's tenure would soon be over. This fear is why the slave states seceded, thus precipitating the Civil War.

The firmness of Lincoln and the Republicans, from the time of Lincoln's election through the conduct of the war, should be an example for Republicans today. Lincoln could probably have prevented the war by compromising his position that slavery could continue in the South but would be barred from extending into the new territories. Several such compromises—including the so-called Crittenden Compromise—were advanced to avert the danger of secession and war.

The Crittenden Compromise guaranteed the permanent existence of slavery in all states and territories demarcated by the Missouri Compromise line. It also affirmed popular sovereignty as the mechanism by which new territories could become slave states or free states. Historians recognize that perhaps the only way to avert the Civil War in that late stage was for Lincoln to embrace the Crittenden Compromise or something akin to it.

Yet Lincoln refused to do this, and in this sense he refused to do the one thing that could have avoided the war. Lincoln would not bend even one iota on his position—he refused to concede any ground to the Democratic doctrine of popular sovereignty. Lincoln argued that for him to do so would be to negate the very result of the 1860 election.

In effect, Lincoln would be allowing the very people who lost the election to win it simply by making their demands the necessary condition for them staying in the union. Lincoln would be selling out the American people in order to appease disgruntled Democrats. This he would not do.

In 1863, Lincoln signed his Emancipation Proclamation freeing slaves in the Confederacy. Solid Republican majorities in the House and the Senate supported this proclamation. The Copperheads or Peace Democrats opposed it, making it clear they favored maintaining the union but not freeing the slaves. The slogan of the Copperhead Democrats was, "The Union as it was, the Constitution as it is." In other words, let's keep the union and let's also keep slavery.

Today's progressives blast Lincoln and the Republicans for the limited scope of the Emancipation Proclamation, sarcastically noting it freed slaves not under union control, while at least for the present keeping in captivity slaves who were. Once again, Lincoln's actions can be understood as preserving union power. For Lincoln to have freed slaves in the border states would have risked further secession or at least widespread political division. Lincoln's challenge was to keep the union forces together so that the war could be prosecuted to a successful conclusion. Winning the war was the sine qua non of permanently abolishing slavery.

Throughout the war, Lincoln's Democratic opponents in the North—the Copperheads or Peace Democrats—sought to undermine him and the Republicans. The Copperheads sought to weaken Lincoln so that he could not be reelected. They called him a "nigger in principle" and urged

Americans to defeat his "negroism."[22] This was the vocabulary in which the Democratic campaign of 1864 was conducted.

FIRE IN THE REAR

Lincoln recognized the threat from the Copperheads. He called these Peace Democrats the "fire in the rear" and he regarded them as just as dangerous as the armies of the Confederacy. If Lincoln had been defeated, the Copperheads would undoubtedly have sought to reconcile with the Confederacy, largely on Confederate terms. Lincoln's reelection sealed the fate of the Peace Democrats, and also the fate of slavery.

But even after the surrender of the Confederacy—a surrender that presaged the final destruction of slavery—there were Democrats who refused to accept the outcome. One of them, John Wilkes Booth, decided to take action. Booth was a Confederate sympathizer from Maryland. Earlier Booth had joined a volunteer militia of Democrats in attendance at the hanging of abolitionist John Brown. Booth and the Democrats came armed to prevent abolitionists from rescuing Brown from the gallows.

Two days after Lee's surrender, Lincoln gave a speech at the White House in which he suggested that some blacks should get the vote. That did it for Booth, who gathered a group of likeminded Democrats who resolved to assassinate not only President Lincoln but also the vice president and the secretary of state. This was nothing short of an attempted coup.

The coup failed. Booth did kill Lincoln, who became the first president in American history to be assassinated. But the co-conspirators did not kill Vice President Johnson or Secretary of State Seward—although Seward was gravely injured. There was a national backlash against the conspirators. Booth was killed in a shootout with the authorities, and eight co-conspirators were tried and four were hanged.

Thus the last effort of Democrats to save the institution of slavery ended in ignominy. But the Democrats were not finished. They were down but not out. Soon, as we will see in the next chapter, the Democrats moved on to a new nefarious scheme of oppression and theft, one that was almost as despicable as slavery.

CHAPTER 4

SEGREGATION NOW, SEGREGATION FOREVER

HOW DEMOCRATS USED LAWS—AND LAWLESSNESS— TO KEEP BLACKS IN THEIR PLACE

This is a white man's country—let the white man rule.
—Official Democratic Party slogan, 1868 presidential campaign

I n 1969, twenty-one-year-old Hillary Rodham was selected to give the commencement address on behalf of graduating seniors at Wellesley College. Hillary came prepared with an address that included the familiar 1960s cocktail of left-wing idealism and pure blather. None of it is worth our attention. Here I want to focus on what Hillary said impromptu, once she had heard the speaker who preceded her.

The speaker was Senator Edward Brooke, a Republican from Massachusetts and the first black senator to be popularly elected in American history. Brooke was a political moderate, as suggested by the title of his autobiography, *Bridging the Divide*. He had been chosen to receive an honorary degree by Wellesley that year.

Upon receiving the award, Brooke spoke briefly, expressing his empathy with the idealism of young people on issues such as the Vietnam War and civil rights. At the same time, Brooke cautioned them that they should stay within the law and not engage in "coercive protest" because that would risk alienating people otherwise sympathetic to their cause.

Brooke's unobjectionable remarks stirred Hillary into high dudgeon and she ascended the podium. Attempting to speak for her generation, Hillary said, "We're not in the positions yet of leadership and power, but we do have that indispensable task of criticizing and constructive protest."

Responding directly to Brooke, she added, "Part of the problem with empathy with professed goals is that empathy doesn't do us anything." Hillary went on to say, "We've had lots of empathy; we've had lots of sympathy." Hillary didn't say it but her implication was clear: we've heard enough from you, old black man!

Hillary added that her generation had been asked to wait for too long, and now it was feeling used. "We feel that too long our leaders have said politics is the art of the possible. And the challenge now is to practice making what appears to be impossible, possible." Hillary didn't say whether Brooke was a false friend using young people, or whether he was, as a supporter of Richard Nixon and the war in Vietnam, himself a case of a black man being used. The audience could draw its own conclusions about that.

Hillary concluded her address by reading a poem that referred to "the hollow men of anger and bitterness" who must be left behind. Senator Brooke took offense to that, recognizing it as a reference to him. Hillary's point didn't escape anyone in the audience. She and like-minded young people were ready and willing to take over the country from the likes of Senator Brooke.

Hillary's speech was met with a thunderous ovation by her fellow students, and her professors enthusiastically joined in. The *Boston Globe* reported the next day that Hillary had upstaged Brooke. Hillary was profiled that year in a *Life* magazine feature, "The Class of '69," that highlighted student speakers across the country. Clearly the young star had struck a chord, and her career was on its way.

Even today, young leftists claim to draw inspiration from what Hillary said more than thirty-five years ago. And Hillary herself has never repudiated her remarks; on the contrary, returning to Wellesley during her husband's presidency, Hillary said that her original commencement speech "reflected the hopes, values and aspirations of my classmates." Then she confessed, "It is uncanny to me the degree to which those same hopes, values and aspirations have shaped my adulthood."[1]

LETTING THE BLACK MAN HAVE IT

Ponder the extraordinary spectacle that young Hillary created at her graduation address. Here was a white girl, scarcely in her twenties, delivering a public scolding and tongue-lashing to a highly accomplished fifty-year-old black man. Hillary lectured him with a tone of evident contempt and from a position of presumed superiority. Yet Hillary had no accomplishments that could compare with Brooke's; her superiority was clearly not based on anything that she had done. Where, then, did it come from?

It came from history. Hillary placed herself squarely on the "right side" of history and, by implication if not outright assertion, placed Senator Brooke on the "wrong side." Hillary didn't quite say it, but both in her tone and in her remarks, she left the clear impression that Brooke was a kind of Uncle Tom. He was a sellout to the system—to the existing way of doing things—while she represented a moral challenge to the system.

Here Hillary did not merely assert the obvious, if tedious, truism that the future belongs to the young. Much more than that, she appealed to a progressive consensus that she could rely on. That consensus declared that left-leaning Democrats are the good guys and Republicans—even moderate Republicans—are the bad guys. Consequently, white liberals should feel no qualms about giving it to black Republicans, fully confident that academia will applaud and the media will cheer.

Let's examine the main themes and story line of the progressive consensus. According to this story line, America has a long history of racism that was especially virulent in the South. Although Republicans may have played an important role in ending slavery, the South basically created new institutions of racism in the postbellum period. This southern oppression is epitomized by the Black Codes, segregation, lynching, and the Ku Klux Klan.

Who—the progressive story line continues—fought to end this oppression? The progressive Democrats! It was a Supreme Court dominated by progressives that ended segregation beginning with *Brown v. Board of Education*. The Democratic Party took Martin Luther King's lead and championed the cause of civil rights, first for blacks, and then for women and other minorities. A Democratic president, Lyndon Johnson, pushed through the Civil Rights Act of 1964. The Johnson administration also convinced a Democratic Congress to pass the Voting Rights Act of 1965 and the Fair Housing Bill of 1968.

Meanwhile, according to the progressive story line, conservatives and Republicans have proven themselves the consistent enemy of civil rights. The Republican South, in particular, is the home of American racism. No wonder blacks and other minorities vote for Democrats in overwhelming numbers. African Americans and other persons of color aren't stupid; they know who their friends are. Here, in sum, is the fund of moral superiority that Hillary Clinton drew on when she gave it to Senator Brooke.

The central issue, therefore, is which is the party of racism and which is the party of civil rights? This question cannot be answered simply by invoking the Civil Rights Movement of the 1950s and 1960s. That movement was itself parasitic on an earlier civil rights movement that took place a century earlier.

Didn't know there were two civil rights movements? That's because the progressives don't say much about it. They focus on the later movement and pass over the earlier one. The earlier civil rights revolution is downplayed today because it has become politically problematic. It disrupts the progressive party line. Even in the second civil rights revolution, however, the roots of the first one are clearly apparent.

Let's enumerate the rights supposedly conferred by the Civil Rights Movement of the 1950s and 1960s. The *Brown* decision, in ending school segregation, allegedly established the right of blacks to freely avail themselves of public facilities without legal restriction or prohibition. In other words, it was a freedom decision.

The Civil Rights Act of 1964 famously guaranteed blacks, women, and other minorities the right not to be discriminated against in jobs and government contracts. The Fair Housing Bill of 1968 extended this antidiscrimination provision to housing. So these two pieces of legislation provided equal rights under the law. They were social justice provisions.

The Voting Rights Act of 1965 guaranteed to blacks and other minorities full enfranchisement, in other words, the same right to vote that whites enjoyed. It was an equality provision.

WHERE THESE RIGHTS COME FROM

Yet what was the constitutional basis for these actions? Desegregation and anti-discrimination laws both relied on the notion that blacks weren't slaves any longer; rather, they were free and could make their own choices. This freedom, however, had been secured for blacks by the Thirteenth Amendment to the Constitution which permanently abolished slavery. Thus, the Thirteenth Amendment was the original freedom charter for African Americans.

The desegregation court rulings and the anti-discrimination provisions of the Civil Rights Act and the Fair Housing Bill were also based on the "equal protection" clause of the Fourteenth Amendment. This Amendment granted citizenship to blacks and established equal rights under the law. It was the original social justice manifesto for blacks, women, and other minorities.

Finally, the Voting Rights Act attempted to secure for blacks full enfranchisement, the right to vote. But blacks already had the right to vote. That right was specified in the Fifteenth Amendment to the Constitution. This amendment declared that, as citizens, blacks had the same prerogative to cast their ballots as whites and all others. The 1965 Voting Rights Act merely sought to enforce an equality provision that had been constitutionally affirmed much earlier.

The Thirteenth, Fourteenth, and Fifteenth amendments were passed in the aftermath of the Civil War. They were passed by the Republican Party. The Republicans enacted these measures then to secure the freedom, equality, and social justice that Democrats keep harping on today. To further promote these goals, Republicans also implemented a series of Civil Rights laws: the Civil Rights Act of 1866, the Reconstruction Act of 1867, and the Ku Klux Klan Act of 1871.

The Republican ethos underlying these landmark provisions was aptly framed by the great abolitionist Republican, Frederick Douglass. Douglass said, "It is evident that white and black must fall or flourish together. In light of this great truth, laws ought to be enacted, and institutions established—all distinctions, founded on complexion, and every right, privilege and immunity, now enjoyed by the white man, ought to be as freely granted to the man of color."[2]

This was the clarion cry taken up by the GOP in the aftermath of the Civil War. Virtually all the black leaders who emerged from that era were Republicans who supported the GOP's call to remove race as the basis of government policy and social action. Historian Eric Foner writes that black activists of the antebellum era embraced "an affirmation of Americanism that insisted blacks were entitled to the same rights and opportunities that white citizens enjoyed."[3]

Notice that the GOP program—articulated by Douglass and affirmed by black leaders—is none other than the color-blind ideal outlined in Martin Luther King's famous "dream." King envisioned a society in which we are judged by the content of our character, not the color of our skin. This is substantially what Douglass and other black Republicans called for, more than a century earlier.

How interesting that the Democrat, Martin Luther King, is identified with a principle that the Republican, Frederick Douglass, expressed even more eloquently so much earlier. How bizarre that the Democrats are presumed to be the party of civil rights when the very content of civil rights was formulated and developed by the GOP.

Very few young people know this history. Most of them haven't even heard about Douglass; who hasn't heard of Martin Luther King? Am I suggesting that the scandalous neglect of Douglass and the excessive praise heaped on King is part of the progressive whitewash? You bet I am.

But, say the Democratic and progressive historians, wait a minute! While King's program moved forward and was enacted into law,

Douglass's program was halted in its tracks. We cannot forget about the backlash!

Yes, indeed. The Democratic storytellers are right that there was a powerful backlash against blacks in the South, so that the constitutional provisions of freedom, equality, and social justice became a dead letter. The Civil Rights laws were stymied, and even the provisions that passed were ignored. Blacks were reduced to new forms of subjugation not identical with, but reminiscent of, slavery. This re-enslavement of blacks was enforced by a juggernaut of violence epitomized by that institution of domestic terrorism, the Ku Klux Klan.

This part of the story is true enough. What the storytellers omit, however, is that the Democrats are the ones who caused the backlash! They are the ones who from the beginning opposed black freedom and black equality, undermining voting rights and equal treatment under the law. They were the true enemies of racial and social justice.

Moreover, the Democrats did those things not just through political and legal measures but also through domestic terrorism. Indeed, the Ku Klux Klan was a licensed instrument of terror and intimidation unleashed by Democrats and operating for the benefit of the Democratic Party.

Consequently, it was Democrats who, from the 1860s through the 1960s, prevented blacks as a group from enjoying their rights through political opposition and violent acts of terror. Democrats now claim credit for allowing blacks to have the civil rights that they themselves violently prevented for a hundred years.

BLAMING THE SOUTH

Today's Democrats try to shift blame from themselves by blaming "the South." The South is supposedly responsible for espousing racist views and implementing racist practices. Yet the detractors of the South neglect to point out that after Reconstruction, the Democratic Party was the dominant, almost the sole, political party in the South.

One prominent Democrat, South Carolina governor (and later senator) Ben Tillman, explained how this came about. "Republicanism means

Negro equality, while the Democratic Party means that the white man is superior. That's why we Southerners are all Democrats."[4]

How did the South become so uniformly Democratic? Basically the Democrats used racist ideas and practices to establish a lasting political hegemony there. So racism wasn't incidental; it was an essential part of the Democratic Party's strategy. The Democrats won the South by appealing not just to the former planter class but also to poor whites.

How did they do this? The great postbellum invention of the Democratic Party was the institution of white supremacy. After the war, writes historian George Fredrickson, "The one thing that held the Democratic Party together was a commitment to maintaining white supremacy."[5] White supremacy is an elaborate ideological structure for justifying racism, in the same way that the "positive good" school was an elaborate ideological justification for slavery.

Now I am obviously not suggesting that the Democrats invented racism, any more than I am suggesting that they invented slavery. Obviously slavery existed for a long time before the Democrats made their "positive good" arguments in favor of it. Similarly racism existed long before the Democrats developed the comprehensive ideology of white supremacy.

The purpose of an ideology is to reinforce a practice by defending and systematizing it. The "positive good" defense strengthened slavery by giving it an ideological foundation, and white supremacy did the same for racism. In fact, the supremacist ideology did more for racism than the "positive good" ideology did for slavery. "Positive good" arguments, after all, didn't create the plantation system. That system already existed, and the "positive good" school was simply a southern Democratic rationalization for it.

By contrast, white supremacy created a whole new set of laws and practices that became the institutional embodiment of racism: the Black Codes, Jim Crow, segregation, and a network of terrorist organizations such as the Ku Klux Klan. Together these institutions created what historians bluntly refer to as the "re-enslavement" of blacks.

The term "enslavement" is an important one that will recur in this book. As I said in the last chapter, enslavement isn't slavery—it is a transmission belt for moving people in the direction of slavery. Enslaved people are not property but they are in captivity.

By historical analogy, serfs were not slaves because they weren't literally owned by their masters. On the other hand serfs were so captive to their masters in every aspect of their lives that we can fairly describe serfdom as a kind of enslavement. Having previously specialized in slavery, the Democratic Party soon specialized in enslavement—a strategy the party employs to the present day.

The institutions of black enslavement and white supremacy did not exist before Democrats in the South created them. The very same institutions then became the mechanisms that Democrats used to build their power, and also to repel and defeat attempts by Republicans to extend rights and opportunities to black Americans.

A NEW RACKET

After slavery, the Democrats needed something new in order to continue their tradition of theft, oppression, and power-seeking. They found a replacement for slavery in the form of white supremacy. Once Democrats were no longer allowed to buy and sell people and force them to work for free, racism and white supremacy became the preferred mechanism for Democrats to exploit black people, recruit new supporters, and secure the party's power and control in the South.

But how? How did racism and white supremacy consolidate the Democrats as the ruling party of the region for nearly a century, from the 1860s through the 1960s? White supremacy may be a racket, like slavery, but we all know how slavery pays—it pays in the form of getting other people to work for you for free. How does white supremacy pay? What do the people who support it get out of it?

Let's consider the situation facing the poor white man in the South. What does this guy stand to gain from segregation—from forcing blacks to drink from separate water fountains or to use separate restrooms? What would make a man who would seem to derive no economic benefit from it nevertheless join that institution of Democratic terror, the Ku Klux Klan? To put it bluntly, what's in it for him?

We can resolve this conundrum by answering a similar question that historians have raised about the Civil War. Why did poor whites, the vast majority of whom didn't own slaves, fight on the Confederate side? Of course we know why the slave owners fought—to protect the value of their "property." But how did they convince the non-slaveholding whites to join them? Seemingly these poor whites had nothing to gain by extending the life of the "peculiar institution." What, then, were they fighting for?

A clue to this question is provided in an address delivered in 1860 by South Carolina planter John Townsend. Speaking on behalf of secession to a group called the 1860 Association, Townsend directly addressed the issue of how the southern plantation system benefited whites who didn't own slaves.

> The color of the white man is now, in the South, a title of nobility in his relations to the Negro. Although Cuffy or Sambo may be immensely his superior in wealth, may have his thousands deposited in the bank, as some of them have, and may be the owner of many slaves, as some of them are, yet the poorest non-slaveholder, being a white man, is his superior in the eyes of the law, may serve and command in the militia, may sit upon juries, to decide upon the rights of the wealthiest in the land, may gave his testimony in court, and may cast his vote, equally with the largest slaveholder, in the choice of his rulers.
>
> In no other country in the world does the poor white man occupy so enviable a position as in the slaveholding states of the South. In countries where Negro slavery does not exist, as in the Northern states of this union and in Europe, the most menial and degrading employments in society are filled by the white poor, who are hourly seen drudging in them. Poverty, then, in those countries, becomes the badge of

inferiority, and wealth, of distinction. Hence the arrogant airs which wealth there puts on, in its intercourse with the poor man.

But in the Southern slaveholding states, where these menial and degrading offices are turned over to be performed exclusively by the Negro slave, the status and color of the black race becomes the badge of inferiority, and the poorest non-slaveholder may rejoice with the richest of his brethren of the white race, in the distinction of his color. The poorest non-slaveholder thinks and feels and acts as if he was, and always intended to be, superior to the Negro.[6]

A RACIAL CASTE SYSTEM

Here we see beautifully enumerated the social and psychological benefits that poor whites derived from white supremacy. White supremacy created a racial caste system in which the poorest, meanest, and stupidest white guy belonged to an aristocracy of color that elevated him above the most intelligent, decent, and productive black man.

George Orwell saw the same phenomenon in Burma (now Myanmar) when he served as a colonial officer there. Relaxing at the whites-only club, Orwell saw arrogant British twenty-somethings ordering and kicking around dignified Asian Indian servants in their fifties and sixties.

I remember hearing similar accounts from my grandfather, who suffered the indignity of hearing white-skinned youths call him "coolie" and "boy." My grandfather was a mechanical engineer in his forties. As a consequence of his humiliating experiences at the hands of uncouth Britishers, he became embittered for life against white people.

These uncouth Britishers, Orwell knew, were losers in their own country. They were at the bottom of the British caste system. In fact, they had been dispatched to India and Burma largely to get rid of them. In India and Burma, however, they found that their social level had been raised.

As a consequence of the colonialist distinction between the ruling class and the ruled, the low men on the British totem pole became the

high men on the Indian and Burmese totem pole. Suddenly their whiteness made them members of an elite and privileged caste. They could
now have fun kicking other people around.

Yet—and this is the most amazing part—Orwell noticed that these
very same abusive jerks would sound off to each other about how they
were in India for the benefit of the Indians. Orwell termed this "the lie
that we're here to uplift our poor black brothers instead of to rob them."
Orwell concluded that, "We Anglos could be almost bearable if we'd
only admit we're thieves and go on thieving without any humbug."

Even as an Englishman, Orwell was appalled at the condescending
hypocrisy he witnessed at the colonial club. Yet he understood it. The
young Englishmen were enjoying the twisted pleasures of aristocracy.
They took pleasure in demeaning and lording it over the brown people
below them—even while pretending to be magnanimous toward them—
because in this way they confirmed and ratified their superiority.[7]

Precisely the same benefit that the British government offered to its
white expatriates, the Democratic Party in the United States offered to
its poor white supporters. From the 1870s through the 1960s, the Democrats established their political hegemony in the South by granting
whites the full social and psychological enjoyments of white supremacy.

Blacks paid a costly price for this, because the Democrats unleashed
a fury of violence against them. In fact, had the Democrats been the only
political party in America, it's hard to image what would have become
of the black population of the South. Blacks, however, had during most
of this difficult period a single ally. That ally was the Republican Party.

For nearly a century following the Civil War, the Republican Party
made valiant efforts, often against near-impossible odds, to protect
blacks from the Democratic onslaught and to secure their basic rights.
At times these measures worked; at other times, they proved far too
feeble to control the vicious racists in the Democratic Party.

Nevertheless, in the long run the GOP succeeded. Just as the Founders' constitutional principles eventually supplied the necessary foundation
for America to realize the principle that "all men are created equal," so
too the GOP-sponsored amendments of the 1860s supplied the

indispensable basis for blacks in the 1950s and 1960s to overcome white supremacy and actually exercise their rights. Blacks today owe their basic rights of liberty, equality, and justice to the GOP—rights that Democrats withheld from them for almost a century.

THE ORIGINAL CIVIL RIGHTS REVOLUTION

Let's begin by examining the first civil rights revolution in America—the civil rights revolution of the 1860s. This was a Republican revolution, which is why progressive Democrats ignore it and pretend that the later revolution of the 1950s and 1960s is the only one. Yet of the two civil rights revolutions, the first—the ignored one—is actually more important.

To see why, consider the meaning of the term "civil rights." What is a "civil right" and why are civil rights important? Civil rights are actually distinguished from natural rights. Imagine if you and I lived in the jungle, removed from society. Philosophers call this the "state of nature." In the state of nature, we would have natural rights: the right to defend ourselves, or the right to pick fruit from trees and eat it. These are rights that we have by virtue of being human.

Civil rights, by contrast, are rights that we derive from society. They arise out of a social compact whose legitimacy derives from the consent of the people. While blacks were slaves, they had no civil rights. Even when they were emancipated, this merely returned them to freedom, to the state of nature. Humans have natural rights in the state of nature but they do not have civil rights. Civil rights are derived from membership in a society.

The Republicans who controlled both houses of Congress after the Civil War knew this. They also knew that, before conferring civil rights, they had to once and for all abolish slavery. The Thirteenth Amendment ending slavery was passed by the Senate on April 8, 1864, and by the House on January 31, 1865.

Republican support for the amendment: 100 percent. Democratic support: 23 percent. Even after the Civil War, only a tiny percentage of

Democrats were willing to sign up to permanently end slavery. Most Democrats wanted it to continue.

In the following year, on June 13, 1866, the Republican Congress passed the Fourteenth Amendment overturning the *Dred Scott* decision and granting full citizenship and equal rights under the law to blacks. This amendment prohibited states from abridging the "privileges and immunities" of all citizens, from depriving them of "due process of law" or denying them "equal protection of the law." The Fourteenth Amendment passed the House and Senate with exclusive Republican support. Not a single Democrat either in the House or the Senate voted for it.

Two years later, in 1868, Congress with the support of newly-elected Republican president Ulysses Grant passed the Fifteenth Amendment granting suffrage to blacks. The right to vote, it said, cannot be "denied or abridged by the United States or any state on account of race, color or previous condition of servitude."

In the Senate, the Fifteenth Amendment passed by a vote of 39 to 13. Every one of the 39 "yes" votes came from Republicans. (Some Republicans like Charles Sumner abstained because they wanted the measure to go even further than it did.) All the 13 "no" votes came from Democrats. In the House, every "yes" vote came from a Republican and every Democrat voted "no."

It is surely a matter of the greatest significance that the constitutional provisions that made possible the Civil Rights Act, the Voting Rights Act, and the Fair Housing Bill only entered the Constitution thanks to the Republican Party. Beyond this, the GOP put forward a series of Civil Rights laws to further reinforce black people's rights to freedom, equality, and social justice.

When Republicans passed the Civil Rights Act of 1866—guaranteeing to blacks the rights to make contracts and to have the criminal laws apply equally to whites and blacks—the Democrats struck back. They didn't have the votes in Congress, but they had a powerful ally in President Andrew Johnson. Johnson vetoed the legislation.

Now this may seem like an odd act for Lincoln's vice president, but it actually wasn't. Many people don't realize that Johnson wasn't a

The roots of the Clinton Foundation's corruption can be found in the land-stealing policies of Andrew Jackson, the founder of the Democratic Party. *Library of Congress*

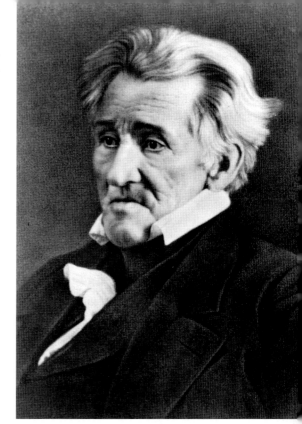

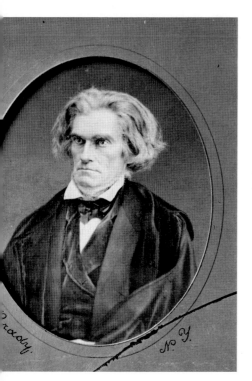

Democrat John C. Calhoun invented the "positive good" school of slavery in which he insisted slavery was good not only for the master but also for the slave. Ever since, Democrats have been exploiting people while insisting that such exploitation is good for the people being ripped off. *Library of Congress*

Abraham Lincoln, America's first Republican President, aptly described the difference between the two parties by saying that one thinks slavery is wrong and ought to be restricted, while the other thinks slavery is right and ought to be extended. *Library of Congress*

Northern Democrat Stephen Douglas, who sought to uphold slavery through his doctrine of "popular sovereignty," gives the lie to the idea that the slavery battle was between the North and the South—actually it was between the Republican and the Democratic parties. *Library of Congress*

While Democrats previously kept blacks "down on the plantation" with lashings and whippings, today they keep blacks on the urban plantation through dependence on the progressive welfare state. Hillary's America *(the film)*

Here's an example of Democratic Party propaganda from the Civil War period—Democrats are portrayed as dignified white men while Republicans are portrayed as blacks with scary, exaggerated features. *Library of Congress*

THE TWO PLATFORMS

Every RADICAL in Congress VOTED for NEGRO SUFFRAGE. Every RADICAL in the Pennsylvania Senate VOTED for NEGRO SUFFRAGE. STEVENS, FORNEY & CAMERON are for NEGRO SUFFRAGE; they are all Candidates for the UNITED STATES SENATE. NO RADICAL NEWSPAPER OPPOSES NEGRO SUFFRAGE. GEARY said in a Speech, at Harrisburg, 11th of August, 1866—"THERE CAN BE NO POSSIBLE OBJECTION TO NEGRO SUFFRAGE."

CLYMER'S
Platform is for the White Man.

GEARY'S
Platform is for the Negro.

READ THE PLATFORMS

CONGRESS says, THE NEGRO MUST BE ALLOWED TO VOTE, OR THE STATES BE PUNISHED.
[POST THIS UP.]

Republican Booker T. Washington, a former slave, inspired the ire of Democratic racists when he dined with Republican President Teddy Roosevelt; Democratic Senator Ben Tillman said, "Now that Roosevelt has eaten with that n*gger Washington, we shall have to kill a thousand n*ggers to get them back to their place." *Library of Congress*

IDA B. WELLS.

Republican crusader Ida B. Wells sought to stop the practice of lynching, but she had mixed success because lynching was protected and promoted by the Democratic Party as a technique of keeping blacks down—and preventing them from voting Republican. *Library of Congress*

By showing the racist film *The Birth of a Nation* in the White House, the progressive Democrat Woodrow Wilson inspired a Ku Klux Klan revival in the South, Midwest, and West. Wilson also segregated all areas of the federal government, telling black leaders that segregation was for their benefit. *Copyright by Harris & Ewing, courtesy of the Library of Congress*

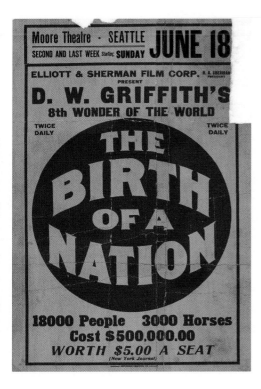

The film *The Birth of a Nation*, a work of propaganda by the Southern Democrat D. W. Griffith, shows valiant Klansmen riding to the rescue of southern maidens who are malevolently abused by lusty black men in league with meddling northern Republicans. *Library of Congress*

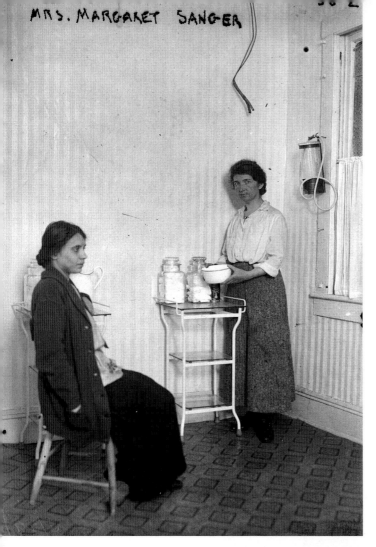

Mrs. Margaret Sanger

Progressive Margaret Sanger—founder of Planned Parenthood and heroine to Hillary Clinton—sought to deal with the "unfit" by keeping them out of the country or killing them. Her "Negro Project" was designed to reduce the size of the black population.
Library of Congress

As part of their national campaign of forced sterilization, progressives sterilized Carrie Buck, and in approving the action, Supreme Court Justice Oliver Wendell Holmes famously declared, "Three generations of imbeciles are enough."
Hillary's America *(the film)*

The Ku Klux Klan was founded in the 1860s and initially focused its terror tactics not on blacks but on white Republicans. *Library of Congress*

Night-riding and cross-burning were two symbols of the KKK. Historian Eric Foner calls the Klan the domestic terrorist arm of the Democratic Party, whose main objective was to enforce white supremacy and to keep the South voting monolithically Democrat. *Library of Congress*

The sexual relationship between bank robbers Bonnie and Clyde was complicated—possibly just as twisted as that of their modern-day counterparts, Bill and Hillary Clinton. But even so, what these cases show is that the couple that steals together, stays together. *Library of Congress*

Mobster Al Capone is the inspiration behind modern progressive techniques of intimidation and political shakedown; he also helps us understand how the Democratic Party, while operating like a crime syndicate, came to be viewed as on the side of the "little guy." *Pennsylvania Department of Corrections/FBI*

Hillary Clinton's political techniques can be traced back through Saul Alinsky to Frank Nitti, the number two man in the Capone mob—seen here as depicted in the film *Hillary's America*. *Hillary's America (the film)*

Segregation laws were passed by Democratic legislatures, signed by Democratic governors, and enforced by Democratic mayors, city officials, sheriffs, and vigilante mobs. Segregation was, from beginning to end, created and sustained by Democrats. *Library of Congress*

Progressive hero Franklin Roosevelt cut a deal with racist Democrats in which he agreed, in exchange for their support of his agenda, to block anti-lynching legislation and to exclude blacks from most New Deal programs. This shows how progressivism didn't displace racism; rather, it incorporated it. *Library of Congress*

One of FDR's closest allies was the notorious racist Theodore Bilbo—FDR's choice to run the District of Columbia—who said, "The n*gger would never vote in Washington. Hell, if we give 'em the right to vote up there, half the n*ggers in the South will move into Washington and we'll have a black government." *Library of Congress*

If my claim of progressive fascination with fascism and Nazism seems far-fetched, consider this: young John F. Kennedy toured Germany in the 1930s and praised Hitler as a "legend," attributing hostility to the Nazis to jealousy of what they had accomplished.
Courtesy of the John F. Kennedy Presidential Library and Museum, Boston

The forced sterilization policies of the Nazis—which at first didn't target Jews but rather "unfit" physical and mental defectives—were based in part on compulsory birth control measures developed in the United States by Margaret Sanger and her progressive allies.
Library of Congress

Progressive Democrats have worked hard to erase this history, but their hero Franklin D. Roosevelt admired Mussolini in the 1930s, and Mussolini returned the compliment, considering FDR to be a fellow fascist. *Office of War Information, Overseas Picture Division, Washington Division, 1944, courtesy of the Library of Congress*

George Wallace, who coined the slogan "Segregation now, segregation tomorrow, segregation forever," is symbolic of the massive intergenerational faction of racist Democrat politicians—numbering over 1,500—of which only fourteen—less than 1 percent—switched and later became Republicans. *Library of Congress*

Originally a member of the southern faction of racist Democrats, Lyndon Johnson saw the Civil Rights Act as a means to keep "n*ggers," as he called them, down on the Democratic plantation. *Library of Congress*

Saul Alinsky—mentor to both Obama and Hillary—was no crusader for social justice; rather, he began his career as a petty street criminal and thief and later learned the art of political intimidation and shakedown at the hands of various Chicago gangs. *Associated Press*

While young Hillary—seen here at Wellesley College—wrote her thesis on Alinsky, she went beyond Alinsky's outsider shakedown approach to develop her own strategy of shaking down the country from the inside, using the coercive instruments of the federal government. *Getty Images*

Young Hillary realized what we all know, that Bill Clinton is a sex addict, and she saw how she could turn his problem to her lifelong advantage. Hillary's America *(the film)*

Here is the charade of the Clinton marriage on full display; in reality this is a bargain in which Hillary gets her "pitch man" and in exchange provides protection and cover for Bill's predatory sexual behavior. *Library of Congress*

My experience spending eight months with hoodlums in a federal confinement center proved indispensable in understanding the criminal and mob-inspired operations of the Clintons and the Democratic Party. Hillary's America *(the film)*

Just as Evita Peron used her philanthropic foundation to take in $200 million for herself and her husband Juan, Hillary uses the Clinton Foundation as a receptacle for hundreds of millions of dollars in "contributions" that are actually bribes in exchange for favors granted through her and Bill's political influence. *Evita Peron photo: Associated Press, Hillary Clinton photo: Getty Images*

Republican; he was a Democrat. Historian Kenneth Stampp calls him "the last Jacksonian."[8] Lincoln put him on the ticket because he was a pro-union Democrat and Lincoln was looking for ways to win the votes of Democrats opposed to secession.

Johnson, however, was both a southern partisan and a Democratic partisan. Once the Civil War ended, he attempted to lead weak-kneed Republicans into a new Democratic coalition based on racism and white privilege. Johnson championed the Democratic mantra of white supremacy, declaring, "This is a country for white men and, by God, as long as I am president, it shall be a government of white men."

In his 1867 annual message to Congress, Johnson declared that blacks possess "less capacity for government than any other race of people. No independent government of any form has ever been successful in their hands. On the contrary, wherever they have been left to their own devices they have shown a consistent tendency to relapse into barbarism."[9] These are perhaps the most racist words uttered by an American president, and no surprise, they were uttered by a Democrat.

Outraged by Johnson's words and his veto of the Civil Rights Act of 1866, the Republican Congress sought to impeach him. The measure passed the House but fell just short in the Senate—just as a century later there were not enough Senate votes to remove Bill Clinton from office. The GOP was, however, successful in over-riding Johnson's veto, so that the Civil Rights Act of 1866 became law over the Democratic president's objection.

Furious at Republican success in passing constitutional amendments and civil rights legislation for blacks, southern Democrats responded with the infamous Black Codes. These were approved through state legislatures and state constitutional conventions held throughout the South in the years following the war. Only whites participated in these sessions. These codes represented a new Democratic form of enslavement; some historians use the term "neo-slavery."

Fairly typical is the code Democrats adopted in South Carolina. Blacks were permitted to work only in certain professions, thus granting whites a labor monopoly in the remaining ones. White masters could whip young black servants. Blacks could not travel freely; if they did, they ran the risk of being declared "vagrants" in which case they could be arrested and imprisoned. Sheriffs could then assign hard labor or hire them out to white employers to work off their sentence. Black children could be apprenticed to white employers against their will.

In addition, blacks could not vote or serve on juries. Their testimony in court was only considered relevant in cases involving other blacks. Many crimes—such as rebellion, arson, and assaulting a white woman—carried the death penalty for blacks, but not for whites. Blacks were not allowed to sell alcohol or carry a firearm. While blacks could now marry, the code made it clear that "marriage between a white person and a person of color shall be null and void."

THE GOP COUNTERATTACK

Indignant at what they perceived as a southern Democratic attempt to nullify emancipation, Republicans struck down the Black Codes and began the process of Reconstruction. Reconstruction was aimed at rebuilding the South on a new plane of equality of rights between the races. It wasn't easy, but essentially Congress was attempting to control the internal affairs of southern states where the local Democratic Party mounted stubborn resistance. Even so, it's remarkable what the Republicans achieved against daunting odds.

The GOP's first step in this regard was to establish the Freedman's Bureau. At one point the bureau considered a reparations bill modeled on one of General Sherman's field directives. Sherman's Directive 15 provided blacks with forty acres of land to farm on their own, plus a retired army mule. The bureau began to implement its reparations plan, settling blacks on the plantations that had been taken over by Union troops.

Today we hear occasional demands for black reparations, and those demands usually come from progressive Democrats. I find it interesting that these Democrats never suggest that they pay reparations for what their party did. Rather, they point the finger at Republicans, when

Republicans are the ones who historically supported and attempted to enact reparations. In a sense the GOP was trying to compensate blacks for their suffering at the hands of the Democratic Party.

Unable by themselves to thwart the Bureau's reparations bill, Democrats appealed to President Johnson. Johnson undercut practical efforts at reparations by issuing pardons galore so that former Confederates could recover their property that had been lost during the war. Blacks who had been granted land by Sherman or the Freedman's Bureau were forced to return it to the former plantation owners.

So the Republican reparations program died an ignominious death. The bureau did, however, open hundreds of schools for blacks. It also provided newly freed blacks with food, health services, and legal protection, and also helped unite the families of former slaves. These measures, although insufficient, showed African Americans that their only political ally in the country was the Republican Party.

The most aggressive move the GOP made under Reconstruction was to appoint military governors throughout the South. These officers had the power to override local authority. Thanks to Republican supervision, more than 1,500 blacks won federal, state, and local offices. A former slave named Blanche K. Bruce became the first black senator from Mississippi to serve a full term. John Langston became the first black congressman from Virginia. Every single one of these blacks was elected as a Republican.

No surprise that these African Americans are ignored in progressive historiography. Rosa Parks is well known to young people simply because she refused to sit in the back of the bus. (Actually this was no spontaneous act. Parks had been put up to it. Her "tired old black woman" story was largely invented to serve the needs of progressive propaganda.)

By contrast, Blanche K. Bruce was the real deal. Born into slavery in Virginia, Bruce was freed by his master and studied at Oberlin College before becoming a successful farmer and landowner. He is the only former slave to have served in the U.S. Senate. His story is vastly more impressive than that of Parks. Progressive historians ignore him because he was not a Democrat.

THE DEMOCRATS AND THE KU KLUX KLAN

The Democrats did play a role in Reconstruction—they worked to block it. The party struck out against Reconstruction in two ways. The first was to form a network of terrorist organizations with names like the Constitutional Guards, the White Brotherhood, the Society of Pale Faces, and the Knights of the White Camelia. The second was to institute state-sponsored segregation throughout the South.

Let us consider these two approaches one by one. The Democrats started numerous terror groups, but the most notorious of these was the Ku Klux Klan. Founded in 1866, the Klan was initially led by a former Confederate army officer, Nathan Bedford Forrest, who served two years later as a Democratic delegate to the party's 1868 national convention. Forrest's role in the Klan is controversial; he later disputed that he was ever involved, insisting he was active in attempting to disband the organization.

Initially the Klan's main targets weren't blacks but rather white people who were believed to be in cahoots with blacks. The Klan unleashed its violence against northern Republicans who were accused of being "carpetbaggers" and unwarrantedly interfering in southern life, as well as southern "scalawags" and "white niggers" who the Klan considered to be in league with the northern Republicans. The Klan's goal was to repress blacks by getting rid of these perceived allies of the black cause.

Once again Republicans moved into action, passing a series of measures collectively termed the Ku Klux Klan Acts of 1871. These acts came to be known as the Force Bill, signed into law by a Republican President, Ulysses Grant. They restricted northern Democratic inflows of money and weapons to the Klan, and also empowered federal officials to crack down on the Klan's organized violence. The Force Bill was implemented by military governors appointed by Grant.

These anti-Klan measures seem modest in attempting to arrest what Grant described as an "invisible empire throughout the South." But historian Eric Foner says the Force Bill did markedly reduce lawless violence by the Democrats. The measures taken by Republicans actually helped shut down the Ku Klux Klan. By 1873, the Klan was defunct, until it was revived a quarter-century later by a new group of racist Democrats.

In 1902 a prominent Democratic writer, Thomas Dixon, wrote a vicious anti-black novel *The Leopard's Spots: A Romance of the White Man's Burden* and followed it up in 1905 with *The Clansman: An Historical Romance of the Ku Klux Klan.* Dixon's book was a massive bestseller in the Democratic South. A few years later, Dixon collaborated with another Democrat, the film producer D. W. Griffith, to make *The Birth of a Nation.* This was one of the first full-length motion pictures ever shown in the United States.

Released in 1915, *The Birth of a Nation* caused a sensation with its dramatic scenes of ruthless northerner carpetbaggers looting the poor, honest families of the South as well as lusty black men preying with impunity on southern maidens. In later interviews, Griffith said he modeled the hero of the story on his own father, who is depicted as heroically if unsuccessfully trying to uphold southern gentlemanliness in the face of northern barbarism.

Interestingly enough Abraham Lincoln is portrayed favorably in the film; he is called the Great Heart and the story implies that Reconstruction would have gone better had he remained in office. The villain of Griffith's story was a northern politician named Austin Stoneman, who was modeled directly on the Republican abolitionist Thaddeus Stevens.

The night-riding Klansmen were the film's heroes, finally taking on the northern malefactors and protecting the honor of the South. The film made no reference to Republicans or Democrats—in a sense, Griffith was the original perpetrator of the progressive myth that party differences were inconsequential and that slavery and segregation were purely a North-South issue.

The Birth of a Nation was strongly protested by northern Republicans such as Harvard president Charles Eliot and the feminist reformer Jane Addams, but also by Republicans in the South, such as the black educator Booker T. Washington. By contrast, the film was vigorously defended by Democrats across the country, including the former chief justice of the Supreme Court, Edward White, who was a member of the original Ku Klux Klan.

In the year of the film's release, the Democratic president, Woodrow Wilson, arranged a private screening in the Oval Office for his cabinet and other invited guests. After the screening Wilson declared that everything in *The Birth of a Nation* was accurate. In Wilson's words, "It's like writing history with lightning, and my only regret is that it is all so terribly true."

The film inspired a Klan revival, spawning Klan chapters not only in the South but also in the Midwest and the West. These Klans featured men in white costumes with titles like Giant, Cyclops, and Grand Dragon, gathering together for vigils and cross-burnings and meetings known as Klonciliums and Klonvocations. Wives too could participate in the Klan's sister organization, the women's division of the KKK.

If there seems to be an element of theater in all these Klan rituals—a kind of perpetual Halloween for participants—the reality for blacks was grimmer. The new Klan focused its hate and violence against blacks, killing thousands over the course of twenty-five years.

Between 1920 and 1925, Klan membership ranged between two to five million, making it one the largest fraternal organizations in American history. Its members included the governors of Texas, Indiana, and Oregon, as well as the mayors of several major cities, and innumerable sheriffs, councilmen, and local judges. The Klan is often described as the face of southern racism, but the group wasn't exclusively southern. Rather, the Klan represented the racist face of the national Democratic Party.

In the fifty-year period starting from the Klan's founding through the late 1920s and early 1930s, every prominent Klan leader was a Democrat. In fact, Democrats were so prominent in the Klan that the group sometimes held its own primaries to decide which Klansman should receive the Klan endorsement in the upcoming election, and the Klan role was so central to the 1924 Democratic National Convention in New York that historians sometimes call it the Klanbake.

The Klan claimed to be devoted to justice, ensuring that blacks who propositioned or raped white women were punished through vigilante action. In reality, scholars of the Klan agree that much of the group's terrorism was aimed at keeping blacks socially subservient to whites, and also in preventing blacks from voting.

To this end, Klansmen raided black workplaces, burned black homes, terrorized black families in nightly raids, and formed lynch mobs in an ongoing campaign of intimidation and terror. As a consequence of Klan mayhem—together with a series of Democratic measures such as poll taxes and literacy tests—black voting declined precipitously throughout the South.

THE TERRORIST WING

Historians now recognize that the Klan wasn't going it alone; rather, it was acting on behalf of the Democratic Party. As I argued earlier, the Democrats attracted poor whites by establishing a fixed racial caste system in which every white, no matter how degraded, had a higher social position than every black, no matter how educated or refined. The Klan was the enforcement mechanism of this inflexible racial hierarchy.

The Klan also enforced a widely-echoed Democratic Party mantra, which is that whites refuse to allow themselves to be governed by Negroes. This position required the suppression of the black vote, not because blacks were the majority in most states, but because white Democrats did not want any blacks to have a say in how they were governed.

Today this may seem to us like an expression of mindless racism, but the Democratic Party didn't see it that way. Democrats realized that the party's political dominance, mainly in the South but also in areas of the West and Midwest, relied on stopping blacks from voting. Black votes, after all, only undermined the Democrats and helped their opposition. In the half-century following the Civil War, the vast majority of blacks who voted did so for the GOP.

The Democrats wanted to be the party of the white man, but they didn't want the Republicans to benefit from being the party that protected the rights of black people. The Democrats were determined to keep Republican influence out of the South, and after Reconstruction, they were largely successful in doing so. Republicans watched in dismay as Democrats used their virtual monopoly in the South to visit terror and destruction upon a vulnerable black population.

The Klan may have been the poster organization of Democratic racism, but it didn't operate by itself. The group's racial terrorism occurred, and was legitimized, within a political context in which racism was the accepted discourse of the Democratic Party. This was an era in which Democratic writers published books with titles like *The Negro a Beast*; *The American Negro as a Dependent, Defective and Delinquent*; *The Negro, a Menace to American Civilization*; and *America's Greatest Problem: The Negro*.[10]

The racist Democrats weren't just out in the culture writing books—they also served in the halls of the U.S. Congress. "What does civilization owe to the Negro?" the racist Democrat from Georgia, Tom Watson once said. His answer, "Nothing!" Watson was later elected to the U.S. Senate as a Democrat in 1920.

Watson, a Klansman himself, deployed the Klan against his political enemies and advocated lynching blacks, Catholics, and nonwhite immigrants. When he died, his memorial service was organized jointly by the Ku Klux Klan and the Georgia Democratic Party.

Another outspoken Democratic racist was James Vardaman of Mississippi, who served both as governor and then U.S. senator. When Republican president Teddy Roosevelt agreed to have dinner with the distinguished black leader Booker T. Washington, Vardaman fumed, "I am just as opposed to Booker Washington with all his Anglo-Saxon reinforcements as I am to the coconut-headed, chocolate-colored typical little coon Andy Dotson who blacks my shoes every morning."[11] Notice how Vardaman maintains the racial caste line so that poor whites among his constituents can feel superior even to Booker T. Washington.

Another Democrat, Senator Benjamin Tillman of South Carolina, offered an even more outrageous response. "Now that Roosevelt has eaten with that nigger Washington, we shall have to kill a thousand niggers to get them back to their place."[12] That's how Democrats talked back then; they want us to forget about it now. We can see from Tillman's threat why Democrats needed and relied on the Ku Klux Klan. The Party needed a domestic militia to carry out its racist projects of mayhem and murder.

THE SEGREGATION SOLUTION

In addition to the Klan, another institution of white supremacy that the Democrats created across the South was state-sponsored segregation. This took longer; while the Klan was in full operation in the 1860s, segregation was institutionalized in the 1880s and comprehensively established only by the early twentieth century.

The Democrats did it because they knew they could get away with it. By the 1890s, the Democrats had consolidated their power in the South and the party was strong enough to prevent the federal government from intervening in the way it did during Reconstruction. Thus Republicans in the North were limited in what they could do. Northern Republicans knew that they could not perpetually rule the South; at some point, the southerners would have to govern themselves.

In 1896, the Supreme Court in *Plessy v. Ferguson* affirmed the constitutionality of segregation. The Court considered a Louisiana railroad segregation statute that was euphemistically titled, "An Act to Promote the Comfort of Passengers." A Democratic legislature passed the law, and a Democratic governor signed it.

Homer Plessy, a Republican who was seven-eighths white, refused to sit in the railroad compartment reserved for blacks and when he was cited for breaking the law, brought suit to challenge the constitutionality of the Louisiana statute. A largely though not exclusively Democratic Supreme Court upheld the law, with the sole dissent coming from Justice John Harlan.

Harlan famously stated that "our constitution is color-blind and neither knows nor tolerates classes among citizens."[13] Here—in the Republican tradition of Frederick Douglass—is a further affirmation of the color-blind ideal, more than half a century before King's "dream" speech. Harlan's dissent is justly famous; less well known is the fact that he was a Kentucky Republican.

Gradually, Democrats in the South segregated everything. Hotels, taverns, and inns were segregated. Schools were segregated, as were public water fountains. Prisons were segregated, as were public theaters, public libraries, and public parks. Hospitals, jails, and cemeteries were segregated. Movie theaters and opera houses were segregated, and also the professions. Black barbers could only cut the hair of other blacks; black plumbers could only do repair work in black homes.

Let there be no doubt about this: all the Jim Crow laws mandating segregation were enacted by Democratic legislatures and signed into law by Democratic governors. Democratic judges upheld those laws, and Democratic sheriffs and public officials enforced them. Segregation was solely and entirely the handiwork of the Democratic Party. The party may as well have adopted the motto of Democratic segregationist Governor George Wallace who notoriously declared, "Segregation now, segregation tomorrow, segregation forever."

Over time, as racism became less defensible and fashionable, some Democrats insisted that segregation laws were not racist; rather, they were neutral on their face. After all, segregation laws merely separated the black world from the white world, while making no explicit statement about which one was better.

This "separate but equal" argument was concocted way back in the late nineteenth century. A Democratic majority on the Supreme Court declared in the *Plessy* decision that if blacks feel inferior as a result of segregation it's because they choose to view it that way, not because of anything in the law itself.

Yet everyone, black and white, who lived under segregation knew that it was an instrument of white supremacy. Separate was not equal. No one knew this better than the Democrats. In fact, the Democrats counted on their white supporters to see it that way. The whole purpose of stamping the black race with inferiority was to enable the Democrats to confer privilege on their white constituents. Yet notice how Democrats consistently claimed that these mechanisms of exploitation were "fair" and "just."

The racist Democrat, James Vardaman, speaking on the floor of the Senate, admitted that "separate" didn't actually mean "equal" and went on to explain why blacks should not be given the same education as whites. "Educating the black man simply renders him unfit for the work which the white man has prescribed. The only effect is to spoil a good field hand, and to make an insolent cook."[14]

Segregation wasn't limited to the South. Following his election, Woodrow Wilson mandated segregation for all the agencies of the federal government. This had never happened before. In a sense, Wilson was burying the ghost of Lincoln, who would have been appalled beyond measure. The black community was apoplectic. Black leaders like Ida B. Wells and Monroe Trotter protested Wilson's racism, but the Democratic president was unmoved.

Wilson indignantly told these black leaders that they had no reason to complain, because segregation was in fact beneficial to blacks. Wilson also echoed the argument from *Plessy* that segregation was just, since whites were being separated from blacks just as much as blacks were being separated from whites.

By now these themes should be familiar: oppression is good for you, and it also promotes social justice. The Democrats had been down this road before. Recall that Andrew Jackson told the Indians that it was good for them that the government was taking their land. Jackson also insisted that his land confiscations were Just—a term that he typically spelled with a capital letter. Of course knowing what we do about how Jackson and his cronies made off like bandits, we may be pardoned in sarcastically quipping that "justice" for Jackson actually meant "just us."

Today, too, Democrats make the same bogus claims when they exploit people by taking their money and turning them into second-class citizens. Naturally Americans get upset about being demeaned and ripped off. The thieving Democrats then inform them that they should feel good about being stolen from, because in this way they are being cured of greed, selfishness, and materialism. Democrats also justify their confiscations in the name of "social justice." Now, as in the past, the Democratic Party counts on its victims to be suckers.

THE PROGRESSIVE LIE

Summing up, we can see from this chapter that Hillary Clinton's arrogance before Senator Brooke was utterly misplaced. Brooke's indignation over the incident was completely justified. Brooke was actually the good guy, and Hillary's attempt to talk down to him was condescendingly racist.

Of course, it was no more racist than Hillary's Democratic ancestors. But this is the point: Hillary was pretending to a different pedigree. She was basing her actions on a progressive narrative that is itself a lie. She was posing as the poster child for civil rights while her actions—and her party's actions—qualify her as a poster child for white privilege and the degradation of blacks and other minorities.

"America" doesn't have a long history of white supremacy, the Democrats do. Democrats are the party of racism while opposition to racism came mainly from blacks and Republicans. From the Civil War onward, Republicans have been the party of equality and civil rights while Democrats have been the party of racism and opposition to civil rights.

Did that change? In the next chapter, we explore this question. Let me just say at this point that the answer will surprise you. For now, we can take it as established that the Democratic Party, through the dark night of slavery and the long period of racism and white supremacy, has been the systematic oppressor of blacks. Instead of demanding that blacks be grateful, what Democrats owe them is restitution—and an apology.

CHAPTER 5

THE PROBLEM OF USELESS PEOPLE

THE LOW, DISHONORABLE ORIGINS OF MODERN PROGRESSIVISM

We are paying for and even submitting to the dictates of an ever-increasing, unceasingly-spawning class of human beings who should never have been born at all.[1]
—Margaret Sanger, *The Pivot of Civilization*

In 2009, Hillary Clinton came to Houston, Texas, to receive the Margaret Sanger award from Planned Parenthood. Sanger was the founder of Planned Parenthood and the award is its highest prize. In receiving the award, Hillary said of Sanger, "I admire Margaret Sanger enormously, her courage, her tenacity, her vision. I am really in awe of her. There are a lot of lessons we can learn from her life and the cause she launched and fought for and sacrificed so greatly."[2]

What was Margaret Sanger's vision? What was the cause to which she devoted her life? Sanger is known as a champion of birth control, of providing women with the means to avoid unwanted pregnancies. But the real Margaret Sanger was very different from how she's portrayed in Planned Parenthood brochures. The real Margaret Sanger did not want women in general to limit their pregnancies. She wanted white, wealthy, educated women to have more children, and poor, uneducated, black women to have none. "Unwanted" for Sanger didn't mean unwanted by the mother—it meant unwanted by Sanger.

Sanger's influence contributed to the infamous Tuskegee experiments in which poor blacks were deliberately injected with syphilis without their knowledge. Today the Tuskegee Project is falsely portrayed as an example of southern backwardness and American bigotry; in fact, it was a progressive scheme carried out with the very eugenic goals that Margaret Sanger herself championed.

In 1926, Sanger spoke to a Women's Chapter of the Ku Klux Klan in New Jersey about her solution for reducing the black birthrate. She also sponsored a Negro Project specifically designed, in her vocabulary, to get rid of "human beings who should never have been born." In one of her letters Sanger said, "We do not want word to get out that we are trying to exterminate the Negro population."[3]

The racists loved it; other KKK speaking invitations followed. Now it may seem odd that a woman with such views would be embraced by Planned Parenthood—even odder that she would be a role model for Hillary Clinton. Why would they celebrate Sanger given her racist philosophy? In this chapter I intend to show that their enthusiasm for Sanger is not despite but because of her philosophy. As Planned Parenthood and Hillary recognize, Sanger's philosophy is actually the foundation for modern progressivism. With slight tactical modification, it represents what modern progressives still believe.

This chapter is about the roots of the modern progressivism championed by Hillary Clinton and the Democratic Party. What is this progressivism and where did it come from? Here we begin with the progressive myth. The progressive myth is that progressivism is simply another word for progress. In this view, progressivism is nothing less than a philosophy of the future. Its critics are stuck in the past.

Progressivism is allegedly about civil rights, human rights, human dignity, and social justice. The other side, progressives say, opposes civil rights and human rights and advocates social injustice. If this is true, it follows that all good people in America should be progressives and vote for the party—the Democratic Party—that embodies progressive ideals. Republicans are bad guys and bad guys are, naturally, attracted to the Republican Party.

Now it seems odd that a party that championed slavery and segregation for centuries can plausibly claim to be the party of civil rights and social justice. Progressive Democrats, even while they evade and downplay their party's role in past oppression, have to admit that most of their forbears were vicious racists. When confronted with the evidence, they do admit it. Then they counter: but that was then, and this is now.

THE SO-CALLED BIG SWITCH

Progressive historiography relies on the claim that there was an historic big switch: Democrats saw the light and became champions of equality, while the racists in the Democratic Party became Republicans. Look, progressives say, at a segregationist like Strom Thurmond. Thurmond once ran for president on the Dixiecrat platform. Then he switched parties and became a Republican. Here is a classic example of the switch in action.

The switch narrative is supported by two important pieces of evidence. First, blacks, who used to vote Republican, now vote Democratic. This would seem to prove that whatever its past, the Democratic Party is now the party of racial justice. Second, the Civil Rights Movement was championed by a Democratic president, Lyndon Johnson, and supported by progressives like Martin Luther King. From this perspective, Republicans are, at least since the 1960s, enemies of civil rights.

The switch narrative, plausible at first glance, becomes problematic when we realize that the Thurmond case is anomalous. The Dixiecrats emerged from the Democratic Party and they returned to it after the presidential election of 1948. Thurmond did not become a Republican until 1964, and he was virtually alone among his Democratic colleagues in changing parties.

Southern Democrats throughout the 1960s remained the party of segregation, and three of the most nationally prominent southern Democrats of the postwar era, President Harry Truman, Supreme Court Justice Hugo Black, and Senate Majority Leader Robert Byrd, were former members of the Ku Klux Klan.

Later I'll say more about Black, but here I want to focus on Truman and Byrd. Some historians today downplay Truman's Klan membership, insisting that he did little more than pay his membership fee and quit the group shortly thereafter, reportedly because of its antagonism to Catholics.

This attempt to exculpate Truman is too hasty, however. In researching Truman, historian William Leuchtenburg recently uncovered some very interesting statements by the former Democratic president. In 1911, Truman wrote his future wife Bess, "I think one man is just as good as another so long as he's honest and decent and not a nigger or a Chinaman."

Truman added, "Uncle Will says that the Lord made a white man from dust, a nigger from mud, then He threw up what was left and it came down a Chinaman. He does hate Chinese and Japs. So do I. It is race prejudice, I guess. But I am strongly of the opinion Negroes ought to be in Africa, yellow men in Asia, and white men in Europe and America."

More than twenty-five years later, as a U.S. senator from Missouri, Truman wrote a letter to his daughter calling White House waiters "an army of coons." In another letter to Bess in 1939, Truman used the phrase "nigger picnic day." In an interview with a reporter in 1963, he asked, "Would you want your daughter to marry a negro?" This is the same Harry Truman who gets credit from progressives for desegregating the armed forces, typically without any mention of what he really thought about blacks.[4]

Byrd joined the Klan at age twenty-four. In the early 1940s he organized a 150-member chapter or Klavern in Sophia, West Virginia, and was chosen as its leader. In later years, Byrd admitted it was Joel Baskin, Grand Dragon of the Klan, who advised him to go into politics. "Suddenly lights flashed in my mind," Byrd later wrote. "Someone important had recognized my abilities."

During World War II, Byrd wrote Senator Theodore Bilbo of Mississippi that he would not join the U.S. military because he refused to fight alongside black people. "I shall never fight in the armed forces with a Negro by my side. Rather I should die a thousand times, and see Old

Glory trampled in the dirt never to rise again, than to see this beloved land of ours become degraded by race mongrels, a throwback to the blackest specimen from the wilds."[5]

Byrd's racist past wasn't a youthful flirtation. More than two decades later, he filibustered the Civil Rights Act of 1964 by speaking on the Senate floor for fourteen hours. Byrd also opposed the Voting Rights Act of 1965. Yet Byrd became a revered figure in Democratic politics, endorsing Obama and eventually winning a 100 percent approval rating from the NAACP. When he died in 2010, media reports made only a bare mention of his KKK membership and opposition to civil rights. Hillary Clinton issued a statement praising her "friend and mentor" Robert Byrd.

Bill Clinton and Obama were at his memorial service. Obama emphasized how much Byrd learned and changed, noting that "the arc of his life bent toward justice." Here is another version of the progressive switch narrative. Byrd is presented as a living example of a bad southerner who became a good Democrat. He grew. He learned. He became one of us. To a point, I agree. But what exactly Byrd learned Obama did not specify. In this chapter, I will.

Bill Clinton, the only speaker to directly address Byrd's KKK association, dismissed it. "What does that mean? I'll tell you what it means. He was a country boy from the hills and hollows of West Virginia. He was trying to get elected." This is revealing. Clinton admits that in some states Klan membership was a political asset—perhaps even a political requirement—for success in the Democratic Party.[6]

Yes, people can change. But I find it bizarre, to put it mildly, that men like Byrd made such a seamless transition from being in the Klan to being champions of civil rights. It's equally strange that a party long devoted to owning and subjugating blacks and other minorities would suddenly become the dedicated advocate of equal rights and social justice. When reversals of this magnitude occur—and they do occur—some sort of moral accounting is required.

Consider the example of Whittaker Chambers, who used to be a communist but then became an anti-communist. Chambers didn't just leapfrog from one to the other. He produced a massive work, *Witness*, in which he searchingly examined what attracted him to communism, what he saw in the Communist Party, how he became disenchanted, why he left the party, how he exposed Alger Hiss as a communist spy, and why ultimately he feared, wrongly as it turned out, that he was joining the "losing side."

Where are the comparable accounts for why Truman, Black, and Byrd went from being Klansmen to being champions of civil rights? Where is the Democratic Party's story of how it went through soul-searching in order to achieve moral conversion? These accounts simply do not exist. There seems to have been no soul-searching, raising the question of whether there was in fact a conversion. This too-easy progressive switch story raised my suspicion. I decided to look into it, and discovered it was largely bogus.

PROGRESSIVE RACISM

In this chapter I'll show that the Democratic Party never abandoned racism—it figured out a way to integrate it into its new progressive philosophy. Progressivism didn't replace racism; rather, northern progressivism worked in tandem with southern racism to create a successful Democratic coalition that pushed through the New Deal and the Great Society.

I'm not alone in thinking this; progressive historian Ira Katznelson admits as much in a powerful recent book, *Fear Itself*. Katznelson focuses his indictment on the central figure of modern progressivism, Franklin D. Roosevelt. I expand the indictment to the other two central figures: Woodrow Wilson and Lyndon Johnson. And of course we see the same general trend in the entire Democratic Party. Through this investigation, we'll discover what Byrd learned that enabled him to make the easy transition from being a racist Democrat to being a progressive Democrat.

It may seem heretical to link the three great progressive champions of the twentieth century—Wilson, FDR, and Johnson—with racism. But the indisputable fact is that all three were either racist themselves or made their peace with racism. Progressive historiography has had to work overtime to conceal the actual facts.

There is some debate about whether Wilson was himself a member of the Ku Klux Klan. Whatever the truth about that, Wilson was unquestionably a Klan sympathizer. By showing *Birth of a Nation* at the White House, Wilson contributed to the Klan revival of the early twentieth century. FDR didn't despise blacks in the way Wilson did, but he did serve as Navy Secretary in the Wilson administration, never objecting to the de jure segregation that Wilson had imposed throughout the federal government.

When FDR became president, he made a bargain with racist southern Democrats that required him to block anti-lynching legislation and exclude blacks from New Deal programs. A surge in lynching during the 1930s had no effect in altering FDR's commitment to the pact. One might expect to see FDR liberalize on race relations over his multiple terms, but he never did. His bargain with the worst racists in the Democratic Party endured throughout his presidency, from 1932 to 1945.

Lyndon Johnson was himself a member of the racist group of southern Democrats that FDR worked with and cut deals with. Johnson vociferously opposed civil rights in the early part of his career. Later Johnson appeared to change, but in this case the appearance was deceiving. Even as president—during the very period he was promoting the Civil Rights Act of 1964—Johnson called blacks "niggers" and spoke of civil rights legislation as tactical measures for keeping blacks on the Democratic plantation.

What about the Republicans? I will show in this chapter that Republicans throughout the 1950s and 1960s supported civil rights, while the main opposition to the Civil Rights laws came from Democrats. Blacks, starting in the 1930s, did switch from voting Republican to voting Democrat, but this was not on account of racism. On the contrary, blacks in joining the Democratic Party found themselves in the same camp with the segregationists and the Ku Klux Klan. Far from escaping racism, blacks threw themselves into the party of racism.

Why did they do it? The best insight into this question comes from Mary Boykin Chesnut's Civil War journal. Chesnut observed that even though all the able-bodied white men were away fighting the Yankees, the slaves had not left the plantations. Chesnut found this odd because the slaves were alone with the women and children. They could leave if they wanted; there was no one to stop them. "If slavery is as disagreeable to negroes as we think it," she wrote, "why don't they all march over the border where they would be received with open arms?"[7] Chesnut implies that whatever their antipathy to slavery, the slaves must have liked the security provided by the plantation.

Another person who understood the tempting security of plantation life was the Republican abolitionist Frederick Douglass. Douglass, however, railed against it. In an 1865 speech to the Massachusetts Anti-Slavery Society, Douglass addressed the question: What must be done for the former slaves? Douglass replied, "Do nothing with us! Your doing with us has already played the mischief with us. If the Negro cannot stand on his own legs, let him fail. Let him alone. If you will only untie his hands and give him a chance, I think he will live."[8]

Douglass's speech was titled, "What the Black Man Wants." For Douglass, what the black man wanted was freedom—the freedom to make his own future. But the Democrats of the 1930s thought differently. Democrats knew that blacks as much as anyone were suffering financial hardships from the Great Depression; and those hardships gave Democrats—the party of slavery, segregation, and Jim Crow—a new opportunity.

AN OFFER THEY COULDN'T REFUSE

So the Democrats made the black leaders a tempting offer. In effect, the Democrats said to them: You may now be free, but what does freedom really amount to? Life for the free black means unemployment and insecurity. This is the "freedom" the Republicans are offering you. We know you don't trust us—our record with you is a bit spotty—but we have figured out a way to correct that. We can offer you something that will make your life better, something very practical, here and now.

Remember life on the plantation? True, the work was excruciating and unending and you didn't get paid for it. But in other respects, it wasn't so bad. We gave you food and a place to live. If you got sick, we called the doctor. We looked after you in your old age. We took care of the children, even when they were too young to work. Plantation life wasn't much, to be sure, but it was better than living in starvation and fear.

So here's our deal. We'll give you a living, and you don't even have to work for it. In fact, we'd prefer you didn't work. If you worked and earned money, we'd have to stop paying you. We'd rather have you dependent on us. We'll look after you, and have other people pay for it. We just want one thing in exchange. You must keep voting for us so that we can keep getting you stuff for free. What do you say?

The answer was yes. This is why blacks—many of them deeply reluctant to leave the party of Lincoln and join the party of the Ku Klux Klan—became Democrats. The black leadership made a Faustian bargain—they sold their souls to the progressives for cash benefits. They traded emancipation and freedom—the right to determine one's own destiny—for secure dependence on the progressive state. Blacks returned to a new type of plantation run by the same people who used to run the old ones.

I understand how people living during hard times might take this deal. Over time, however, the Democratic payout simply became an entitlement. Black leaders eventually treated opposition to the entitlements as itself a form of racism. Today when black leaders accuse Republicans of opposing civil rights, they are simply playing the progressive game. All they mean is that Republicans aren't willing to provide the same plantation benefits that Democrats do. For the most part, the African American community today is a ward of the progressive Democratic state.

This remarkable story of the emergence of modern Democratic progressivism begins with Margaret Sanger, who is not merely the founder of Planned Parenthood but one of the founding foremothers of the progressive movement. We cannot understand Sanger by projecting onto her modern progressive talking points. Empowerment! Free choice! Spacing out pregnancies! These weren't Sanger's goals at all. Rather, she had a novel solution to what may be termed the problem of useless people.

Useless people abound in every society. India, for example, has plenty of them. That fact is somewhat camouflaged in America, where the success of Indian Americans persuades many that Indians are all smart and productive. "You Indians are so bright and so enterprising." I get this all the time. The truth is that only smart, enterprising Indians can figure out how to get to America.

Long-distance immigration is a highly selective process; it's not simply a matter of climbing a fence or wading across the Rio Grande. It is a sociological truth—I call it D'Souza's Law of Immigration—that the quality of the immigrant is directly proportional to the distance traveled to get here. So the Indians in America are not typical Indians. Typical Indians—the type I grew up with—include lots of useless, unproductive people.

MY USELESS UNCLE BHARAT

One such useless person I knew well was my uncle Bharat. This fellow—my mother's youngest brother—was only ten years older than me. A college dropout, he never seemed capable of finding a job. When he did find a job, he couldn't keep it. When I was around twelve, Uncle Bharat was employed by an advertising agency. Each week he would take me out for ice cream. We'd head to the ice cream place on his bicycle, with me riding on the back seat.

As we had our ice cream, he would tell me what product he was working on and ask me to come up with witty lines and jingles to help sell that product. Initially I was reluctant, since I was only twelve, but he seemed to really like my ideas. "I really feel, Dinesh," he told me, "that you are my secret weapon, because you know a lot of words." My off-the-top-of-my-head suggestions, I'm firmly convinced, made up the bulk of his work product for the week. It was a good deal for me, since I got ice cream out of it. But I knew even then that I was in the company of a useless person.

We never knew what to do with Uncle Bharat. He remained a dependent all his life, living with his parents until they died, and then sponging off relatives, until he eventually died of a heart attack. He was a leech, I have to admit, but the tragedy of his life was not merely that he lived off other people. Rather, it was also that he knew he was a useless person and his was a life unlived. He was never an autonomous individual who experienced the earned satisfaction of having made something of himself.

In the late nineteenth and early twentieth centuries, the Democratic Party also had a problem with what they considered to be useless people—namely African Americans—and progressivism became its solution for dealing with that problem. The problem for Democrats emerged only at the end of the Civil War. That's because, from the Democrats' perspective, before the war all the useless people were usefully employed as slaves.

Incredibly, many Democratic masters even considered the slaves to be useless people. They routinely complained about how lazy, shiftless, and unproductive the slaves were. We learn from Mary Chesnut that a constant refrain on the plantation was, "They don't do any work." It never seemed to occur to the people making such complaints that in fact the slaves did all the work. The masters were the ones who did nothing. While the slaves toiled, the Democratic master class employed itself in such pursuits as mint julep sipping, croquet on the lawn, and dueling.

Even so, the slave owners' allegation that slaves avoided work did have a basis in fact. Frederick Douglass acknowledged this. He made the obvious point that since slaves couldn't keep what they earned, they had no incentive to work hard. Still, on balance, Democrats knew that slaves were useful—at least to them. Even indolent slaves produced more than it cost to keep them.

Slavery may have been an unprofitable institution for society—discouraging work on the part of both slave and master, and thus contributing to a slothful, unproductive culture in the Democratic South—but it was unquestionably profitable for the masters. From the Democrats' point of view, the truly useless people were those who opposed slavery, namely abolitionists and Republicans.

After slavery, the Democrats had a new problem: What to do with the blacks who were now free? The same Democrats who complained that slaves were useless people now insisted that black people were useless unless they were slaves! One Democratic columnist from Charleston warned that free blacks were like animals walking around without owners—this was not good for the animals, he insisted, and it was also bad for society.

After considering what to do with free blacks in the South, the Democratic Party came up with three solutions: Jim Crow, segregation, and the Ku Klux Klan. Through such measures, southern Democrats simultaneously kept black people down and rallied the votes of white people. For several decades, from the 1870s to the 1930s, this solution worked, sustaining the Democrats as the majority party in the South.

Even so, the Republican Party dominated the rest of the country, and blacks in the North and the South voted overwhelmingly for Republicans. Immigrants too, though initially drawn to the Democratic Party, tended to move to the GOP as they became more established and more successful. Nationally, the GOP was without question the majority party and won most presidential elections from 1865 through the 1920s. The Democrats realized that they needed something new, something that went beyond Jim Crow, segregation, and the Klan.

STOP THEM BEFORE THEY'RE BORN

Margaret Sanger came up with an original proposal: let's prevent these useless people from even existing. Let's stop them even before they are born. This was the whole point of "birth control," and it became one of the foundation stones of early progressivism. The progressives recognized the value of Sanger's cause. So did the leadership of the Democratic Party. If useless people aren't born, we don't have to segregate them, nor do we have to chase them down and kill them. People who don't exist can hardly pose a problem. For one thing, they can't vote Republican.

Sanger's Klan appearance, together with her Negro project, show she shared the special antipathy to blacks that was a trademark of the Democratic Party in the South. Sanger did regard blacks as the most backward, unintelligent subset of the population. She seemed to regard a large percentage of the black population as borderline retarded. Sanger's general view was that ignorant, uneducated people should be convinced through propaganda to practice birth control, but if they refuse they should be forced. As for the "retarded" and "feeble-minded," Sanger advocated compulsory sterilization.

Sanger set up her Negro Project to give special attention to keeping blacks from multiplying. She wanted black clergymen to sell them on birth control because she thought that blacks listened only to their ministers. If the minister said it was okay, then blacks wouldn't get the paranoid idea that some white person was trying to wipe out their numbers—even though Sanger was in fact a white person who was trying to wipe out their numbers!

"The most merciful thing that a large family does to one of its infant members" Sanger said, "is to kill it."[9] Sanger's implication is that she—not the family itself—knows what is best for them. It is not a matter of the parents choosing for themselves; she insists they must choose prevention. Sanger routinely spoke of the "unwanted and the unfit" but by this she meant unwanted by her, unfit according to her standard.

Sanger also suggests it is merciful—an act of compassion—to kill an unwanted child. Do children see it that way? Is there a significant population alive today who would rather their births had been prevented? What interests me here is Sanger's appeal to compassion. It reminds me of how Andrew Jackson claimed he was being kind to the Indians in driving them from their homes, and how Democratic slave owners viewed themselves as apostles of compassion in providing food and lodging to their slaves.

Today's Democrats, too, have created horrible living conditions for American Indians on reservations and for blacks in inner cities. People there wallow in miserable dependency, lacking jobs, lacking prospects, and lacking hope. Pretty much every child born there is illegitimate; in other words, bastardy is the normal condition of life in the city. Sanger would have been horrified; she would regard the very existence of these populations as a failure of birth control.

Yet today's Democrats aren't so different from Sanger, even if they have found a different solution to the problem of useless people. Like Sanger, today's Democrats deprive others of dignity and opportunity while viewing themselves as apostles of caring and empathy. Like Sanger, today's Democrats unceasingly praise their own "compassion" and regard anyone who criticizes their policies as "lacking compassion."

Sanger was a eugenicist, but of a special type. The term itself means "well born" and eugenics refers to the selective breeding of human populations. Just as animal breeders can engineer certain traits in a dog or horse, eugenicists seek to engineer certain traits in human society. Today we think of eugenics as a single thing, but in the early twentieth century, eugenics came in two versions: positive eugenics and negative eugenics.

In 1925, Sanger attended the Sixth International Malthusian and Birth Control Conference in New York. She writes about this experience in her autobiography. Here Sanger encountered a group of eugenicists who spoke of their philosophy of "race betterment." Sanger agreed with them; she was enthusiastically on board with the idea of racial progress.

But then she heard these eugenicists—men like C. B. Davenport, director of the Cold Spring Harbor for Experimental Evolution—call for "more children from the rich." This is positive eugenics. Sanger was unimpressed; she didn't think it would work. She went around asking these men how many more children they themselves wanted to have. Most of them said, "None."

These replies confirmed Sanger's suspicion that wealthy, educated people didn't want large families and no amount of convincing would change their mind. Sanger became convinced that eugenics, to be successful, should have a different emphasis: negative eugenics rather than positive eugenics. As Sanger puts it, "The eugenicists wanted more children for the rich. We sought to stop the multiplication of the unfit."[10]

Eugenics was all the rage in America in the early twentieth century, as suggested by the names of influential organizations: the American Breeders Association, the Eugenics Record Office, and the National Conference on Race Betterment. Yes, these were real organizations.

Intellectually, eugenics was fueled by social Darwinism. Darwin's doctrine of evolution was described by the sociologist Herbert Spencer as "survival of the fittest." This is where Sanger got the term, and it became a mantra of a newly emerging progressivism.

For Darwin, survival of the fittest was a description of the natural order—of the way things are. But eugenicists interpreted the term to reflect their aspiration for the social order, for the way things ought to be. They demanded that society be designed so that the "fittest" reproduce and multiply, and the less fit disappear from the face of the earth.

UNDER THE KNIFE

Progressivism is closely associated with eugenics and social Darwinism. This is not to say that all of progressivism can be reduced to these two things. In its origins progressivism was a broad movement that even included some Republicans. Teddy Roosevelt, for example, was a Republican who once ran for president under the banner of the progressive (Bull Moose) party.

But Republican progressives generally focused on reforming government, dismantling political machines like New York's Tammany Hall. They also sought, like TR, to break up what we might now call crony capitalism, the collusion of large corporations with the government. TR sometimes used a racially tinged Darwinian vocabulary, but he was too much of an enthusiast for large families to support any kind of eugenics. As we saw in the last chapter, he befriended Booker T. Washington in a manner that once again confirms Republicans—not Democrats—as the party of a color-blind society.

Even though a progressive himself, TR railed against the kind of progressivism that Woodrow Wilson represented, and it is this kind of progressivism that became the dominant force in the Democratic Party. This is what we mean by progressivism today, and this is the progressivism that became closely intertwined with racism. For these progressives, eugenics and social Darwinism became the vehicle for moving society onward and upward.

The eugenicists and social Darwinists had a vision for society that was rich, educated, and white. Yet they feared that, without their intervention, the poor would outbreed the rich, and society would become increasingly poor, uneducated, and dark-skinned. Progress, in this context, had a specific meaning. It meant reducing the number of poor, uneducated, dark-skinned people.

Many progressives supported forced sterilization. In 1907, Indiana became the first state to adopt a sterilization law. By 1915, a dozen states had passed similar measures to sterilize women dubbed "unfit" or "retarded." These statutes resulted in tens of thousands of American women being forcibly sterilized. Decades later, some of these laws remained on the books. The eugenic legacy of progressivism is hardly a phenomenon of the distant past.

In an infamous 1927 case, the Supreme Court ordered the sterilization of a young woman named Carrie Buck. Buck was white, but the State of Virginia classified her as "retarded" and ordered her forcibly sterilized. A group of progressive experts, without having met Buck, found her "shiftless, ignorant and worthless." Buck had given birth to an illegitimate child, and this seemed to be the main basis for the assessment. Later, however, Buck would show she wasn't retarded; she went on to live a normal life, demonstrating adequate intellectual and social capacity.

The Supreme Court, however, upheld Virginia's sterilization law, sealing Buck's fate. Writing for the majority, progressive Justice Oliver Wendell Holmes justified his decision in progressive social Darwinist terms. "It is better for all the world, instead of waiting to execute degenerate offspring for crime, or to let them starve for their imbecility, society can prevent those who are manifestly unfit from continuing their kind." Echoing Sanger, Holmes crisply commented, "Three generations of imbeciles are enough!"[11]

It may seem from the case of Carrie Buck that progressive sterilization schemes weren't necessarily racist because Buck, after all, was white. But in reality progressive sterilization was aimed at minorities. So how did Carrie Buck qualify? Because she was a white person that progressives somehow managed to lump together with non-whites.

This seems bizarre today, but as progressives of the time saw it, even white people from certain parts of Europe didn't count as white. Olive-colored southern Europeans, for instance, failed to make the grade. Carrie Buck, white as they come, was demoted from whiteness because she was regarded by progressives as feeble and degenerate just like blacks and other minorities.

We can see from this that progressivism thoroughly incorporated racism, expanding its reach from blacks to other minorities—not only brown people but also white people who were not perceived as "acting white." No wonder that the Democratic Party, racist to its core, admired and effortlessly adopted this new way of thinking.

There was no dramatic "switch" from racism to progressivism. Rather, Democrats adopted progressivism as an innovation and continuation of their racist philosophy. Progressivism in a way enlarged racism by extending it beyond blacks to include Mexicans, Asians, and even southern and eastern Europeans. In progressivism, the Democrats saw an opportunity to extend their empire of subjugation to cover a bigger range of people.

Progressivism had something else going for it, as far as Democrats were concerned. Progressives distrusted the free institutions of society to bring about the results they sought. From the beginning, they proposed centralized planning as the mechanism for moving society forward. For the job of planners, the progressives proposed...well, themselves! They considered themselves eminently qualified to run things.

This top-down approach also appealed to the leadership of the Democratic Party. The Democrats, remember, relied on the federal government to protect slavery by returning runaway slaves. In the South they institutionalized state-sponsored segregation. In other words, Democrats had a history of imposing government supervision of people's lives.

Now here was progressivism proposing a new system of regimented government control. Once again, this appealed to Democrats because, as they had seen in the past, governments operate through coercion rather than consent. From the Democrats' point of view, what better way was there to control people and exploit them? The Democrats took a hard look at progressivism, and what they saw, they liked.

WOODROW WILSON'S PROGRESSIVE BIGOTRY

At first, the Democrats saw no cause to abandon southern segregation for northern progressivism. Rather, they simply held on to the one while embracing the other. These two forms of bigotry came together in the person of Democratic president Woodrow Wilson. "During the Wilson years," historian Ira Katznelson writes, "the composite of racism and progressive liberalism came to dominate the Democratic Party."[12]

Earlier we saw how Wilson promoted segregation and the Ku Klux Klan. This might suggest Wilson was the prototypical racist southern Democrat. Wilson, however, was a man of the South who had gone north to become the president of Princeton University and also governor of New Jersey. There Wilson was exposed to northern progressive ideas. He became a zealous convert to social Darwinism.

Wilson now spoke in terms of a natural hierarchy in which black and brown people were simply less evolved than whites. The case of Orientals—the yellow people—was complicated: Wilson considered them an advanced race, but for reasons unexplained this group had "degenerated," basically lowering them into the black and brown category.

In order to reduce the numbers of these groups, Wilson championed the same type of eugenic birth control policies that Sanger advocated. As New Jersey governor, Wilson signed legislation that formed a Board of Examiners of the Feebleminded, Epileptics and Other Defectives. The law enabled the state to regulate procreation for women with a criminal record, women living in poorhouses, and women broadly classified as "feebleminded" or "defective."

Wilson's progressivism can be seen in the way he championed centralized power in Washington, D.C., and repudiated the South's traditional political doctrine of states rights. As president, Wilson openly advocated that America's founding principles be replaced by centralized planning. Wilson recognized that the Founders had created a federal system that divided power between the national government and the states. But this formula, Wilson insisted, was out of date. "We are not bound," Wilson said, "to adhere to the doctrines held by the signers of the Declaration of Independence."[13]

This is a remarkable statement; no previous American president spoke like that. Previous presidents might quarrel over the meaning of the founding, but none before Wilson scornfully dismissed the founding. Wilson denounced the Founders in the name of progressive centralization of power. For Wilson, centralized planning and power were the way of the future; they represented progress. Those who espoused such ideas he cherished as fellow progressives; those who opposed them he considered regressive.

FDR'S RACIST BARGAIN

While Wilson balanced racism and progressivism, maintaining a kind of equilibrium between the two, Franklin Roosevelt tilted the scales decisively in favor of progressivism. Even so, FDR didn't replace racism with progressivism; rather, he maintained his governing coalition through a bargain with racism that lasted throughout his three-term presidency.

The facts are laid out in historian Ira Katznelson's book *Fear Itself.* Katznelson writes that Roosevelt's New Deal relied on "an intimate partnership with those in the South who preached white supremacy." Racist Democrats, Katznelson says, "acted not on the fringes but as an indispensable part of the governing political party." Roosevelt's progressivism relied for its success on a pact with bigotry. Without racism, in other words, there would never have been a New Deal.

Following his election in 1932, FDR sought to create a Democratic majority in American politics. To do so, he needed the support of the "solid South," which is to say the Democratic South. FDR pitched his progressive platform to the southern Democrats, and they immediately saw how nicely progressivism dovetailed with their existing racist schemes. The southern Democrats recognized that they too could use entitlements for some to extract money from the general population, and also that this process gave government something important to do, thus consolidating its power over the productive sector.

But the southern Democrats had no intention of giving up their existing racist racket. They wanted progressivism, but they wanted it in addition to racism, not as a substitute for it. So the southern Democrats told FDR they would come on board under two conditions. First, FDR must make no effort to overturn segregation or lynching. Indeed, FDR must oppose desegregation measures and block the anti-lynching schemes of blacks and Republicans. Moreover, FDR must not hold it against Democrats if they belonged to white supremacist organizations like the Ku Klux Klan.

FDR agreed to this first condition and upheld his end of the bargain. At the White House, he continued Wilson's policy of segregation among the household staff. He banned black reporters from White House press conferences. Throughout his presidency, he continued Wilson's segregation of the armed forces.

When Republicans during World War II called for integrated fighting units, FDR said that to change the existing structure of segregation would "produce situations destructive to morale." Working with his Democratic majority in Congress, FDR ensured that anti-lynching bills were defeated; he even pressured northern Democrats to table or oppose such measures.

As Katznelson points out, some of Roosevelt's closest allies in the Senate were notorious racists like Hugo Black of Alabama; Theodore Bilbo of Mississippi; James Byrnes of South Carolina; and Claude Pepper of Florida. All were progressives on economic issues, and staunch backers of Roosevelt's New Deal policies. Pepper was so left-wing on issues other than race that his nickname was "Red" Pepper. Still, these were the Democrats who filibustered anti-lynching legislation. Roosevelt made sure that their filibusters were successful and that such bills never became law.

In 1934 a black man accused of rape and murder was caught by a posse and murdered in front of a crowd of four thousand people, including women and children. The victim was castrated and burned, and his body hung from a tree. Outraged at this expression of mob justice, Republicans once again tried to push an anti-lynching measure through Congress. Roosevelt remained silent on the issue, one of his spokesmen saying that the president believed that lynching was undesirable but it remained a matter for the states to decide for themselves.

The southern Democrats launched a procedural adjournment move to kill the anti-lynching bill. This maneuver could have been defeated had northern Democrats allied with Republicans. They did not. "What is striking about this," Katznelson writes, "is not the overwhelming support of southern Democrats or the comparable degree of opposition by Republicans. It is, rather, the critical support for adjournment provided by non-southern Democrats, almost half of whom voted to support the South's procedural move."[14]

Among the racist southern Democrats who were FDR's allies, Bilbo was probably the most notorious. FDR backed Bilbo's selection as chairman of the Senate Committee on the District of Columbia, effectively making him mayor of the city. Listen to how this man talked. "You know folks, I run Washington. I'm Mayor there. Some niggers came to see me one time to try to get the right to vote there. Their leader was a smart nigger. Of course he was half white. I told him that the nigger would never vote in Washington. Hell, if we give 'em the right to vote up there, half the niggers in the South will move into Washington and we'll have a black government."[15]

SOME OF HIS BEST FRIENDS ARE KLANSMEN

FDR appointed two members of his racist cabal, James Byrnes and Hugo Black, to the Supreme Court. What made Black's appointment controversial was that he was a former Ku Klux Klan member. His law partner Crampton Harris, Cyclops of the Birmingham Klan, had introduced Black to the Klan. Black became an active member, marching in parades and addressing Klan rallies throughout Alabama.

Black was also known as a Klan lawyer, both representing Klansmen and making effective appeals to Klan-dominated juries. In court cases,

Black specialized in appeals to racial prejudice, asking questions in court like, "Was he standing at the door where this nigger woman came in?" When Black ran successfully for the Senate, his campaign manager was James Esdale, Grand Dragon of the Alabama Klan.

Republicans protested Black's nomination. Echoing Bill Clinton's justification for Robert Byrd, Black protested that he simply joined the Klan in order to advance his career. "The Klan," he said "was in effect the underground Democratic Party in Alabama."[16] Here Black was telling the truth, and what a telling truth it is!

One might expect northern Democrats to be outraged at this candid confession of Black's participation in the Klan for self-advancement. This, however, was not the case. Democrats across the country backed Black's nomination. One of them, Senator William King of Utah, said he saw no reason why membership in the KKK should disqualify someone for elevation to the Supreme Court.

FDR did not directly address the issue, but the president's private feelings were later revealed by Black himself in a 1968 memo. "President Roosevelt told me there was no reason for my worrying about having been a member of the Ku Klux Klan. He said that some of his best friends and supporters were strong members of that organization. He never in any way, by word or attitude, indicated any doubt about my having been in the Klan nor did he indicate any criticism of me for having been a member of that organization."[17]

The southern Democrats had a second demand for FDR. They demanded that a disproportionate share of New Deal programs be steered toward the South and that blacks, who mainly worked as domestic servants and farm laborers, be excluded from those programs. No "New Deal" for the blacks!

Again, FDR agreed. As Katznelson describes, he wrote his New Deal legislation in such a way that the South received a large fraction of the goodies. A telling example was the TVA Act, which involved the construction of huge power and navigation dams on the Tennessee River. The program benefited Missouri, Tennessee, Alabama, Georgia, North Carolina, Kentucky, and Virginia. An elated Mississippi Democrat, John

Rankin, boasted that TVA would produce "power that will exceed the amount of physical strength of all the slaves freed by the Civil War."[18]

Keeping up his end of the bargain, FDR also ensured that the two main occupations involving blacks, namely domestic and farm labor, were excluded from federal benefits. This is a fact that progressive historiography usually omits, because of its devastating significance. Most blacks were excluded from New Deal programs! The grim consequence of FDR's diabolical pact with the racists was that millions of blacks were ineligible to receive Social Security, unemployment, and a host of other benefits that were being offered to workers in every other type of industry.

One might think that blacks, seeing all this, would indignantly repudiate FDR and his progressive pact with bigotry. But during the 1930s blacks were desperate. The Depression hit blacks harder than anyone else. So the black leadership decided that the crumbs being offered by the progressive Democrats were at least more than they were getting before.

New Deal programs like the National Industrial Recovery Act (NIRA) and the Civilian Conservation Corps (CCC) were segregated and offered the best jobs to whites. Even so, blacks saw they at least offered employment to tens of thousands of blacks. The administration denied FHA loans to blacks seeking to move into white neighborhoods, but they did assist blacks in buying homes in black areas. Other federal projects backed by the Works Project Administration (WPA) also alleviated black unemployment.

Recognizing that FDR was steering benefits their way, blacks during the New Deal era moved steadily toward the Democratic Party, in a sense selling their votes for a mess of pottage. By 1936, 75 percent of blacks became Democrats. This trend has only continued since then, so that today around 90 percent of blacks vote Democratic and only 10 percent vote Republican. From 1865 to 1936, the trend was exactly the reverse: approximately 90 percent of blacks voted Republican and only 10 percent voted Democratic.

So this was a switch: blacks switched from Republican to Democrat. Democrats could scarcely believe their good fortune. They found that they could continue to exclude, exploit, and subjugate blacks, and still get the black vote. Democratic strategists at the time expressed their amazement and delight that blacks votes came so cheap. In subsequent decades, progressive Democrats recognized that they could secure a virtually permanent hold on the black vote by creating plantation-style dependency on the state.

Later, Obama added a finishing touch to this macabre picture of welfare dependency by offering people free Obamaphones. This way, you see, he could even text you messages about how to support progressive Democrats and keep the benefits flowing in your direction.

LYNDON JOHNSON'S UPPITY NEGROES

The third member of this progressive troika—building upon Wilson and FDR—was Lyndon Johnson. During Johnson's tenure the Democratic Party completed the tilt away from old-style racism toward progressivism. In his early career, Johnson was a typical racist southern Democrat. But over time Johnson evolved.

What shape did this evolution take? Johnson came to understand that keeping blacks and other minorities in the Democratic camp required him to be more creative, more flexible. Not that Johnson became a convert to the idea of black improvement. On the contrary, he was convinced that keeping blacks poor and dependent was essential to maintaining long-term Democratic supremacy.

Why was this? Part of the reason was to retain the black vote. If blacks became independent they would have no more reason to vote Democratic. There was also a second reason. Black suffering gave Democratic progressivism a continuing claim to "social justice." In other words, black hardship provided a fund of moral capital that Democrats could use to cajole and intimidate voters into supporting a centralized progressive state and keeping progressive Democrats in power.

Johnson and his fellow Democrats cynically recognized that as long as blacks were beholden to them—as long as they stayed on the Democratic plantation—anyone who dissented from the progressive program could then be accused of being anti-black. Republicans who opposed progressivism could be charged with being racist! Blacks themselves—politically beholden to their providers—could be counted on to make these accusations. They could also be counted on to keep other blacks on the progressive plantation.

In an incredible twist, black conservatives and the party of black emancipation and of civil rights could now be tarred with the charge of bigotry and being against civil rights. Of course black leaders needed help to sustain these charges, especially with young people. So progressive historians and pundits kept up a drumbeat of progressive Democratic propaganda. To this day, they continue to recite those mantras, hoping that young people will swallow their story line about Republican perfidy and Democratic virtue.

What Lyndon Johnson actually thought about blacks was something else entirely. Here's what Johnson actually said, in a conversation with Democratic Senator Richard Russell of Georgia: "These niggers, they're getting pretty uppity these days and that's a problem for us since they got something now that they never had before, the political pull to back up their uppityness. Now we've got to do something about this, we've got to give them a little something, just enough to quiet them down, not enough to make a difference." Otherwise, Johnson concluded, blacks may start voting Republican and "it'll be Reconstruction all over again."[19]

This was not the only time Johnson—even after his evolution from a racist Democrat to a progressive Democrat—used the N word. Traveling on Air Force One with two Democratic governors, Johnson told them how important it was to him that they vote for the Civil Rights Act of 1964. The governors asked why. Johnson replied that it was part of his long-term strategy. "I'll have them niggers voting Democratic for two hundred years."[20]

We can see from this statement that Johnson—hailed as a progressive civil rights hero—remained a thoroughgoing racist. I don't mean to place him in a special category; rather, he belongs in the same category as a multitude of other Democrats. The significance of Johnson's statement is not in his predictable bigotry, but in his recognition that, for the first time, Democrats needed the black vote.

Previously Democrats sought to prevent blacks from voting in the South, and maintained Democratic majorities by monopolizing the white vote. This was done, as we saw, through boisterous appeals to racism and white supremacy. But as the South became more prosperous economically during the 1950s and 1960s, the racist appeal lost its currency and white southern Democrats realized that they had more in common with the Republican Party. They identified with the GOP idea of controlling your own destiny and improving your own life.

In a remarkable book, *The End of Southern Exceptionalism*, Byron Shafer and Richard Johnston make the case that white southerners switched to the Republican Party not because of racism but because they identified the GOP with economic opportunity and upward mobility. As the agrarian South became more industrial and then post-industrial, white southerners switched parties not because of race but because of economic prospects. Interestingly, whites moved to the Republican Party for the same reason blacks moved to the Democratic Party: both groups saw the journey as congruent with their economic self-interest.

Shafer and Johnston show how Democrats tried, and failed, to keep southern whites in the fold by appealing to racism. Southern whites, however, migrated to the GOP as the party that better represented their interests and aspirations. Shafer and Johnston supply reams of data to substantiate their claim that the poorest, most racist whites remained Democratic, while more prosperous whites who were not racist were more likely to become Republicans. To the horror of the Democratic Party, the South moved in the Republican direction as white southerners embraced the GOP as the non-racist party of economic opportunity and patriotism.[21]

Johnson grew up in rural Texas; he fully understood the politics of the South. He knew that if the Democratic Party were to maintain its viability in the region, it would have to rely on the black vote as never before. This is the basis of Johnson's insistence that the Democrats, however reluctantly, offer blacks something. Johnson wanted to give as little as possible—he needed the blacks poor and dependent, rather than self-reliant and upwardly-mobile—but he was candid that the rules had changed and blacks had to be bought off with new benefits in order to keep them on the Democratic plantation.

Now we can understand Johnson's motive for championing the Civil Rights Act of 1964. Johnson fought hard for it because his party depended on it. He also knew that the main resistance would come from his own party, as indeed it did. A later generation of progressives would rewrite textbooks creating the false impression that the Republicans were the ones in opposition. Johnson knew better. He actively recruited Republicans across the aisle to help him defeat his fellow Democrats who feverishly tried to block the landmark laws of the Civil Rights Movement.

WHICH PARTY OPPOSED CIVIL RIGHTS?

The voting rolls of the Civil Rights laws speak for themselves. The Civil Rights Act of 1964 passed the House with 153 out of 244 Democrats voting for it, and 136 out of 171 Republicans. This means that 63 percent of Democrats and 80 percent of Republicans voted "yes." In the Senate, 46 out of 67 Democrats (69 percent) and 27 out of 33 Republicans (82 percent) supported the measure.

The pattern was similar for the Voting Rights Act of 1965. It passed the House 333–85, with 24 Republicans and 61 Democrats voting "no." In the Senate, 94 percent of Republicans compared with 73 percent of Democrats supported the legislation.

Here's a revealing tidbit: had Republicans voted for the Civil Rights laws in the same proportion as Democrats, these laws would not have passed. Republicans, more than Democrats, are responsible for the second civil rights revolution, just as they were solely responsible for the first one. For the second time around, Republicans were mainly the good guys and Democrats were mainly the bad guys.

Here's further proof: the main opposition to the Civil Rights Movement came from the Dixiecrats. Note that the Dixiecrats were Democrats; as one pundit wryly notes, they were Dixiecrats and not Dixiecans.

The Dixiecrats originated as a breakaway group from the Democratic Party in 1948. For a time, the Dixiecrats attempted to form a separate party and run their own presidential ticket, but this attempt failed and the Dixiecrats reconstituted themselves as a rebel faction within the Democratic Party.

Joined by other Democrats who did not formally ally themselves with this faction, the Dixiecrats organized protests against desegregation rulings by the Supreme Court. Dixiecrat governors refused to enforce those rulings. Dixiecrats in the Senate also mounted filibusters against the Civil Rights Act of 1957 and the Civil Rights Act of 1964. Johnson's Democratic allies in Congress required Republican votes in order to defeat a Dixiecrat-led filibuster and pass the Civil Rights Act of 1964.

Leading members of the Dixiecrat faction were James Eastland, Democrat from Mississippi; John Stennis, Democrat from Mississippi; Russell Long, Democrat from Louisiana; Strom Thurmond, Democrat from South Carolina; Herman Talmadge, Democrat from Georgia; J. William Fulbright, Democrat from Arkansas; Lester Maddox, Democrat from Georgia; Al Gore Sr., Democrat from Tennessee; and Robert Byrd, Democrat from West Virginia. Of these only Thurmond later joined the Republican Party. The rest of them remained Democrats.

The Dixiecrats weren't the only racists who opposed civil rights legislation. So did many other Democrats who never joined the Dixiecrat faction. These were racists who preferred to exercise their influence within the Democratic Party, which after all had long been the party of racism, rather than create a new party. Richard Russell of Georgia—who now has a Senate Building named after him—and James Eastland of Mississippi are among the segregationist Democrats who refused to join the Dixiecrat faction.

Now the GOP presidential candidate in 1964, Barry Goldwater, did vote against the Civil Rights Act. But Goldwater was no racist. In fact, he had been a founding member of the Arizona NAACP. He was active in integrating the Phoenix public schools. He had voted for the 1957 Civil Rights Act.

Goldwater opposed the 1964 act because it outlawed private as well as public discrimination, and Goldwater believed the federal government did not have legitimate authority to restrict the private sector in that way. I happen to agree with him on this—a position I argued in *The End of Racism*. Even so, Goldwater's position was not shared by a majority of his fellow Republicans.

It was Governor Orval Faubus, Democrat of Arkansas, who ordered the Arkansas National Guard to stop black students from enrolling in Little Rock Central High School—until Republican President Dwight Eisenhower sent troops from the 101st Airborne to enforce desegregation. In retaliation, Faubus shut down all the public high schools in Little Rock for the 1958–59 school year.

It was Governor George Wallace, Democrat of Alabama, who attempted to prevent four black students from enrolling in elementary schools in Huntsville, Alabama, until a federal court in Birmingham intervened. Bull Connor, the infamous southern sheriff who unleashed dogs and hoses on civil rights protesters, was a Democrat.

Progressives who cannot refute this history—facts are stubborn things—nevertheless create the fantasy of a Nixon "Southern strategy" that supposedly explains how Republicans cynically appealed to racism in order to convert southern Democrats into Republicans. In reality Nixon had no such strategy—as we have seen, it was Lyndon Johnson who had a southern strategy to keep blacks from defecting to the Republican Party. Johnson, not Nixon, was the true racist, a fact that progressive historiography has gone to great lengths to disguise.

Nixon's political strategy in the 1968 campaign is laid out in Kevin Phillips's classic work *The Emerging Republican Majority*. Phillips writes that the Nixon campaign knew it could never win the presidency through any kind of racist appeal. Such an appeal, even if it won some converts in some parts of the Lower South, would completely ruin Nixon's prospects in the rest of the country. Nixon's best bet was to appeal to the rising middle classes of the Upper South on the basis of prosperity and economic opportunity.[22] This is exactly what Nixon did.

There are no statements by Nixon that even remotely suggest he appealed to racism in the 1968 or 1972 campaigns. Nixon never displayed the hateful, condescending view of blacks that Johnson did. The racist vote in 1968 didn't go to Nixon; it went to George Wallace. A longtime Democratic segregationist, Wallace campaigned that year on an independent ticket. Nixon won the election but Wallace carried the Deep South states of Arkansas, Louisiana, Mississippi, Alabama, and Georgia.

Nixon supported expanded civil rights for blacks throughout his career while Johnson was—for the cynical reasons given above—a late convert to the cause. Nixon went far beyond Johnson in this area; in fact, Nixon implemented America's first affirmative action program which involved the government forcing racist unions in Philadelphia to hire blacks.

To sum up, starting in the 1930s and continuing to the present, progressive Democrats developed a new solution to the problem of what they saw as useless people. In the antebellum era, useless people from the Democratic point of view were mainly employed as slaves. In the postbellum period, southern Democrats repressed, segregated, and subjugated useless people, seeking to prevent them from challenging white supremacy or voting Republican. Meanwhile, northern progressives like Margaret Sanger sought to prevent useless people from being born. Today's progressives, building on the legacy of Wilson, FDR, and Johnson, have figured out what to do with useless people: turn them into Democratic voters.

CHAPTER 6

PROGRESSIVISM *ÜBER ALLES*

THE SECRET PACT BETWEEN PROGRESSIVISM AND FASCISM

I am much interested and deeply impressed by what he has accomplished. I don't mind telling you in confidence that I am keeping in fairly close touch with that admirable Italian gentleman.[1]
—Franklin Delano Roosevelt on Mussolini

Hillary Clinton has a big idea that she intends to be the centerpiece of her 2016 campaign. She wants to turn college education into a new entitlement, like health care. To this end, she has an ambitious proposal to help cover the costs of higher education. "Under my plan," she says, "tuition would be affordable for every family. Students should never have to take out a loan to pay for tuition at their state's public university."[2]

Hillary's proposal is not "free college" but rather "debt-free college." For "free college"—or at least free public university education—we have to turn to Bernie Sanders. Hillary is offering the discount program while Bernie comes closest to offering the free program. Bernie's plan offers no tuition and no fees at public universities. While Hillary's plan is estimated to cost $350 billion over ten years, Bernie's plan would cost $70 billion a year.

Under Hillary's proposal, students and their parents would still pay according to their ability. The federal government would dispatch money to the states to subsidize public universities, which would be pressured to lower costs. So students at state-run universities would presumably get a debt-free education. A fully free education would only be available to some students: low-income students and students who enrolled in government programs like Americorps.[3]

Critics of Hillary's program, such as Douglas Holtz-Eakin of the American Action Forum call these plans "Obamacare for higher education." Obama I think would approve of this label. A couple of years ago, Obama himself offered a $60 billion proposal to make community college free. Even though Obama's plan languished in the Republican-dominated Congress, Bernie and Hillary build on it, even though they intend to take it much further over the next several years.

Both Hillary and Bernie's plans appeal to a lot of young people. College debt is a serious problem—it totals $1.3 trillion at last count—so debt-free sounds good. Even more attractive is the idea of not paying for college at all. Young people have historically responded well to offers of "free food" and "free drinks." Why then should they not respond equally well to the idea of a free college education?

Of course it would never occur to these same young people to work for free when they graduate. And, they would surely realize if they thought about it, college isn't actually free. Obviously there are buildings to construct and maintain, facilities to operate, faculty to pay, and innumerable other costs to bear. Someone has to foot the bills for all this.

If students and their families are not the ones who are paying, who is? Hillary and Bernie both answer: the taxpayer. The government will pay. College isn't free, but it's free to you. Your entitlement comes at someone else's expense.

The government will pay, but the government, it turns out, doesn't have the money. Over and above existing allocations for Pell Grants and other federal subsidies, there are no discretionary funds lying about that can be used to fund young people's college education.

Hillary and Bernie both want to get the money for their college subsidy programs from Wall Street. That means Congress would have to approve higher taxes. If Congress doesn't do this, there is only one other way to pay: the government would have to borrow the money. The United States government is $19 trillion in debt and counting. So under Hillary's plan, $350 billion would be added to the national debt over the next decade. Bernie's plan would add even more.

What happens to that debt? Ultimately it has to be paid. If this generation isn't going to pay it, then it is going to be passed down to the next generation. It goes, in other words, to young people. They inherit the debt and the accumulated interest from their profligate predecessors. In the end, the national debt is a claim upon the future earnings of the younger generation.

What Hillary's proposal amounts to, objectively considered, is a transfer of income from the future to the present. She is reaching into the back pockets of young people, taking out their own future earnings, and using those earnings to pay for young people's education today. This isn't robbing Peter to pay Paul; it's robbing Paul to pay Paul. This entitlement isn't free at all.

The genius of Hillary's idea is that she gives young people the false impression that she is providing free education when, as we just saw, young people end up paying their own freight plus interest. With some innovative financing, they could have themselves arranged to borrow against their future earnings. Hillary is not "giving" them anything.

But she is counting on suckers to believe that she is. The real beneficiary in this whole deal is Hillary herself. If she pulls it off, she is viewed as the person who made higher education free, in the same way that Obama is viewed as the person who provided health care for all Americans. Isn't it wonderful to gain a reputation for such magnanimity without putting out a penny? This is the basic scam of progressive politics.

Hillary's real objective isn't to help students; it is to establish government control—which is to say progressive control—over higher education. The progressives already dominate elementary and secondary education, because public schools are an arm of the state. If Hillary succeeds, she will have brought another major arm of the private sector into the federal orbit that will turn out Democratic voters for decades to come.

COLONIZING THE PRIVATE SECTOR

This continues a trend under Obama in which major industries have, one by one, been colonized by the federal government. The process began in 2009 with banks and investment houses being taken over in the aftermath of the 2008 market crash. Next, the government established control over the automobile sector through bailouts, paying the unions, and stiffing the bondholders.

Next came health care. Through Obamacare, the federal government became the boss of every insurance company, every hospital—that amounts to one-sixth of the U.S. economy. Next stop is the energy sector. Through EPA regulations, the government can control what type of energy Americans are allowed to use and how much can be used per day. Higher education would be the next prize in this ongoing usurpation of the private sector, further tightening federal control which is already exercised through regulations and grants.

Three features of his progressive expansion of power stand out. The first is entitlements: progressives advance by declaring that people are entitled to something without having to work for it or earn it. Second, there is typically an element of fear. Progressive control over banking and investment firms came about in the aftermath of the 2008 panic. Obamacare played on fears that people who got sick would not have access to hospitals and doctors. Third, the progressive move is not to actually take over and manage the private sector but to direct and regulate it from the outside; in other words, state-run capitalism.

Where do these ideas come from? We are accustomed to linking progressivism with socialism but none of the three features of modern progressivism come from socialism per se. Socialism doesn't involve "entitlements." Marx never appealed to fear. He did predict that class conflicts would generate a socialist revolution in which the workers overthrow the capitalists, but that prophecy has long been discredited.

Finally, state-run capitalism is not socialism. Socialism is not about the state relying on private industry to create resources and then staking its claim to steer and direct those resources. Rather, socialism is about nationalization, which means the government actually takes over an industry like oil drilling or health care and manages it. We have seen nationalization in Russia, China, India, Venezuela, Cuba, and other socialist regimes.

Obama and Hillary are not socialists in that sense. In fact, they are too lazy to be socialists. They have no interest in actually running companies or factories. They don't intend to build automobiles or computers or figure out how to extract oil from the ground. Neither do the vast majority of American progressives. They don't know how to do any of this, nor do they want to. Rather, they want the private sector to produce resources, and then they want to direct the use of those resources. This isn't socialism; it's something else.

Perhaps Hillary and Obama's approach can be understood in terms of another version of socialism—socialism in the classic sense. Socialism in the classic sense means that workers control the means of production. An automobile company, for instance, would be owned and controlled by its workers. Apple would be owned and governed not by shareholders or management but by the people who work at Apple. Clearly classic socialism is not what Obama and Hillary are about. They haven't even *proposed* that workers in American companies own or run those companies. Again, socialism per se isn't going on here.

So what's going on? In the previous chapter I showed the association of progressivism with racism. But people who know history may feel that I am leaving something out. How can you say, they might protest, that progressivism derived all its central themes from racism? Here the critics are right. I never meant to suggest that modern progressivism was solely based on racism. As I intend to show, it also drew its inspiration from another important twentieth-century movement: fascism.

LEARNING FROM FASCISM

Most people today have no idea what fascism means. They think it means the Holocaust. Actually, that's not correct. Fascism preceded the Holocaust. While the German fascists hated Jews and perpetrated the Holocaust, fascists in Italy and other countries did not do this and opposed it. As Jonah Goldberg reminds us, fascism by itself has nothing to do with anti-Semitism or gas chambers.[4]

Fascism actually means putting the resources of the individual and of industry at the service of the state. This means that the state defines what individual aspirations are about, and the state controls the resources of private industry. Fascism also confers entitlements on citizens and uses these to justify state power and state control. Finally, fascism draws on an atmosphere of perpetual fear—sometimes accompanied by perpetual conflict—to keep citizens apprehensive and make them look to the state for protection and care.

This is how fascism is defined and this is how fascism has been implemented in the countries that have implemented it. The actual definition is not obscure, notwithstanding postwar progressive efforts to obscure it. So given what fascism means and how it is actually put into practice, who can deny that Obama and Hillary's vision for the federal government most closely resembles fascism? It is, I suggest, a new fascism for the twenty-first century.

If this is so, however, it's hardly a new departure for the Democratic Party. The progressive Democrats have shown an affinity for fascism—both of the German and Italian type—since at least the early 1930s. Moreover, Italian and German fascists drew on the ideas of American progressives going back to the 1910s and 1920s. European fascism and American progressivism are old friends, even if progressive intellectuals have worked hard to disavow the association.

At this point I can almost hear progressives erupt with outrage. Fascism! Nazism! The Holocaust! How dare you associate our movement and our party and our iconic leaders with thuggery and mass murder?

Well, let's see. John F. Kennedy is an icon of the Democratic Party. He was a progressive but a relatively moderate one; even some conservatives today admire JFK. In 1937 as a young man, JFK toured Germany in the early years of Adolf Hitler. What he saw greatly impressed him. "Fascism?" JFK wrote in his diary. "The right thing for Nazi Germany."

JFK visited Hitler's Bavarian holiday home as well as a teahouse that Hitler had constructed on a mountaintop. "Who has visited these two places," JFK observed, "can easily imagine how Hitler in a few years will emerge from the hatred currently surrounding him as one of the most important personalities that ever lived." In a later journal entry, JFK continued in the same mode, remarking that Hitler "had something mysterious about him. He was the stuff of legends."

Touring the Rhineland, JFK echoed Nazi propaganda at the time. "The Nordic races certainly seem to be superior to the Romans." Hostility to Nazi Germany, JFK added, stems largely from jealousy and fear of German superiority. "The Germans really are too good—therefore people have ganged up on them to protect themselves."[5]

JFK went on to serve as a Navy Lieutenant in World War II. He had no illusions about Hitler after the war. Even so, JFK's pre-war fascination with Hitler is revealing because he was not alone. Other noted progressives at the time admired Hitler and the Nazis. The feeling was reciprocal; Hitler and the Nazis admired them.

In 1933, for example, the main Nazi paper *Volkischer Beobachter* confessed that the Nazi movement had a lot to learn from the New Deal. "We National Socialists are looking toward America." The publication found FDR's policies "thoroughly inflected by a strong national socialism" and noted that "many passages in his book *Looking Forward* could have been written by a National Socialist."[6]

Many more progressives admired fascism—not so much Nazi-style fascism as the fascism of Italian strongman Benito Mussolini. New Deal progressives lionized Mussolini, and left-leaning journals like *The New Republic* praised his policies. As the quotation at the beginning of this chapter suggests, FDR was quite a fan of Mussolini. Mussolini, for his part, was also a fan of FDR.

A SECRET PACT

The secret pact between American progressivism and European fascism is perhaps the most closely guarded secret in politics today. Fascism showed progressives how to use "entitlements" to create dependent classes not just of blacks but of Americans of all colors. Fascism also provided a model for how to organize the progressive state: basically as a quarterback directing the wealth and resources of private industry. How, then, have progressives gotten away with hiding their deep connection with the twentieth century's most odious political movement?

The reason is as follows. During the 1930s, FDR and American progressives drew heavily from multiple strands of European fascism. They borrowed from the fascist style of charismatic leadership, from fascist monumentalist architecture, and from fascist techniques of political propaganda. Progressives especially loved the forward-looking emphasis of fascism, encapsulated in the slogan of the Hitler youth song featured in the movie *Cabaret*, "Tomorrow belongs to me."

Progressives did far more than emulate the style of fascism; they also adopted its ideas. Progressivism was in line with fascist social policy, which mainly involved killing off undesirables and excluding immigrants. Progressives also embraced fascist economic policy—instituting citizen entitlements and then using those to justify state control over the private sector—which shaped the contours of the New Deal.

After World War II, fascism—to put it mildly—fell into bad repute. It became politically impossible in decent company to profess an ideology that took on the odor of the Holocaust. So progressives dumped many of the social and political features of fascism—no more compulsory sterilization or racist immigration policies—while retaining fascist economic policy.

Progressives quickly got rid of the fascist label and, in a creative move, they publicly pretended that fascism was the very antithesis of what they had always been about. Now they portrayed fascism as somehow a conservative, right-of-center phenomenon. To this day, without bothering to define what they mean, progressives routinely accuse conservatives of being "fascists."

The prime progressive candidate to be a fascist is, of course, Donald Trump. The online magazine *Slate* even interviewed a supposed expert on fascism to explore how closely Trump fits the fascist label. The expert, Robert Paxton, found "some echoes of fascism" by noting that Trump is a nationalist, Trump appeals to people of low education, and he "even looks like Mussolini in the way he sticks his lower jaw out."[7]

But if progressives consider Republicans to be fascist because fascism is "right wing," this is not how the fascists themselves saw it. The fascists themselves always knew they were left-wingers. We are blinded to this today because we think of socialism and fascism as opposed to each other, and we tend to liken progressivism to socialism. In reality, socialism and fascism are closely linked. That's why, at least in one stage of World War II, it was natural for Hitler and Stalin to ally with each other; both believed they were fighting on the same side.

The link between fascism and socialism can also be seen in the way the Nazis described themselves. They called themselves National Socialists. The Nazi program involved nationalization of trusts, government control of industry, confiscations of amassed wealth, shared profits with labor, a whole range of entitlements. Fascism, in other words, was a branch of socialism and was recognized as such by its champions and adherents.

Progressivism, Communism, and Fascism are today considered to be the three alternative systems of government that emerged in the twentieth century. But in fact all three are expressions of collectivism—of a powerful centralized state. Collectivism is the big idea of the twentieth century. It gained power as a consequence of the Great Depression, which many saw as proof of the collapse of capitalism. As a result of this erosion of confidence, people proved willing to put their faith in collectivist solutions.

Progressives today insist that progressivism—as manifest in FDR's New Deal—"saved" capitalism. This is part of the progressive postwar story, and it's pure bunkum: progressivism no more "saved" capitalism than fascism or communism did. These were from the outset systems to replace and subvert capitalism. The fact that capitalism survived and even thrived was not due to progressivism but due to the failure or inadequacy of progressive efforts to subvert capitalism.

To compare progressivism with fascism is not to equate FDR, Mussolini, and Hitler. All three were charismatic leaders, but there are obvious differences between them. Partly they reflected cultural differences between their three respective countries. They were also different people. FDR wasn't a mass murderer, as Hitler was. Neither was FDR an outright dictator, like Mussolini became. Rather, FDR for the most part used the democratic process to achieve goals that reflected his version of fascism—fascism, one may say, American-style.

Yet if FDR was freely elected, so was Hitler. Both came to power through a democratic process. If FDR embodied the spirit of the American people, so did Mussolini and Hitler respectively embody the Italian and the German spirit. Hitler and Mussolini jettisoned democracy immediately upon taking power, but FDR too assumed virtually dictatorial wartime powers.

Even in peacetime, FDR sought to circumvent the constitutional system of checks and balances by packing the Supreme Court. Fortunately, this packing scheme didn't work, but FDR achieved his greater purpose when the court changed its tune and became a pliant supporter of the New Deal.

Hitler was a racist in a way that Mussolini wasn't, with FDR occupying a position somewhere between the two of them. FDR was not an anti-Semite, as Hitler was, but he did share Hitler's low view of Asians and blacks. During World War II, FDR ordered that many Japanese Americans, under suspicion of disloyalty, be interned in camps. There is, of course, an argument in wartime for holding captive those who pose a security risk. My point, however, is that FDR made no similar arrangements for Italians and Germans in the United States.

So there was a clear racial element in FDR's approach to security. FDR was culpable for doing exactly what progressive Democrats accuse Donald Trump of doing when he threatens to target violent Islamists. Yet Trump doesn't single out radical Muslims while exonerating other groups who act like them. FDR, by contrast, treated Japanese Americans in a way he didn't treat German Americans or Italian Americans.

That, I'm suggesting, is because FDR, even during World War II, retained a soft spot for German and Italian fascism. Also FDR wasn't turned off by the fascist idea of a racial hierarchy; indeed, here was FDR implementing one himself. Incidentally Japanese internment is another crime that Democrats blame on "America" when their own hero, FDR, is the one who ordered it.

FDR, Mussolini, and Hitler all denounced the free market and blamed the problems of their society on private business. All vowed to use the state to combat the power of business, and offered themselves as the true manifestation of the collective good. If one ended as the enemy of the other two, it shouldn't blind us to their earlier mutual admiration.

THE EUGENIC LINK

We may think that the progressive association with fascism begins with Mussolini and Hitler but actually it begins much earlier, in the eugenics movement championed by Margaret Sanger. In the previous chapter I focused on Sanger's views of blacks, but Sanger, it turns out, had a much bigger list of undesirables that she wanted to see wiped off the earth.

Sanger was a eugenicist who saw birth control and sterilization as the means to create what she called "a race of thoroughbreds." This required making women she termed "reckless breeders" stop producing "human weeds." Sanger drew a sharp line not so much between black and white as between "fit" and "unfit." By fit she admittedly meant whites, but only educated, upper-class whites. By "unfit" she meant pretty much everyone else. Sanger viewed birth control as a mechanism to multiply the numbers of the fit while reducing the numbers of the unfit.

As we saw earlier, she preferred to use social pressure and propaganda but, if those failed, she wholeheartedly supported compulsory sterilization. (Abortion was not an issue during that time; later Planned Parenthood would become a zealous promoter and performer of abortions.) If Sanger had lived longer I'm sure she would have become an abortion enthusiast—at least for "unfit" populations. For Sanger, what mattered was not the means but the result. As she put it on the cover of her magazine *Birth Control Review*, "More children from the fit, less from the unfit—this is the chief aim of birth control."[8]

Sanger was also an early advocate of the Nazi sterilization laws as setting a global example in this area. Sanger corresponded with psychiatrist Ernst Rudin, director of the Kaiser Wilhelm Institute and chief

architect of Hitler's sterilization program. In 1933, she also published
Rudin's article, "Eugenic Sterilization: An Urgent Need" in her *Birth
Control Review*. The earliest of the Nazi sterilization laws were, by
Rudin's admission, modeled on American laws drafted by Sanger and
her associates at the American Birth Control League.[9]

Sanger's like-minded associates, Madison Grant and Lothrop Stoddard, also maintained good personal ties with the Nazis. Grant received
letters of praise from the German chancellor, and his book *The Passing
of the Great Race* was personally inscribed by Hitler as "my bible" on
the subject of eugenics. Stoddard met with Hitler and praised him in
1940 for "weeding out the worst strains in the Germanic stock," adding
that the Jew problem in Germany is "settled in principle and soon to be
settled in fact by the physical elimination of the Jews themselves."

Progressives like Sanger weren't just concerned with limiting the births
of nonwhite people; they were also concerned with limiting their immigration to the United States. What these people feared was the browning of
America. They fought it on two fronts. First they tried to construct a legal
blockade to keep the brown people out, and if they got through the blockade, to restrict their breeding. The two methods worked together, in a kind
of scissors motion, toward the same racially restrictive end.

Progressives like Edward A. Ross, Lothrop Stoddard, and Madison
Grant—all associates of Sanger—were leading champions of laws
restricting immigration. Ross was an academic advisor to Sanger.
Employing with full gusto the social Darwinist rhetoric of early twentieth century progressivism, Ross described immigrants from central and
southern Europe as "hirsute, low-browed, big-faced persons of obviously
low mentality. Clearly they belong in skins, in wattled huts at the close
of the Great Ice Age. These ox-like men are descendants of those who
always stayed behind."[10]

Stoddard, who served on the board of Sanger's Birth Control
League—the forerunner to Planned Parenthood—was the author of *The
Rising Tide of Color Against White World Supremacy*. He was, during
the 1920s, the most famous racist writer in the United States. The Ku
Klux Klan regularly cited his work and so did the Nazis. Stoddard wrote

that immigrants were a kind of virus and "just as we isolate the bacterial invasion, and starve out the bacteria, so we can compel an inferior race to remain in its native habitat."[11]

Madison Grant was president of the New York Zoological Society and one of Sanger's heroes; she listed his book *The Passing of the Great Race* as required reading on the eugenics list of her *Birth Control Review*. Grant warned that what he called Nordic civilization was being swamped and vitiated by inferior Alpine and Mediterranean strains from central and southern Europe. These darker Europeans were really "Western extensions of Asiatic species," Grant insisted, while Nordics were Aryans, "the white man par excellence."[12]

KEEPING OUT THE "UNFIT"

Although we hear many progressive laments today about how Republicans are against immigrants—an allegation supported by nothing more than opposition to illegal immigration—in reality no one has attacked immigrants with the venom of progressives. In fact, the progressive assault on immigrants in the 1920s was unprecedented and had far-reaching consequences.

America had long been considered a magnet for immigrants. Hundreds of thousands of Irish, Italians, and Jews came to America in the nineteenth century, and these groups helped build America. Immigration levels were just as high in the early twentieth century. More than four hundred thousand immigrants came to America each year from 1900 to 1920.

But progressives hated immigration largely because they hated the types of immigrants whom they saw entering the country. Sanger's main cause was birth control, but she too eagerly backed immigration curbs for "unfit" populations. Sanger argued that America should "keep the doors of immigration closed to the entrance of certain aliens whose condition is known to be detrimental to the stamina of the race, such as the feebleminded, idiots, morons, the insane, syphilitic, epileptic, criminal, professional prostitutes, and others."[13]

Progressive influence was instrumental in the passage of the Immigration Act of 1924. From the outset Sanger supported the law, but her public endorsement of restrictive immigration came later, in a speech in 1932 titled "My Way to Peace." Nevertheless, for the first time in American history, laws were passed that systematically barred people from entry and established quotas based on race and national origin. White immigrants were preferred over immigrants of color, and northern Europeans were preferred over southern Europeans.

Of course there were laws that restricted Chinese immigration in the nineteenth century. These were anomalous, however, and there were no laws that curtailed immigration from Europe. The 1924 law put even most Europeans on the unwanted list. The effect was immediate. In the period from 1925–1939, immigration levels dropped to around twenty-five thousand a year, an astonishing 95 percent decline from earlier levels. Progressive "reform" had won the day.

This "reform," however, had dangerous consequences. During the 1930s there were last-ditch efforts to waive some of the restrictions of the 1924 Immigration Act in order to grant asylum to Jews whose lives were in mortal danger from the Nazis. These were not Jewish applications that came through the mail from Germany. The issue was far more pressing. Almost a thousand German Jews waited desperately in a ship off the coast of Florida, seeking a life-saving approval of their immigration papers.

Progressives like Harry Laughlin—a director of the Birth Control League and close ally of Sanger—resolutely opposed entry to the U.S. by these Jews. In his report, *Immigration and Conquest*, Laughlin sought to prove that Jews were hard to assimilate and that they would cause a "breakdown in the race purity of the superior stocks."[14] In a sense, American progressives like Laughlin were tacitly collaborating with the Nazis who obviously did not want the Jews to escape to the United States. As a consequence of progressive resistance, the Nazis got their wish and the ship was sent back to Germany.

Progressive support for eugenics and hostility to immigration were both rooted in social Darwinism, with its accompanying idea of higher and lower races. The social Darwinists developed a social program that they said was modeled on Darwin's concept of natural selection: "survival of the fittest." Basically they sought to plan and design society so that "fit" groups could prosper and "unfit" groups could be exterminated. (Recall Sanger's reference to the "extermination" of the Negro population.)

This extermination rhetoric would prove immensely appealing to the fascist movement emerging in Germany. As historian Richard Weikart shows in two important books, *From Darwin to Hitler* and *Hitler's Ethic*, Hitler himself was a social Darwinist. Hitler's speeches and writings are suffused with social Darwinist rhetoric. He used that rhetoric to justify his racialist and eugenic policies.

Case in point: Hitler promoted and subsidized childbirth for what he considered "fit" Nordic and Aryan types. At the same time, he supported abortion and sterilization for Jews, gypsies, and other "unfit" groups. Hitler was, then, anti-abortion for the "Master Race" and pro-abortion for everyone else. Hitler's discrimination between Aryans and non-Aryans is very much along Sanger's racial lines. For Hitler, as for Margaret Sanger, birth control meant "more children from the fit, fewer from the unfit."

COVERING THEIR TRACKS

Thanks to its association with Hitler, social Darwinism became taboo. At this point, progressives moved quickly to camouflage their association with it. Historian Richard Hofstadter in his 1944 book *Social Darwinism in America* spearheaded the academic cover-up. The progressive claque hailed Hofstadter's book as a masterpiece because it blamed social Darwinism on the free market. Later scholars have largely discredited Hofstadter's thesis, but even so that thesis remains the basis for the conventional wisdom about social Darwinism.[15]

In Hofstadter's analysis, social Darwinism in America was a movement to promote capitalist and laissez-faire ideals. Hofstadter could only find two individuals who represented his thesis, and one of them was an

Englishman, Herbert Spencer. Spencer could only in an antiquated sense be termed a Darwinian, since he preceded Darwin. He did, however, coin the term "survival of the fittest" which was later adopted by Darwin. The only American free market advocate who spoke in Darwinian terms was sociologist William Graham Sumner.

What about the economists and actual businessmen—did their support for free market values arise out of a commitment to social Darwinism? In general, no. Many American economists supported laissez-faire but they defended their principles by appealing to Adam Smith, not Darwin. Most American businessmen simply accepted free markets as what commerce was all about. Darwin and Darwinism had nothing to do with it.

It was leftists, progressives, and Marxists who frequently invoked Darwin, and they did so to justify higher taxes, government regulation, and socialism. Marx, for example, wrote in 1861 that Darwin's work "is most important and suits my purpose in that it provides a basis in natural science for the historical class struggle."[16] Marx liked Darwin because he saw Darwin as overthrowing the idea of a natural order in society.

Other socialist and leftist intellectuals—Thorstein Veblen, H. G. Wells, George Bernard Shaw—also employed Darwin's ideas to support their own statist economic and social theories. Hofstadter knew all this—he quoted the line from Marx that I have given above—but he downplayed it. He also downplayed the role of social Darwinism in advancing progressive causes like eugenics and racially based immigration controls.

Hofstadter's goal was to use the cudgel of social Darwinism to attack the free market. (Hofstadter was a progressive who understood the importance of covering up the tracks of the progressive movement. He was also a member of the American Communist Party for a brief period in 1938.) Thus Hofstadter twisted social Darwinism to make it into something it wasn't, and he submerged the actual themes of social Darwinism, giving them only a passing mention. In this way Hofstadter successfully dissociated American progressivism from its eugenic and racist association with fascism and Nazism.

As the enormity of Hitler's crimes became apparent, progressives were forced to abandon Nazi-sounding eugenic schemes and racially based immigration policies. On immigration, progressives adopted essentially the same solution that they had earlier discovered for blacks. They went from being opponents of legal immigration to becoming champions of illegal immigration. By offering the newcomers free stuff, progressives hope to convert these populations they formerly considered undesirable and unfit into highly-desired and fit Democratic voters.

While progressives jettisoned old-style eugenics, they didn't altogether stop caring about the subject. They continued to champion birth control, but now as a means of personal choice and population reduction. In other words, the explicit eugenic racial element was removed. No more talk about more children from the fit, fewer from the unfit. No more references to wiping out the black population!

Nevertheless, it cannot escape notice that progressive groups like Planned Parenthood even today concentrate their propaganda in the inner cities. They champion birth control as just another free "entitlement," like free education and free health care. Today 40 percent of the women having abortions are black and, in places like New York City, abortions outnumber births in the black community. How proud Margaret Sanger would be if she had been around to see it.

So what happened to Planned Parenthood's Negro project? It still exists! Today it is simply called...Planned Parenthood. The group's propaganda efforts are now concentrated in black and minority communities, and largely invisible everywhere else.

A MUTUAL ADMIRATION SOCIETY

While progressives were forced to modify their fascist social policies, they never gave up on fascist economic policy. The progressive fascination with fascist economics goes back to the early 1930s, when FDR came to

office with virtually no plan to deal with the Great Depression. Ambitious, confused, and a little desperate, FDR looked abroad.

There he saw what the new governments were doing in Europe. He
was impressed. Yes, what caught FDR's eye was fascism. Both in Italy
and Germany, FDR witnessed charismatic strongmen who harnessed
the fear caused by the global depression. They directed that fear against
the business class and the entrepreneurs who were previously the most
powerful people in society. They drew on that fear to increase the power
of the state to control industry and control people. FDR's reaction was:
Hey, if this is fascism, what's not to like?

Today, of course, the idea of a revered figure like FDR admiring
fascist leaders like Mussolini seems far-fetched bordering on absurd.
What could FDR have seen in that cartoon dictator? But as historian
Wolfgang Schivelbusch points out, the image of Mussolini as a cartoon
dictator is a post–World War II creation. After the war, progressives
remade Mussolini into that figure. Viewed retrospectively, Mussolini's
fascism—what he termed the Corporate State—became a bad joke.

Before the war, however, these same progressives viewed Mussolini
quite differently. As Schivelbusch points out, before World War II progressives emphasized not the differences between FDR's New Deal and
Mussolini's Corporate State but the similarities. These similarities were
evident not only in America but in Europe as well. As we will see, FDR
and Mussolini recognized them themselves.

In 1932, the progressive writer H. G. Wells gave a telling speech at
Oxford University. The speech was titled, "Liberal Fascism." Wells
argued that liberals in the West were mostly trying to copy Soviet-style
socialism but actually the fullest, finest form of socialism was fascism.
Basically, according to Wells, progressives needed to overcome their
inhibitions and move in the fascist direction. Wells ended his speech with
a resounding call "for a Liberal *Fascisti*, for enlightened Nazis."[17] This
is not a speech you are likely to find today in a progressive reader.

While Wells puts fascism out in front, he seems to recognize that
FDR's welfare-state liberalism and Soviet Communism were movements
running in the same direction. Schivelbusch remarks that the similarities

between these movements were widely noticed on both sides of the Atlantic prior to World War II. His book comparing them is called *Three New Deals*. All of them centralized power; all put a new class of planners in charge of the productive wealth of the society, restricting the operations of the free market; and all used modern propaganda techniques to rally the masses in the name of collective solidarity.[18]

These are movements that drew upon each other, and learned from each other. FDR assembled a "brain trust" of intellectuals and media figures around him, just as Mussolini and Hitler did. The Italian and German fascists used academia and the media as allies in establishing their domination over the business class, and FDR followed suit. In fact, he began the practice of progressive presidents calling on these "brain trusts." JFK subsequently had a brain trust, as did Lyndon Johnson. Obama seems to prefer czars, his tastes apparently favoring Russian autocracy over the Germanic type.

In the grim aftermath of World War II and the Stalinist purges, the term "totalitarianism" has become a bad word. But for progressives before the war, Jonah Goldberg points out, it was a good word. "Totalitarianism" was a term used by Mussolini in a positive, descriptive sense. It meant giving total allegiance to the state; it meant a state that took care of people's physical, emotional, and aspirational needs. Totalitarianism implied an exhilarating unity of thought and action. [19]

Totalitarianism, in this sense, was the shared aspiration of fascists, Nazis, and progressives. Schivelbusch writes, "The New Deal Fascist Italy and Nazi Germany all profited from the illusion of the nation as an egalitarian community whose members looked out for one another's welfare under the watchful eyes of a strong leader."[20] Progressives across Europe and America in the 1930s relished the idea of the totalitarian society in which they could impose this unity, in other words, to supervise and control people's lives.

Does totalitarianism in this sense seem unfamiliar? It shouldn't be. Recall President Obama's propagandistic "Julia" videos. Essentially the Obama administration promised this hypothetical young woman cradle-to-grave protection. Absurdly, the package of benefits offered by the government under Obama would be worth more than the wages of a typical forty-hour work week.

"Under President Obama" Julia would get education subsidies, minimum wage, food stamps, and free health care. "Under President Obama" Julia even decides to bear a child. To me, it's a bit unnerving. But this is progressive utopia: citizens are all brought into complete subordination and submission to an all-powerful state.

HILLARY'S FASCIST STREAK

We find the same totalitarian overtones in Hillary Clinton's statist vision for children represented in her book *It Takes a Village*. Let's see how. Her book is based on the African proverb, "It take a village to raise a child." As the Africans mean it, raising children is not merely a job for parents; the whole culture of the village must be supportive. In this sense, I agree: my own childhood on the outskirts of Mumbai was enriched by extended family, a wide circle of friends, the subcultures of church and school, sporting and civic associations, a whole ecosystem of support.

This, however, is not what Hillary means by the title of her book. What she means is "It takes a central government." In Hillary's view all associations from the family to the church to the civic group are ultimately submissive to the state. Children, ultimately, are wards of the state. They may be under the provisional care of parents, but parents are answerable to the state, which has the right to step in at any time and take over if it chooses.

If this seems like an extreme view, the extremism is not in my analysis but in Hillary's own views. In 1973, Hillary published an article titled "Children Under the Law" in the *Harvard Educational Review*. In that article, she advocated liberating "child citizens" from their parents and especially from what she termed the "empire of the father."

In Hillary's view, children are not competent to defend their rights. But, she argued, children should have all the rights guaranteed to adults under the Constitution. We cannot simply trust that parents will protect the rights of their children; that there is an identity of interest between parents and children. In the past, Hillary points out, children were considered "chattels of the family," just like slaves.

Hillary argues that the state has every right to second-guess the family about how to raise children. "The pretense that children's issues are somehow above or beyond politics endures and is reinforced by the belief that families are private, non-political units whose interests subsume those of children." Hillary's own view is: Not so. The family is a political institution, and subject to state control.

Hillary's article concludes with the claim that dependency relationships of the kind fostered by the family are bad. "Along with the family," she writes, "past and present examples of such arrangements include marriage, slavery, and the Indians reservation system." Yet Hillary leaves us with the idea that while dependency on others is a bad thing, dependency on the state is a good thing.

In 1977, Hillary wrote an essay titled "Children's Rights: A Legal Perspective" which was published in a book titled *Children's Rights*. Here she made the startling claim that even for minors, "Decisions about motherhood and abortion, schooling, cosmetic surgery, treatment of venereal disease, or employment, and others where the decision or lack of one will significantly affect the child's future should not be made unilaterally by parents." So who should make them? Hillary's answer is: state-run institutions can do so, supposedly taking into account the welfare of the children who are affected by those decisions.[21]

That same year, Hillary was recruited by Marian Wright Edelman to work with the Carnegie Council on Children to prepare a book-length report. This report, *All Our Children*, recommends that "child ombudsmen" be installed in public institutions and some type of insurance be provided for children to hire their own attorneys to represent their interests not only against their parents but also against private corporations. For example, children could file class action lawsuits against companies for future damages their goods and services might cause.

In the words of the report, "The critical point is to expand our concept of children's protective services. Child protection should go far beyond the traditional model of social workers looking for neglected or poorly-fed children to embrace a federal children's consumer and environmental watchdog agency that screens the practices of private industry and government alike for their effects on children. In the long run, nuclear power, disruption of the ozone layer, chemical additives, prescription and over-the-counter drugs, and industrial pollution may well represent more pressing legal problems for whole generations of children than a relatively small number of neglectful or abusive parents."[22]

Notice how little attention Hillary and her collaborators devote to the actual developmental needs of children. Instead, they use children and their welfare—as interpreted by ombudsmen and child advocates— to justify a massive progressive expansion of power.

In a sense, progressives become the child's ventriloquist. Children's entitlements serve as a pretext for progressives to gain control over a whole range of industries. These industries are subject to regulation because their products supposedly endanger children, even though no one—neither child nor adult—is compelled to buy or use any of these products.

Hillary's scholarly output on the subject of children—from her *Harvard Educational Review* article to *All Our Children*—reflects a totalitarian conception of the relationship of children to the state. Her whole literature is quite literally fascist in tone and content. If we translated it into German, put a German author name on it, and dated it to the 1930s, scholars would have difficulty separating it from the Hitler youth propaganda generated by the Nazis. Interestingly Hillary has never repeated these views since their original publication, but neither has she ever repudiated her creepy conclusions.

A HARD SELL

In the 1930s, however, totalitarianism of the type that Hitler and Mussolini represented was a hard sell in the United States. In Italy, Mussolini could get away with it because he presented himself as a necessary alternative to Italian political chaos and anarchy. In Germany there was an autocratic tradition going back to Bismarck that made progressive centralization more palatable in that country.

In America, however, FDR had to build for the first time a coalition that would support a stronger federal government—a greater centralization of power—than had ever been seen before in American history. How to do this?

Mussolini supplied the answer. Mussolini gave fiery speeches promising the Italians "rights." They had a right to this, and a right to that. In a way, Hitler also promised rights—the right to *lebensraum* or greater living space—but his list wasn't as expansive as Mussolini's. Mussolini of course didn't provide these rights; he didn't have the resources, and it's not even clear he intended to. But he won applause for placing himself on the side of these promises. They became *entitlements*—you had a right to them even if the government didn't actually provide them.

FDR alerted his brain trust to check out Mussolini's implementation of fascism. He dispatched members of his staff to Italy to study fascist administrative methods. One of his leading advisers, Rexford Tugwell, found Italian fascism to be "the cleanest, most efficiently operating piece of social machinery I've ever seen. It makes me envious." This was pretty much in line with FDR's own assessment of Mussolini, whose methods FDR found "admirable." FDR was "deeply impressed with what he has accomplished."

The admiration between FDR and Mussolini was mutual. Mussolini reviewed FDR's 1933 book *Looking Forward* for an Italian publication. He loved it. Mussolini had special praise for Roosevelt's National Recovery Administration, which was formed to enforce production and price controls on American industry. Basically Mussolini decided that FDR was a fascist in the same mode as he was. The methods of the New Deal, Mussolini said, "resemble those of fascism." Mussolini concluded of FDR, hey, this guy is one of us!

FDR, of course, never described himself as a fascist. Drawing on Mussolini's ideas, however, FDR sought to develop an American version of the things that he admired most in Italian fascism. The consequence of these reflections was FDR's famous "second Bill of Rights." The basic idea is that people have a right to food, a right to education, a right to a job, a right to a home or place to live, a right to health care, a right to provision for retirement, even what FDR called a right not to be fearful. Americans, being Americans, are entitled to these things.

Now admittedly earlier generations of Americans would have found this concept incomprehensible. What does it mean to have such rights and entitlements? For FDR, it meant licensing the power of the state to seize the wealth and income of others in order to guarantee the various rights to all citizens. In other words, your rights are realized by picking someone else's pocket, a Democratic Party constant to this day.

If we reflect on this, we can see how progressive rights contrast markedly with the rights guaranteed by the American Founders, and listed in the original Bill of Rights. Most of the provisions in the Bill of Rights begin, "Congress shall make no law." Congress shall make no law restricting freedom of speech, or establishing religion, or preventing the free exercise of religion, or outlawing free assembly, and so on. Basically, we secure our rights against the government—by limiting the power of the government.

Progressive rights, by contrast, are rights against our fellow citizens, and they are secured by expanding the power of the federal government. After all the government is the coercive power that robs Peter to pay Paul, and in this way it secures Paul's allegiance and support. Progressive government relies on multiplying the population of beneficiaries. Through this mechanism, Democratic politicians, intellectuals, and media types gain power over the entrepreneurial sector and establish increasing control over the institutions of American wealth and power. This is not what the Founders wanted.

So FDR continued Wilson's repudiation of the founding, although he was much cleverer than Wilson in not doing so openly. Wilson denounced the Founders in speech, while FDR repudiated them in deed. As a practical matter, FDR founded the progressive state. He also established the Democratic Party as the party of progressivism, which it remains to this day.

Johnson's Great Society, although continuous with FDR's New Deal, would take things to a new level. While the New Deal was at least an emergency response to a genuine crisis, the Great Depression, the Great Society was a response to nothing in particular. It was just a progressive power-grab. Similarly, Obama and Hillary's progressivism uses the bogus chants of "inequality" and "social injustice" to implement wealth-confiscation and power-grabbing schemes much more expansive than anything previously attempted.

In listening to Hillary and reading the blueprints of the progressives, we can see where this is going in the future. There is a movement among progressives today to look back to those halcyon FDR days in which the state had virtually dictatorial powers over the lives of citizens, presumed security risks like Japanese Americans could be tossed into confinement centers, income tax rates were over 90 percent, and even wealth was subject to appropriation and confiscation.

What FDR justified as wartime measures, anchored in the real fear that Americans had of the Nazis and a potential Japanese invasion, today's progressives support as peacetime measures that they seek to justify by creating artificial panics. "You never want a serious crisis to go to waste."[23] Adolf Hitler could easily have uttered those words, which were uttered in 2008 by Obama aide Rahm Emanuel. We see that fear, entitlements, and state appropriation of the powers of the private sector—the three defining features of fascism—continue to inspire progressives today.

I have laid out the low, dishonorable roots of modern progressivism and shown how that progressivism incorporated racism to become the ideological foundation of today's Democratic Party. This is the vile, shameful tradition that Obama and Hillary are part of, even as they shamelessly lie about that tradition to escape accountability for what their party has done, and what their movement stands for. Now it is time to dig deeper into the secret history of these two, the one who has done so much damage to this country, the other who aspires to do far, far more.

CHAPTER 7

THE EDUCATION OF A MAFIOSA

WHAT HILLARY LEARNED FROM ALINSKY AND THE MOB

Life is a corrupting process; he who fears corruption fears life.[1]
—Saul Alinsky, *Rules for Radicals*

n the 1980s and 1990s Barack Obama made multiple trips to Chicago—to attend conferences, work summer jobs, take his first job after college, and again after Harvard Law School. This by itself is curious. Obama wasn't from Chicago. He grew up in Hawaii and Indonesia. Obama did, however, learn about Chicago—first from one of his early mentors, Frank Marshall Davis, and then from radical activists at Columbia, where Obama attended undergraduate college.

What Davis and his Columbia buddies told Obama was that Chicago was the training ground of Saul Alinsky, the radical activist par excellence. The more Obama studied Alinsky, the more he grew intrigued. This was a man he could learn from. This was the only man who could teach him what he needed to know. As Obama later put it, "All the strands of my life came together and I really became a man when I moved to Chicago."[2]

What Obama means is that he learned his trade by becoming an Alinskyite. Call it politics or community organizing or (as I prefer) professional thievery, Obama learned it through his apprenticeship with the Alinskyites. Never mind that Alinsky died in 1972; Alinsky's organizations were still around. Surely there were other Alinskyites who could train Obama to become what he aspired to be.

When Obama made his various pilgrimages to Chicago, however, he had no idea that Hillary Clinton had beaten him to Alinsky's door. When he found this out much later, Obama must have felt like the British explorer Robert Scott, who rushed to the South Pole only to find out to his dismay that his Scandinavian rival Roald Amundsen had already gotten there first. Hillary didn't have to hang out with Alinsky hangers-on; she knew Alinsky. In a sense, she discovered Alinsky as much as he discovered her.

Hillary met Alinsky in high school and she realized right away that this man was unique. The Democrats in the 1960s talked a good game, but Alinsky was someone who knew how to deliver for the cause. And Hillary also saw that he knew how to collect, which is to say, to make himself the main beneficiary of his causes. Hillary was magnetically drawn to Alinsky, and he, apparently, to her. Alinsky seems to have seen in Hillary a younger version of himself.

Once a Republican "Goldwater girl," Hillary moved sharply left at her alma mater, Wellesley college, and Alinsky was a catalyst for this transition. As an undergraduate, Hillary invited Alinsky to speak at Wellesley, and decided to write her senior thesis on him. In preparation for it, according to her thesis adviser Alan Schecter, "She read all of Alinsky."[3] Hillary's thesis was titled, "There Is Only the Fight."

Let's take in the significance of this. The current president of the United States, and the aspiring next president of the United States, were both mentored by the same man, Saul Alinsky. Alinsky didn't seek them out; they sought him out. They became his acolytes during a formative period of their lives. If Hillary makes it to the White House, Alinsky's influence, already huge, will have reached mammoth proportions. Surely there is no other mentor in American history that can legitimately claim to have trained two successive presidents.

A POLITICAL GANGSTER

So what is it about Alinsky? What did Obama and Hillary learn from him? This chapter will show that Alinsky was a political gangster, who learned his trade from criminal gangs, notably the Al Capone mob. Obama and Hillary are two con artists who came to Alinsky to learn his con-man techniques. Alinsky taught them the art of the shakedown. Obama studied well under Alinsky, eventually becoming an instructor of Alinskyite techniques. Hillary, however, went beyond Alinsky. As we'll see, she figured out how to take Alinskyism to a new level.

Before we dive into Alinsky, it's worth noting that Alinsky's public press is almost entirely positive. He is portrayed as a champion of social justice. He fought for the working man, he fought for civil rights, and he took on the powerful forces of corporate America and government on behalf of the downtrodden. If he went overboard or got carried away, it was for human dignity and social justice. This is the general progressive story line, and quite a "story" it is, very much in line with the other tales of progressive whitewash that we have encountered in this book.

A case in point is Sanford Horwitt's book *Let Them Call Me Rebel*. This is supposed to be the authoritative biography of Alinsky. It is an unbelievably boring book. Yet Alinsky was not a boring man; oddly enough, the author omits all the juicy details about Alinsky. Now why would a good biographer do that? The short answer is that he's not doing biography. In fact, Alinskyite foundations funded his book. It is not a work of history, but of propaganda.[4]

Fortunately there is a good source from which we can get the real story: Alinsky himself. It may seem that the best place to get Alinsky's account is his two books *Reveille for Radicals* and *Rules for Radicals*. In those books, however, Alinsky gives strategic advice. Part of Alinsky's counsel, however, is for radicals to be deceptive in the Machiavellian sense. Radicals should camouflage who they truly are. Naturally we would expect Alinsky to follow his own advice, and he does. Consequently, he says little of genuine value about himself in these books.

Alinsky did, however, give a series of interviews in which he spoke very candidly and at length about his life. Here I focus on two sets of interviews, the first with *Harper's* magazine, published as a two-part series in June and July 1965. The second was with *Playboy*, appearing in March 1972—the year Alinsky died. From these interviews we discover a totally different Alinsky than appears in Horwitt's biography and other works of progressive hagiography.[5]

Born in 1909, Alinsky grew up on the South Side of Chicago. His parents were Orthodox Jews who had emigrated from Russia. His father was a tailor, ran a deli, and then opened a cleaning shop. "We were poor," he says. "As a kid I remember always living in the back of a store. My idea of luxury was to live in an apartment where I could use the bathroom without one of my parents banging on the door for me to get out because a customer wanted to get in."

The era from 1909 to 1929 was a prosperous one for America, but it was also harsh for those at the bottom who were struggling to make it. Alinsky's father never did, and as a consequence Alinsky seems to have developed contempt for his father. According to Alinsky, the two of them barely spoke; mostly they exchanged the words "hello" and "good-bye."

Alinsky's father, for his part, did not seem to hold young Saul in high esteem. Alinsky recalled that at one point during the Great Depression, when he had moved away from home, "I had exactly four bucks between me and starvation, so in desperation I sent a registered letter to my father, asking him for a little help, because I didn't even have enough for food. I got the receipt back showing he'd gotten the letter, but I never heard from him. He died in 1950 or 1951 and I heard he left an estate of $140,000. He willed most of it to an orchard in Israel and his kids by a previous marriage. To me, he left $50."

Alinsky didn't just despise his father; he also despised the capitalist system that, in his view, draws the life out of you while never delivering on its promise of success and leisure. "As a kid I don't remember being bothered by a social conscience," Alinsky recalled. In fact, what he didn't get from his father he decided to take from others. As a teenager, Alinsky was "shacking up with some old broad of twenty-two" and learning the art of petty thievery on the slum streets of Chicago.

THIEVERY 101

Alinsky enrolled as an undergraduate at the University of Chicago, where, despite receiving a scholarship, he looked for ways to take advantage of the university. With evident relish, Alinsky described his scam for eating full meals in the university cafeteria system while only paying for a cup of coffee. He would go up to the cashier and order coffee; at that time, it cost just a nickel. The cashier would write him a ticket listing the price, and he would take the coffee and keep the ticket.

Then he would go to another university cafeteria—part of the same chain—and order a full meal. "I ate a meal that cost about a buck forty five," Alinsky recalled, "and believe me in those days you could practically buy the fixtures in the joint for that price." The waitress would then give him his check for the meal. In those days, customers didn't pay the waitress; rather, they went up to the cashier and paid. So Alinsky would pocket the bill for his meal, and submit his nickel ticket to the cashier. By switching checks, Alinsky ate full meals and paid just for his cup of coffee. "I paid the five-cent check and then I left."

This is the kind of scam one can see any cunning, impoverished slum kid pulling off. What makes Alinsky original is that he developed a whole system based on this scam. "All around the university I saw kids who were in the same boat I was. So I put up a sign on one of the bulletin boards inviting anyone who was hungry to a meeting. Well, some of them thought it was a gag. But they came. The place was really jumping.

"I explained my system, using a big map of Chicago with all the chain restaurants spotted on it." Pretty soon he had teams of students signed up. "We got the system down to a science," he recalled, "and for six months all of us were eating free."

Unfortunately for Alinsky and his pals, the university changed its payment system and the scam didn't work anymore. Asked whether he had moral qualms about ripping off the university, Alinsky erupted, "Are you kidding? There's a priority of rights, and the right to eat takes precedence over the right to make a profit." Even here, we see in the young thief that familiar progressive sense of entitlement. He feels justified in gaming the system, and takes pride in teaching others how to do it.

This is a point worth pausing over. Alinsky isn't just a thief; he is also a theft educator, somewhat akin to the pickpocket Fagin in *Oliver Twist*. Alinsky's educational program would ultimately guide a whole political movement, progressivism, and inspire two of the most important figures on the American, and world, stage. It is strange to contemplate that modern progressivism may have found its basic modus operandi in a petty rip-off scheme to get meals in college without paying for them.

Alinsky's defense of his actions—his argument about the priority of rights—reveals another important technique that he bequeathed to modern progressives. He parades his crooked scheme behind the moral banner of social justice. In other words, he isn't just a lowlife thief; he is a thief with a conscience.

Alinsky confesses that the concept of a priority of rights wasn't his original idea. He got it from the labor leader John Lewis, who organized union strikes in the Midwest during Alinsky's college days. Lewis was asked about strikers who were breaking the law by trespassing and destroying private property. Lewis retorted, "A man's right to a job transcends the right of private property."

Alinsky noticed this response shut the interviewer up. The reporter was stumped by the social justice rationale. Alinsky recognized right away that in some situations one could get away with illegal and otherwise-indefensible actions if they came wrapped in a noble-sounding justification.

GETTING IN WITH THE GANGS

Alinsky knew, however, that he didn't want to spend his life on petty rip-off schemes. So he changed his academic focus to criminology, not so much, it seems, to reform crime as to understand how to be a more effective thief. He proposed to his professors a unique project: an in-depth study of Chicago's criminal gangs. At first his teachers were skeptical that Alinsky could penetrate those gangs, but ever the schemer, Alinsky was fully up to the task.

He began with the smaller gangs, like the Sholto gang and the 42 Mob, where he was able to befriend hoodlums and convince them to tell him their "life histories." Alinsky asked gang members to write down their recollections about when they first stole or had their first encounter with the police. These detailed personal histories would prove useful not only for getting him academic credit but also for learning how people stole stuff and got away with it.

The gang that Alinsky really wanted to get in with was the Al Capone mob. Alinsky admired those guys. "When Capone showed up at a Northwestern football game on Boy Scout Day," he said, "three thousand Scouts got up and yelled, 'Yea Al.'" I mentioned a similar incident in an earlier chapter to liken the popularity of Al Capone with that of Andrew Jackson.

Most of all, Alinsky admired the Capone mob's political clout. "They owned City Hall," he recalled. "Why, when one of those guys got knocked off, there wasn't any court in Chicago. Most of the judges were at the funeral and some were pallbearers."

Far from viewing the Capone operation with revulsion, Alinsky said, "I came to see the Capone gang as a huge quasi-public utility serving the population of Chicago." From Alinsky's viewpoint, the public wanted illegal booze, gambling, and prostitution and the Capone crew supplied them.

Capone himself took this view, saying on more than one occasion that he was merely offering what people wanted. For this, he groused, he should receive more credit but instead he had become a hunted man. Alinsky sympathized. More subtly, by observing Capone's connections with political figures, he saw that crime and politics were related, so that a mobster could be understood as not so different from a "public servant."

With single-minded determination, Alinsky set out to get in with Capone's mobsters, to learn their techniques. As Alinsky recounted the experience, "My reception was pretty chilly at first—I went over to the old Lexington Hotel, which was the gang's headquarters, and I hung around in the lobby and the restaurant. I'd spot one of the mobsters whose picture I'd seen in the papers and go up to him and say, 'I'm Saul Alinsky, I'm studying criminology, do you mind if I hang around with you?' And he'd look me over and say, 'Get lost punk.' This happened again and again, and I began to feel I'd never get anywhere.

"Then one night I was sitting in the restaurant and at the end table was Big Ed Stash, a professional assassin who was the Capone mob's top executioner. He was drinking with a bunch of his pals and he was saying, 'Hey you guys, did I ever tell you about the time I picked up that redhead in Detroit?' and he was cut off by a chorus of moans. 'My God,' one guy said, 'do we have to hear that one again?'

"I saw Big Ed's face fall—mobsters are very sensitive, you know, very thin-skinned. And I reached over and plucked his sleeve. 'Mr. Stash,' I said, 'I'd love to hear that story.' His face lit up. 'You would, kid?' He slapped me on the shoulder. 'Here, pull up a chair. Now, this broad, see…' And that's how it started.

"We became buddies. He introduced me to Frank Nitti, known as the Enforcer, Capone's number two man, and actually in *de facto* control of the mob because of Al's income-tax rap. Nitti took me under his wing. I called him the Professor and I became his student.

"Nitti's boys took me everywhere, showed me all the mob's operations, from gin mills and whorehouses and bookie joints to the legitimate businesses they were beginning to take over. Within a few months, I got to know the workings of the Capone mob inside out."

PAYING TOO MUCH FOR MURDER

Alinsky had no problem with the mob murdering people; in fact, he argued with mobsters about the most cost-effective way to get the job done. "Once, when I was looking over their records," Alinsky recalled, "I noticed an item listing a $7500 payment for an out-of-town killer."

Alinsky approached Frank Nitti. "I called Nitti over and I said, 'Look, Mr. Nitti, I don't understand this. You've got at least 20 killers on your payroll. Why waste that much money to bring somebody in from St. Louis?'

"Frank said patiently, 'Look kid, sometimes our guys might know the guy they're hitting, they may have been to his house for dinner, taken his kids to the ball game, been the best man at his wedding, gotten drunk together.

'But you call in a guy from out of town, all you've got to do is tell him, Look, there's this guy in a dark coat on Sate and Randolph; our boy in the car will point him out; just go up and give him three in the belly and fade into the crowd.

'So there's a job and he's a professional, he does it. But if one of our boys goes up, the guys turns to face him and it's a friend, right away he knows that when he pulls that trigger there's gonna be a widow, kids without a father, funerals, weeping—Christ, it'd be murder.'"

Alinsky recalls that when he stuck to his guns about using a local guy and saving money, even a hardened criminal like Nitti was shocked and regarded Alinsky as "a bit callous." We might expect the student, Alinsky, to be shocked by the callousness of the high-level mobster, but in fact it is the high-level mobster who is shocked by the callousness of Alinsky.

Alinsky admired how the Capone gang could shake down various merchants and commercial establishments and essentially extort from them or rob them at will. He summed up the effectiveness of the Capone operation. "They had Chicago tied up tight as a drum. Forget all that Eliot Ness shit; the only real opposition to the mob came from other gangsters, like Bugs Moran or Roger Touhy."

Alinsky wasn't a mob operative himself, so he didn't get to enjoy the full rewards of being a member. "I was a nonparticipating observer in their professional activities," he says, "although I joined their social life of food, drink and women. Boy, I sure participated in that side of things. It was heaven." Heaven! Here Alinsky gets to witness, and partly participate, in the fruits of crime. He's "in," and he's hooked.

I'm reminded here of the opening scene in the movie *Goodfellas* where young Henry Hill watches the mobsters at their revelries. How cool they seem, how brazen in their disregard for the law. Right away he decides that that's the life he wants. It's a better life, Hill says, than even being president of the United States.

Resolving to become a professional shakedown artist himself, Alinsky became a student of mob extortion. One could say that he sets his sights on becoming a kind of Don Fanucci. Fanucci, you'll recall, is the Black Hand in the movie *The Godfather*. He forces immigrant businessmen to pay him protection money but it's not so much protection against other gangsters—it's protection from Fanucci himself.

Fanucci is not a reckless shakedown man. He realizes that the Italian immigrants in New York at the turn of the century are a violent lot. He has to be careful with them, and this requires that he not take too much. He only wants, he emphasizes, a small portion of the take, enough to "wet his beak."

We meet Fanucci in the novel because he intends to collect from Vito Corleone and his two friends Tessio and Clemenza after the three of them have pulled off some petty robberies. Fanucci approaches Corleone almost gently. "Ah young fellow," he says, "People tell me you're rich. But don't you think you've treated me a little shabbily? After all, this is my neighborhood and you should let me wet my beak."

Corleone does not answer. Then Fanucci smiles and unbuttons his jacket to show the gun he has tucked away in the waistband of his trousers. Then he moderates his demands. "Give me five hundred dollars and I'll forget the insult."[6] Fanucci was merely doing what worked for him. Most people paid his ransom; they figured it was better than tangling with Fanucci.

THE LITTLE LIGHT BULB

There was only one problem with Alinsky's career goal to emulate criminals like Capone and Fanucci in their shakedown schemes: shakedown men sometimes get knocked off. In *The Godfather*, Fanucci tries to shake down Vito Corleone and his two accomplices and gets murdered. Organized crime is high risk, high reward.

Alinsky wanted to figure out how to keep the reward but reduce the risk. He intended to emulate the mob's shakedown operations without getting killed. He said to himself, "Here I am, a smart son of a bitch, I graduated cum laude and all that shit." He knew he could figure a way. "And then," he says, "it came to me, that little light bulb lit over my head."

Basically, Alinsky realized that the answer was: politics. In politics, you can extract money from people without getting knocked off. In politics, there is such a thing as *legal* theft. What better way to wet your beak? So Alinsky moved on to politics, yet he patterned his political operations on what he had learned from the Capone gang. In a revealing quotation, Alinsky told *Playboy*, "I learned a hell of a lot about the uses and abuses of power from the mob, lessons that stood me in good stead later on, when I was organizing."

For Alinsky, politics is the art of intimidation from the outside. This is basically what a community organizer does. As Alinsky explains, a community organizer must first identify the target, which may be a local business, a national retail chain, a public school system, even the mayor's office. The target must have resources, or money, or jobs to hand out. Extracting those benefits without working for them now becomes the organizer's mission.

Power, Alinsky writes, never gives in without a fight. The only way to get stuff from the people who have it is to make it easier for them to give it to you than to fight you. "Very often the mere threat," Alinsky says, "is enough to bring the enemy to its knees." Getting the target to the point of submission—forcing it to pay up—is the supreme challenge of a political organizer.

Before attempting the extortion, the organizer must recruit allies. In Alinsky's words, "To f*ck your enemies, you've first got to seduce your allies." These allies may be unions, disgruntled workers, 1960s leftists, activist clergy, homeless bums, inner-city gang members, professional malcontents, anyone you can get. Alinsky's strategy was to convince these people that their wants and demands—more money, more power—did not represent mere selfish claims but rather moral entitlements. They had a *right* to this stuff.

Moreover, they should not consider themselves to be asking for gifts or charity. Rather, as Alinsky candidly put it, "They only get these things in the act of taking them through their own efforts." In a sense, Alinsky empowered people to become his co-conspirators in theft while feeling very good about themselves in doing so.

Sometimes Alinsky was able to recruit effective allies in unlikely places. Although a nonpracticing Jew, Alinsky struck up a working alliance with powerful people in the Catholic Church. While the church in that city was politically liberal, Alinsky knew that many priests wanted to stay away from the kind of hardball extortionist politics that he had in mind. He also decided that he could not bring them into his fold with an appeal to Christian charity.

Alinsky explains, "Suppose I walked into the office of the average leader of any denomination and said, 'Look, I'm asking you to live up to your Christian principles, to make Jesus' words about brotherhood and social justice realities.' What do you think would happen? He'd shake my hand warmly and said, 'God bless you, my son,' and after I was gone he'd tell his secretary, 'If that crackpot comes around again, tell him I'm out.'

"So in order to involve the Catholic priests, I didn't give them any stuff about Christian ethics, I just appealed to their self-interest." Basically Alinsky told them that if they backed him he would make sure that more money flowed in their direction through government grants for the church and donations for its charitable activities.

"Now I'm talking their language," Alinsky crowed, "and we can sit down and hammer out a deal. That's what happened in Back of the Yards, and within a few months the overwhelming majority of the parish priests were backing us, and we were holding our organizational meetings in their churches."

A RESENTMENT ORGANIZER

While the church helped Alinsky in Chicago, he realized that on the national scale the biggest challenge was to recruit and radicalize members of the white middle class. This, he frequently said, was the largest and most powerful group in the country. Consequently it could apply strong political pressure to extract benefits both from government and from corporations. At the time Richard Nixon was courting the middle class, and many people considered that group to be politically conservative. But Alinsky felt confident that he could make headway with it.

Of the white middle class, he said, "Right now they're frozen, festering in apathy, living what Thoreau called lives of quiet desperation. They've worked all their lives to get their own little house in the suburbs, their color TV, their two cars and now the good life seems to have turned to ashes in their mouths. Their personal lives are generally unfulfilling, their jobs unsatisfying, they've succumbed to tranquilizers and pep pills, they drown their anxieties in alcohol, they feel trapped in long-term endurance marriages, or escape into guilt-ridden divorces.

"They're losing their kids and they're losing their dreams. They're alienated, depersonalized, without any feeling of participation in the political process, and they feel rejected and hopeless. Their society appears to be crumbling, and they see themselves as no more than small failures within the larger failure. All their old values seem to have deserted them, leaving them rudderless in a sea of social chaos. Believe me, this is good organizational material."

The way to win recruits from this group, Alinsky writes, is not by solving these people's problems but by aggravating them. In Alinsky's words, "The despair is there; now it's up to us to go in and rub raw the sores of discontent." This is done by directing people's frustration not against government but against business. "We'll show the middle class their real enemies: the corporate power elite that runs and ruins this country."

What has this corporate power elite done that is so reprehensible? For Alinsky, this is the wrong question. The real question was a very simple one: Who has the money?

Alinsky realized he could recruit allies and direct their hatred to the corporations by appealing to motives such as envy, resentment, and hatred, but all packaged in the rhetoric of equality and justice. He had no illusion that any of this was related to actual justice.

For Alinsky, justice is a province of morality, and morality is a scam. Morality is the cloak of power. Activists appeal to the language of morality but recognize that it is a mere disguise. As Alinsky puts it, "Ethical standards must be elastic to stretch with the times.... In action, one does not always enjoy the luxury of a decision that is consistent with one's individual conscience.... You do what you can with what you have, and then clothe it with moral garments."[7]

In his book *Reveille for Radicals*, Alinsky takes up the fashionable liberal cause of "reconciliation." He proclaims the very idea totally unrealistic, "an illusion of the world as we would like it to be." In the real world, Alinsky says, "Reconciliation means that one side has the power and the other side gets reconciled to it."[8] Alinsky was determined to have the power on his side, so that his opponents would become reconciled to being shaken down by him.

Alinsky's contempt for traditional morality can also be seen in the way he admiringly cites Lenin. "Lenin was a pragmatist," he writes in *Rules for Radicals*. "When he returned from exile, he said that the Bolsheviks stood for getting power through the ballot but would reconsider after they got the guns."[9] What Alinsky meant by this is that activists should invoke principles like free speech and equality under the law in order to protect themselves, but once they come to power they should ignore these principles and not extend them to their opponents. Modern progressives seem to have taken this lesson to heart.

RIPPING OFF THE GOVERNMENT

While Alinsky attempted to direct middle-class frustration against private corporations, he was not above targeting the government for his shakedown schemes. He gleefully described the way he forced Chicago mayor Richard Daley to give in to some of his extortionist demands. Daley was a very powerful man who regarded Chicago as his personal domain. In this, Alinsky found Daley's Achilles' heel.

Daley was especially proud of the efficiency of Chicago's O'Hare airport. Now in those days, before 9/11, anyone could go through security and enter the main airport. Alinsky's scheme involved deploying several hundred activists to completely immobilize all the airport's restroom facilities. He knew that passengers usually wait to get off the plane before heading for the bathroom.

Alinsky's idea was to have activists take up every stall, armed with, as he put it, "box lunches and reading material to help pass the time." Male activists would be positioned at every urinal, with other activists waiting to replace them as they finished their business and moved to another Men's Restroom. "What were desperate passengers going to do?" Alinsky said. "Is some poor sap at the end of the line going to say, 'Hey pal, you're taking too long to piss?'"

Alinsky was confident that his "shit-in," as he called it, would completely paralyze the airport. "O'Hare would become a shambles." Alinsky didn't even have to carry out the scheme: he leaked it to the press, and Daley caved. The city agreed to increase its hiring and to use Alinsky's network to provide the new recruits.

On another occasion, Alinsky got Daley to give in to another shakedown—this one involving government contracts and jobs funneled throughout Alinskyite organizations—and once again, he didn't actually need to carry it out. "We threatened to unload a thousand live rats on the steps of city hall. Daley got the message, and we got what we wanted."

Alinsky didn't mind that these tactics seemed absurdist or puerile, as long as they worked. His biographer Sanford Horwitt describes an occasion, in the spring of 1972, when Alinsky organized a student protest at Tulane University's annual lecture week. A group of anti–Vietnam War protesters wanted to disrupt a scheduled speech by George H. W. Bush, then U.S. representative to the United Nations, and an advocate for President Nixon's Vietnam policies.

While the students planned to picket the speech and shout anti-war slogans, Alinsky told them that their approach was wrong because it might get them punished or expelled. Besides, it lacked creativity and imagination. Alinsky advised the students to go hear the speech dressed up as members of the Ku Klux Klan—complete with robes and hoods—and whenever Bush said anything in defense of the Vietnam War, they should cheer and holler and wave signs and banners saying: "The KKK Supports Bush."

This is what the students did, and it proved very successful, getting lots of media attention with no adverse repercussions for the protesters.[10]

We see here how Alinsky relies on the progressive canard of the Big Switch. He identifies—and counts on the media to identify—the Klan with Bush's Republican policies, even though, as we have seen, the actual Klan was entirely a vehicle of the Democratic Party.

On another occasion, Alinsky targeted government welfare agencies that in his view were trying to administer programs themselves rather than funnel the money through Alinskyite organizations. Alinsky framed this as an issue of the government deciding for itself what poor people need, rather than trusting the poor to run their own lives. In reality of course, Alinsky wanted himself—rather than government bureaucrats—to allocate the money.

In order to pressure the government to change its approach, however, Alinsky urged black activists to dress in African tribal costumes and greet government officials flying into Chicago from Washington, D.C. This action, he said, would dramatize the "colonial mentality" of the anti-poverty establishment. I learned about this particular Alinsky caper from Hillary Clinton's thesis.[11]

SHAKING DOWN EASTMAN KODAK

Alinsky met with tactical success, not only in tackling government agencies and government representatives, but also in shaking down the private sector. In Rochester, New York—at that time a company town, home of Eastman Kodak—Alinsky organized a campaign called FIGHT and attempted some stunts at the corporate headquarters, but they didn't work. Ostensibly Alinsky was asking that Kodak hire more blacks, but Kodak's president Louis Eilers detected a larger agenda. "It is more and more clear," he said, "that all the talk about unemployment is only an issue or device being used to screen what FIGHT is really doing—and that is making a drive for power in the community."[12]

Eiler was on to Alinsky. But Alinsky was not done with Eastman Kodak. He realized that the city and Eastman Kodak took great pride in the Rochester Philharmonic Orchestra, which the company helped to fund and on whose board top officials of the company sat. Alinsky organized a group of one hundred blacks to attend concert performances. Before the performances, he planned a "pre-show banquet consisting of nothing but huge portions of baked beans."

The plan was basically to have an organized "fart-in." Alinsky found that his activists were excited to participate. "What oppressed person doesn't want, literally or figuratively, to shit on his oppressors?"

But this wasn't just for the psychological benefit of the participants; it was also to force the establishment to back down. Alinsky explains, "First of all, the fart-in would be completely outside the city fathers' experience. Never in their wildest dreams could they envision a flatulent blitzkrieg on their sacred symphony orchestra. It would throw them into complete disarray. Second, the action would make a mockery of the law, because although you could be arrested for throwing a stink bomb, there's no law on the books against natural bodily functions. Can you imagine a guy being tried in court on charges of first-degree farting? The cops would be paralyzed."

With tactics like these, Alinsky brought Eastman Kodak to the negotiating table, and he got most of his shakedown demands met. These demands included the hiring of Alinsky cronies and also the steering of city contracts through Alinsky's activist network.

On another occasion, Alinsky was working in his home base of Chicago to force Chicago's department stores to give jobs to black activists who were Alinsky's cronies. On this issue of course Alinsky was competing—or working in tandem, however we choose to view it—with Chicago's number one racial shakedown man, Jesse Jackson.

Jackson mastered a simple strategy of converting race into a protection racket. He would offer to "protect" Chicago businesses from accusations of racism—accusations that the businesses knew were actually fomented by Jackson himself. The businesses would then pay Jackson to make the trouble go away, and also to chase away other potential troublemakers.

In return for his efforts, Jackson would typically receive hundreds of thousands in annual donations from the company, plus jobs and minority contracts that would go through his network, and finally other goodies such as free flights on the corporate airplane, supposedly for his "charitable work."

Later Jackson would go national with this blackmail approach. In New York, for example, Jackson opened an office on Wall Street where he extracted millions of dollars in money and patronage from several leading investment houses including Goldman Sachs, Citigroup, Credit Suisse, First Boston, Morgan Stanley, Paine Webber, and Prudential Securities.

On the national stage, another race hustler, Al Sharpton, joined Jackson. For two decades these shakedown men in clerical garb successfully prosecuted their hustles. Jackson was the leader at first, but eventually Sharpton proved more successful than Jackson. While Jackson's star has faded, Sharpton became President Obama's chief advisor on race issues.

SEEMS WE'RE IN AFRICA

While Jackson used the blackmail threat of alleging racism or backing race discrimination suits to extract money from corporations, Alinsky had his own distinctive strategy. "One of the largest stores in the city and in the country," Alinsky recounts, "refused to alter its hiring practices and wouldn't even meet with us."

So Alinsky figured out how to teach them a lesson. He lined up several hundred blacks from the inner city to swamp the store. "Every Saturday, the biggest shopping day of the week we decided to charter buses and bring approximately 3,000 blacks from Woodlawn to this downtown store. Now you put 3,000 blacks on the floor of a store, even a store this big, and the color of the store suddenly changes. Any white coming through the revolving doors will suddenly think he's in Africa. So they'd lose a lot of their white trade right then and there.

"But that is only the beginning. At every counter you'd have groups of blacks closely scrutinizing the merchandise and asking the salesgirl interminable questions. And needless to say, none of our people would buy a single item of merchandise. You'd have a situation where one group would tie up the shirt counter and move on to the underwear counter, while the group previously occupying the underwear counter would take over the shirt department.

"This procedure would be followed until one hour before closing time, when our people would begin buying everything in sight to be delivered COD. This would tie up delivery service for a minimum of two days, with additional heavy costs and administrative problems, since all the merchandise would be refused upon delivery."

Once Alinsky had his plan, he said, "We leaked it to one of the stool pigeons every radical organization needs and the result was immediate. The day after we paid the deposit for the chartered buses, the department store management called us and gave in to all our demands. We'd won completely."

This was Alinsky transcending Don Fanucci and acting in true Godfather style. In the vocabulary of Don Corleone himself, Alinsky had made them an offer they couldn't refuse! And when other retail establishments learned of his techniques, they surrendered in advance because they didn't want to risk the kind of mayhem that they knew Alinsky could cause.

"We didn't win in Woodlawn," Alinsky said, "because the establishment suddenly experienced a moral revelation. We won because we backed them into a corner and kept them there until they decided it would be less expensive and less dangerous to surrender to our demands than to continue the fight."

For Alinsky, this was not a matter of coercion. Rather, it was "popular pressure in the democratic tradition. People don't get opportunity or freedom or equality or dignity as an act of charity; they have to fight for it, force it out of the establishment. Reconciliation means just one thing: when one side gets enough power, then the other side gets reconciled to it. That's where you need organization—first to compel concessions and then to make sure the other side delivers. No issue can be negotiated unless you first have the clout to compel negotiation."

One can see here that for Alinsky, democratic politics is basically a mechanism of legal extortion, justified by appeals to justice and equality.

A HANDSOME PROFIT

Alinsky profited handsomely from his rackets. Even Hillary Clinton notes in her thesis that while Alinsky spoke endlessly about poverty and disadvantage, he himself lived very comfortably, far removed from the people on whose behalf he allegedly fought.[13] It was part of Alinsky's shtick and they both knew it.

Toward the end of his life, Alinsky moved to Carmel, California. By this time Alinsky was a millionaire. He enjoyed dining in Carmel's exclusive restaurants, and taking walks on the white-sand beach. It was in ritzy Carmel that Alinsky died of a heart attack in 1972.

His biographer Sanford Horwitt portrays this as a paradox. "This is not the way Saul would have preferred it, not the ending he would have written, not such a prosaic death. And in Carmel of all places! That post-card-perfect oasis where not a speck of the world's troubles was to be found on the soft, white beaches caressed each day by gentle Pacific waters."[14]

Actually, I agree that if Alinsky had his way he would have con-cocted some fantastic report about how he was gunned down by his dangerous enemies, while in pursuit of social justice! But in reality Alin-sky would have known that it was all a big lie. In reality there was noth-ing peculiar about Alinsky dropping dead in affluent Carmel. That's the whole point of being a thief, to get rich.

Would Don Corleone have been in the least bit embarrassed to live in a mansion by the sea? Horwitt may have his own blinders on, but Alinsky had no illusions that at his core he was not a social justice guy; he was a guy who used social justice as part of his business plan. Like mafia dons in the movies and in real life, Alinsky understood that crime is a business in which the godfather's goal is to get rich.

Personally, I wish Alinsky ended up like Henry Hill. At the end of *Goodfellas*, Hill has lost the high life, and he is in the witness protection program. "Today everything is different," he says. "I have to wait around like everyone else." Hill, in other words, is forced to become a normal person again. Alinsky, however, lived like a racketeer and also died like one. He experienced normal life before he hooked up with the mob; it would have been good for his soul to experience it again before he died.

Still, Alinsky's own take was comparatively small. The reason is that throughout his life, Alinsky remained, as he put it, an "outside agitator." He firmly believed that activists should not become part of the government. Hillary Clinton felt differently. Alinsky offered Hillary a job after college, but she turned him down to go to Yale Law School.

Recalling the incident later in her book *Living History*, Hillary wrote, "We had a fundamental disagreement. He believed you could change the system only from the outside," Hillary said. "I didn't. My decision was an expression of my belief that the system could be changed from within."[15]

Hillary's insight was summarized by writer Michael Tomasky: Why remain on the outside when it may be possible to get inside the government? Why fight the power when you can be the power?[16] Outside agitators have limited access and limited resources. But the agencies of government possess enormous coercive authority, including, ultimately, virtually unlimited military firepower.

Control of the government includes control of the Justice Department; you get to decide who gets prosecuted and who doesn't. It includes control of the NSA, where you have access to all kinds of interesting information. Finally, what better instrument of control than the IRS with its terrifying power to audit, confiscate, and prosecute virtually any citizen in the United States? Hillary saw, as Alinsky never did, that government is the best instrument of control, intimidation, and large-scale theft that any community activist could ever wish for.

Alinsky died long before he could see his students ascend to the high corridors of power. Both Hillary and Obama have used the power of the government to shake down the taxpayer and punish their critics, me included; as Alinsky's students, they have one-upped their master. Even so, had Alinsky lived he could take justified pride in being their guiding star, their acknowledged godfather. He was the one who taught progressivism its new and improved contemporary racket.

CHAPTER 8

THE ENABLER

TALES FROM THE CLINTON PLANTATION

Every survivor of sexual assault deserves to be heard,
believed and supported.[1]
—Hillary Clinton, November 23, 2015

This chapter is about the sex life of the Clintons. Many progressives and Democrats regard this as a tedious and unnecessary topic. What's to discuss? Sure, Bill Clinton is a lifelong philanderer, an American Don Juan. Poor Hillary, they suggest, is the victim of these escapades. Even so, she loves Bill and has come to accept—or at least endure—his multiple infidelities. She has accepted the "stand by your man" role. But so what? It's all in the family! The rest of us should butt out. It's their business, not ours.

According to the progressive Democratic narrative, Hillary is running because she wants to be the first woman president. She will symbolize—and dedicate herself to—the cause of women's rights. The Hillary progressives want us to envision is the Hillary who went to the United Nations Conference on Women in Beijing in 1995 and gave a stirring speech on women's rights. That, progressives say, is her actual record; what does any of this personal stuff have to do with Hillary's qualifications to be president?

Hillary herself supported this narrative in an interesting 1979 interview, uncovered by Buzzfeed, in which she addressed the topic of her marriage to Bill. "We have, for me, an excellent marriage. I'm not sure that it would suit other people...but I'm not sure that any marriage doesn't have their own particular kinds of strains, and each couple has to work out an accommodation for whatever reasons there may be. So we've worked out ours and we're very happy and I just hope that other people can work out their strains as well as we have."[2]

So there you have it. The Clintons are just another normal couple, working out "strains." But as anyone with a brain has probably figured out already, these are all clever misstatements of the issue. In fact, they are part of the progressive Democratic cover-up for Hillary. Don't be surprised to see Hillary on the same page; Hillary has always been the original author of the script for that cover-up.

This chapter is not about what the Clintons do in bed, but about what Bill does to other women and how Hillary enables Bill's predatory and abusive behavior, while her feminist and media accomplices cheer her on. The real story is one of horrible abuses of power and even more horrible cover-ups: Hillary's cover-up for Bill, and the progressive cover-up for Hillary's role in covering up for Bill.

Ultimately this is not a chapter about sex, but rather the long Democratic tradition of using power to rape, abuse, and intimidate women and then—if the crimes are exposed—to blame the victims and destroy their lives and reputations. For a party that claims to be a party of justice and women's rights, this pattern of abuse—now carried on jointly and collaboratively by the Clintons—is more than a cruel irony.

BERNIE'S RAPE FANTASIES

Consider, for example, the rape fantasies of Bernie Sanders. These have been grossly under-reported in the media, although they were initially revealed in the leftist magazine *Mother Jones*. The magazine found a 1972 essay that Sanders published in a Vermont newspaper.

Titled, "Man and Woman," the essay begins with Sanders discoursing on his male take on the subject of rape. "A man goes home and masturbates his typical fantasy. A woman on her knees, a woman tied up, a woman abused." Then Sanders turns to the female perspective on the same subject. "A woman enjoys intercourse with her man—as she fantasizes being raped by 3 men simultaneously."

Sanders then raises a broader issue, "Do you know why the newspapers with articles like 'Girl 12 raped by 14 men' sell so well? To what in us are they appealing?" Sanders concludes that "women adapt themselves to fill the needs of men, and men adapt themselves to fill the needs of women."

Imagine the furor if a Republican presidential candidate had published anything like this! The underlying message conveyed by Sanders's essay seems to be that Democrats are expected to be perverts. As with Clinton, we are not talking about fantasies involving *sex* but rather about fantasies involving *rape*.

Now in some puerile sense Sanders in this article is taking a stance against male and female sex roles. But rather than discuss those roles, he makes his point through the medium of rape fantasies. While Sanders attributes the fantasy to a prototypical man and woman, it seems obvious that he is writing about his own fantasies—what he thinks about women, and what he thinks women think about men.

Rape isn't just about sex; it is also about control and dominance. Sanders's rape fantasies involve far more than having women at his imaginative disposal. They also involve controlling and subjugating those women. Symbolically, this is represented in the idea of tying them up, getting them down on their knees, and of course by the coercion implied in the rape itself. For Sanders, as for Bill Clinton, there is a certain progressive pleasure in having the power to dominate other people.

In an obvious attempt to protect Sanders, *Mother Jones* ran a cutline below his essay, saying nothing about the subject of rape fantasies and simply noting, "This 1972 Sanders essay, published in an alternative newspaper, reflected his affinity for Sigmund Freud."[3] In the same vein, mainstream progressive publications have given cursory notice to Sanders's rape imaginings or simply ignored them altogether.

The Sanders campaign dismissed the essay as a "dumb attempt at dark satire" that "in no way reflects his views or record on women." Yet there was nothing satirical about Sanders's essay. And undoubtedly the article did reflect, at the very least, Sanders's view of women at the time that he wrote it.

The question Sanders evades is not whether he supports or advocates rape—he obviously doesn't—but whether the underlying mindset of control and subjugation that produced his article is the same mindset that he has today.

Vice President Joe Biden, we learn, has a habit of swimming nude in his pool. By itself there is nothing wrong with this, except that Biden apparently has female Secret Service agents assigned to him. They have complained about feeling uncomfortable. Biden doesn't care. What his wife thinks about his practice has never been reported.[4]

Biden may have gotten the idea for nude bathing from Lyndon Johnson, who was known to sit nude by the White House pool and dictate letters to his female secretaries. Johnson would also have women brought into the White House and have sex with them while his wife slept in the next room. He also did this on Air Force One, locking himself and his paramours in his stateroom, while Lady Bird was on board.

One of Johnson's secret service agents recalls that Johnson would show his penis to reporters, even female reporters. His motive, the agent reports, was that "he was proud of his organ." Historian Robert Dallek writes about LBJ "urinating in the sink," "inviting people into his bathroom," and even boasting that he had had more women than JFK.[5]

John F. Kennedy—from whom LBJ inherited the presidency—was, according to the various biographies about him, a compulsive womanizer. Kennedy's female conquests included prominent socialites, airline stewardesses, secretaries, and strippers. What we glean from these accounts is that JFK didn't have "relationships." He had no interest in the women themselves; rather, his goal was quantity, not quality.

These affairs continued while JKF was president. JFK reportedly had sex in the White House with Marilyn Monroe and also with Judith Campbell Exner, a socialite known for her connections with mobster Sam Giancana. JFK's wife Jackie reportedly knew about her husband's affairs but was powerless to do anything about them.

Reporters covering the White House, who liked JFK and were sympathetic to his politics, knew about his promiscuity but refused to write about it. I find it telling that there was so much recent hoopla about Trump's references to his manhood while JFK and Johnson's far more vulgar behavior a generation ago inspired no media coverage at all.

A DEMOCRATIC TRADITION

The manipulation, exploitation, and abuse of women is a long Democratic tradition, now camouflaged and enhanced by the women's rights banner behind which progressive Democrats triumphantly march. Feminism not only condones—but provides ideological cover—for Democratic exploitation of women.

The Clintons are the best example of this. The sex abuse jointly carried out by the Clintons has been accepted and even endorsed by contemporary feminists and feminist organizations. We should try and understand why purported champions of women's rights would embrace a serial sex abuser and a woman who routinely blames her husband's female victims.

These are not mere ironies or even double standards. The behavior of the Clintons would be ironic if Democrats had historically behaved differently. We could reasonably speak of double standards if the Democrats actually had a different set of standards. The Democrats, however, have long licensed the systematic abuse of women.

Male predation is not something that stands by itself; it is an institution of enslavement that has historically served the Democratic Party. Women have historically been part of the reward of Democratic institutions of exploitation and subjugation. By using and abusing women,

Democrats showed—and enjoyed—their power and authority. Let us see how this form of exploitation paid off for powerful men.

We have seen in earlier chapters how the Democratic Party was the party of slavery and the party of white supremacy. Both slavery and white supremacy established a hierarchy in which women of color were vulnerable, indeed virtually defenseless, against the depredations of the men who had power over them.

Under slavery and segregation, powerful white men took advantage of powerless black women, stealing from them not only their labor but also their bodies, their dignity. In many cases, the wives of those men had to endure these indignities. They too lacked power, in that there was little they could do to stop their marauding husbands.

In this chapter, we will see that Bill Clinton is in this marauding tradition. He is a horny Democrat who seems to regard his libido as his guiding star, and women as his target. He has used his political positions—as attorney general, as governor, and as president—to hit on, grope, fondle, coerce, and even allegedly rape women who fell within the orbit of his power. He is the Bill Cosby of the Democratic Party.

When his abuses are exposed, he lies repeatedly, effortlessly, even pathologically, seemingly confident that within the culture of the Democratic Party he will never be held to account. While serial lying seems to be a trademark of both Clintons, Bill's defenders say his lies are of minimal significance because they are "only about sex."

Once again the assumption seems to be that Bill is merely engaging in consensual romantic interludes, whereas the reality is that Bill—if his accusers can be believed—is a sex offender. Are criminal sex offenders acceptable to Democrats when their lies revolve around their sex crimes?

Historically, the answer is yes. Bill has many predecessors from plantation owners to white supremacists who did exactly as he did. Then, as now, their fellow Democrats laughed off their offenses. The Democratic Party protected them then, as it protects Bill Clinton today. Since Bill Cosby got no similar protection when his comparable offenses were exposed, we may reasonably conclude that Clinton, like his historical predecessors, is a beneficiary of white privilege.

IN A CLASS OF HER OWN

If Clinton is a familiar type, however—if he is one of a depressingly common genus among Democrats—the same cannot be said of his wife. She is a bizarre specimen. Traditionally white women suffered while their Democratic husbands had their way with vulnerable black women.

Hillary has from time to time struck the longsuffering pose, allowing her supporters to insist that she is in the tradition of female victims. In her book *Living History*, Hillary pretends to be shocked, shocked when Bill told her about his affair with Monica Lewinsky. "I could hardly breathe. Gulping for air, I started crying and yelling at him. I couldn't believe he would do anything to endanger our marriage and family."[6]

Here's how she wants us to react. Poor Hillary! Let's all feel sorry for her!

But in reality Hillary had long known of her husband's women. She had been briefed on the subject by political aides when Bill was governor of Arkansas. She knew about Gennifer Flowers from the 1992 campaign. Months before the Lewinsky affair was exposed, Hillary had been preparing Bill for his grand jury testimony in the Paula Jones case. So Hillary's reaction to the Lewinsky revelation is, quite literally, unbelievable.

Far from being a victim, Hillary is the enabler of her husband's depredations. She covers up for Bill while at the same time going after the women he abuses. She blames the victims while posing as a champion of women's rights. Part of what makes Hillary's marital relationship with Bill so incomprehensible is that never before in American history have we seen this phenomenon: the wife as sexual facilitator and prosecutor. Hillary seems to be in a class of her own.

Keeping Bill and Hillary in mind, let's examine the impact on husbands and wives when masters had their way with slave women on the plantation. Earlier I mentioned Thomas Jefferson's relationship with the slave woman Sally Hemings. Hemings herself was the daughter of a slave woman named Elizabeth and Jefferson's father-in-law John Wayles. Wayles had several other children with Elizabeth.

Wayles was pretty open about his dalliances. Consequently, the Hemingses of Monticello were treated differently than his other slaves.

No member of the Hemings clan was asked to work in the field. Instead, the females worked as house servants, and the males worked as valets, cooks, and skilled craftsmen. This seems to have been Wayles's "payment" for his gratification. His family seems to have known about this.

Uncomfortably, however, this family history suggests that Sally Hemings was actually related to Martha Jefferson. Jefferson bore multiple children with a slave woman who was actually half-sister to his wife. Martha Jefferson may have known about her father siring children with the slaves but there is no evidence that she knew about her husband's relationship with Sally.[7] In this respect, Martha Jefferson was definitely not an enabler.

The southern diarist Mary Boykin Chesnut, wife of South Carolina Senator James Chesnut, was also familiar with what went on at the plantation. Her husband was not one of the guilty parties, but apparently his father James Chesnut Sr. was. "The Colonel," as he was called, apparently sired several light-skinned mulattoes and while everyone else pretended not to notice, his daughter-in-law certainly did.

Chesnut writes that this aspect of plantation life, more than anything else, made her hate slavery. "You say there are no more fallen women on a plantation than in London in proportion to numbers. But what do you say to this—to a magnate who runs a hideous black harem, with its consequences, under the same roof with his lovely white wife and his beautiful and accomplished daughters?

"He holds his head high and poses as a model of all human virtues to these poor women whom God and the laws have given him. From the heights of awful majesty he scolds and thunders at them as if he never did wrong in his life. Fancy such a man finding his daughter reading Don Juan. 'You with that immoral book' he would say, and then he would order her out of his sight.

"The wife and daughters in their purity and innocence are supposed never to dream of what is as plain before their eyes as the sunlight, and they play their parts of unsuspecting angels to the letter. They profess to adore the father as the model of all saintly goodness."

In an earlier chapter I quoted Democratic Senator James Hammond of South Carolina rhapsodizing the virtues of slavery. But Hammond seems to have left out some of slavery's benefits, at least as far as he was concerned. Historian Drew Gilpin Faust notes that Hammond seems to have fathered children by two slave women on his plantation. In a letter to his white son Harry, Hammond confessed his probable paternity, asking Harry to care for these women and their offspring after his own death.

"In the last will I made," he writes, "I left you Sally Johnson, the mother of Louisa, and all the children of both. Sally says Henderson is my child. It is possible, but I do not believe it. Yet act on her's rather than my opinion. Louisa's first child may be mine. Her second I believe is mine. Take care of her and her children who are both of your blood. Do not let Louisa or any of my children or possible children be the slaves of strangers."[8]

So Hammond's two slave concubines are mother and daughter. The daughter was reportedly twelve when Hammond first impregnated her. By the standards of Democrats, Hammond was a considerate fellow; while he didn't want to free his concubines or his children, he did want to keep them enslaved "within the family." I can see Bill Clinton, if he lived at the time, acting the same way and feeling mighty proud of himself for doing so.

Another valuable source on our topic is the abolitionist Republican Frederick Douglass. Douglass recalled during his slave days how masters often produced children with slave women. "This arrangement," he wrote, "admits of the greatest license to brutal slaveholders and their profligate sons, brothers, relations and friends, and gives to the pleasure of sin the additional attraction of profit."

Douglass added, "One might imagine that the children of such connections would fare better in the hands of their masters than other slaves. The rule is quite the other way. A man who will enslave his own blood may not be safely relied on for magnanimity. Men do not love those who remind them of their sins and the mulatto child's face is a standing accusation against him who is master and father to the child.

"What is still worse, perhaps, such a child is a constant offense to the wife. She hates its very presence. Women—white women I mean—are idols in the south, not wives, for the slave women are preferred in many instances; and if these idols but nod or lift a finger, woe to the poor victim: kicks, cuffs and stripes are sure to follow. Masters are frequently compelled to sell this class of their slaves out of deference to the feelings of their white wives."

DEFILERS OF WOMEN

Several themes of consequence emerge from the Chesnut, Hammond, and Douglass accounts. We can see the Democratic slave master as a perfect hypocrite, posing as a champion of virtue while he debases the slave women. Here I am reminded of Bill Clinton, preening as a champion of equality and social justice while he defiles women who are within his power. Apparently the man has no shame, and neither did his Democratic forbears.

From Douglass's description we also see how ruthless the plantation owner can be. He has no qualms about selling off his own children. Here I recall Bill pressuring Gennifer Flowers to get an abortion. These are Democrats, then as now, seeking to avoid accountability and get rid of the evidence of their misdeeds. The circumstances are different, but in terms of the character of these Democrats, not much seems to have changed.

The slave owner is trying to escape what his family will think. Chesnut writes about the plantation daughters whose innocence does not include actual innocence of what their father is up to. They know what's going on, but they pretend not to notice. We cannot say that "ignorance is bliss" because this is feigned ignorance. Feigned ignorance is not bliss—it is actually collusion.

I'm also reminded of the feminists and more broadly progressive and Democratic activists who know at bottom that Bill is a serial abuser. They know Hillary is his co-conspirator. Still, they act like nothing has been really proven. I'm sure the Democrats said some of the same things in the 1830s. "The abolitionists and the Republicans are all lying. None of those things are true."

Then we have the wife, who is disgraced by the husband but endures his atrocities. On the surface that's Hillary, the longsuffering spouse. But only on the surface. When we probe deeper we see that plantation wives had to suffer their husbands' atrocities but they didn't enable them. They didn't cover up for their husbands. They didn't launch public campaigns against the slave women who were defiled.

Not that the plantation wives deserve our complete sympathy. Douglass interestingly points out that the wrath of the plantation wife, instead of being directed against the wayward husband, could sometimes be directed against the child. Douglass is not the only observer to note this; it's a fairly common theme in slave narratives collected by abolitionists in the nineteenth century and by the Slave Narrative Project that interviewed former slaves in the early twentieth century.

In one account, the slave Moses Roper recalled, "I was born in North Carolina, in Caswell County; I am not able to tell in what month or year. What I shall now relate is what was told me by my mother and grandmother. A few months before I was born, my father married my mother's young mistress. As soon as my father's wife heard about my birth, she sent one of my mother's sisters to see whether I was white or black, and when she had seen me, she returned and told her mistress that I was white and resembled Mr. Roper very much.

"Mr. Roper's wife not being pleased with this report, she got a large club stick and knife, and went into my mother's room with a full intention to murder me with her knife and club. But as she was going to stick the knife into me, my grandmother happening to come in, caught the knife and saved my life."

This incident is probably not typical. Most plantation wives, of course, were not murderers. Probably Douglass's account of women instructing that their husband's slave offspring be beaten, punished, or sold is more typical. In any case, this is a very degraded human response: I don't want to confront my husband, so instead I'll take it out on the kid.

Hillary's modus operandi of course is different. She doesn't blame the children, because as far as we know there are no children to blame. But she does blame the women whom her husband has victimized. She hires detectives to threaten them and publicly expose them. She ridicules them, suggesting that they are low-life trash. Rather than admit her husband abused them, she claims that the women are abusing him!

It may seem that in trying to punish or sell illegitimate children, the Democratic plantation wife is far worse than Hillary, who merely sought to discredit, humiliate, and chase off Bill's various women. But in her choice of target, Hillary's behavior is even worse than that of the plantation wife. While the plantation wife lashes out at the child who had nothing to do with the offense, Hillary actually faults the victims of the offense.

DEFENDING A RAPIST

What is the character of a person who becomes a sexual enabler? We get an early glimpse into this question from 1975, when Hillary Clinton defended a man, Thomas Alfred Taylor, who was accused of beating and raping a twelve-year-old girl. A virgin prior to the attack, she spent five days in a coma, several months recovering from her injuries, and years in therapy.

Even people who are accused of heinous crimes deserve criminal representation. Hillary's strategy in defending Taylor, however, was to blame the teenage victim. According to an affidavit filed by Hillary, children who come from "disorganized families such as the complainant" sometimes "exaggerate or romanticize sexual experiences." Hillary suggested the girl was "emotionally unstable with a tendency to seek out older men and engage in fantasizing."

Here Hillary seems to be echoing what Bernie Sanders wrote in his rape fantasy essay. In this case, however, the girl certainly didn't dream up the assault and rape. There was physical evidence that showed she had been violated, and she was beaten so badly she was in a coma. Prosecutors had in their possession a bloodied pair of Taylor's underwear.

But fortunately for Hillary and her client, the forensic lab mishandled the way that evidence was preserved. At the time of trial, the state merely had a pair of Taylor's underwear with a hole cut in it. Hillary plea bargained on behalf of Taylor and got him released without having to do any additional time. A tape unearthed by the *Washington Free Beacon* has Hillary celebrating the outcome. "Got him off with time served in the county jail," she says.

Did Hillary believe that, in this case, justice was done? Certainly not. On the tape, Hillary admits she never trusted her client. "Course he claimed he didn't, and all this stuff." So she decided to verify his story. "I had him take a polygraph, which he passed—which forever destroyed my faith in polygraphs."

Clearly Hillary knows her client is guilty, and this fact doesn't bother her. The most chilling aspect of Hillary's voice is her indifference—even bemusement—at getting a man off after he raped a twelve-year-old. The episode is a revealing look into the soul of an enabler. In fact, it reminds me of Alinsky protesting to Frank Nitti about the wasted expense of importing an out-of-town-killer. Hillary, like Alinsky, seems to be a woman without a conscience.[9]

Yet this is the same Hillary who was honored in September 2013 by the Children's Defense Fund for being a "tireless voice for children." One begins to see here what such awards actually mean. Hillary's actual prize should have been for the facilitation of adult abuse of women and young girls. Her rape case turned out to be excellent preparation for her lifelong advocacy of a single sex offender—Bill.

A KIND OF PIMP

The puzzle of the enabler is what would cause someone to become one. At first glance, we may be tempted to consider Hillary to be a kind of pimp, similar perhaps to the Mayflower Madam. The Mayflower Madam, Sydney Biddle Barrows, ran a prostitution agency with expensive girls and high-paying clients. She boasted that she used modern marketing techniques to win clients and procure "talent." But we know what she got out of the deal: money.

If Hillary were a pimp, she would be a special kind of pimp, renting out a single gigolo who happens to be her husband. Yet Bill is not a gigolo: he doesn't charge for his services. Moreover, Hillary neither procures Bill's sexual partners nor does she directly profit from them. So the pimp analogy, tempting though it is, doesn't really work. We still have to figure out why Hillary has devoted her life to enabling Bill's sex crimes and offenses.

What does it mean to be an enabler? The conventional wisdom is that enablers are indulgent people who make it possible for others to act upon their weaknesses or addictions. Think of the mother who knows her son is an alcoholic and feels sorry for him. Even though she knows that it's bad for him to drink, she lets him, and this of course sustains his addiction and makes his condition worse.

In the psychological literature, this is known as a passive or indulgent enabler. But there is another type of enabler, one that actually creates addictions. This is the active or initiating enabler. Think of a mother who doesn't want her son to leave home. She knows that in the ordinary course of things, he is likely to get a job, meet a woman, and move out of the house.

She knows he likes to drink, so she regularly has alcohol in the house. She encourages him to have one, and then another, and then another. Her goal is to *make* him into an alcoholic. Why? Because then she knows he cannot move out. He is unlikely to be able to find a woman and hold a job. He becomes forever dependent on her, and this is the way she wants it.

Now which type of enabler is Hillary Clinton? Again, the progressive answer is: the first kind, the indulgent enabler. In this scenario Bill is the bad guy. He has a problem, and Hillary, because she married him, has to endure that problem. So Hillary makes the best of it, trying to curb Bill's excesses while still holding together their marriage.

In this view Hillary is the devoted wife, fiercely protective of her flawed husband. Even if she is guilty of some sort of complicity, Hillary is, at worst, a passive enabler. "Tolerating Bill's weakness," says Hillary's pal Susan Thomases, "has always been part of her relationship with him."[10]

Thomases knows that passive enabling does not imply inaction; it sometimes requires the enablers to play a theatrical role. When Bill's abuse of another woman is publicly discovered, for example, Hillary must pretend to be outraged, though in reality she always knew about Bill's conduct.

She must also refuse to be seen with him, showing her "normal reaction" to his supposed betrayal. Even Chelsea and the family dog must be photographed practicing Bill avoidance. Hillary, Chelsea, and the dog are seen together, and Bill is seen all by himself, with a very forlorn expression. This may be called the "leaving Bill in the doghouse" or "taking Bill to the woodshed" phase.

Finally, the two of them must walk hand-in-hand on the beach, signifying reconciliation. They may even dance a few steps together, the loving couple somehow getting through it all. The press goes along with it, in the sycophantic manner reminiscent of courtiers before the French Dauphin. But no one actually believes it; most people know they are witnessing the pathetic, hypocritical performance of the passive enabler.

But a second possibility—never considered—is that Hillary is an active enabler. She doesn't just endure Bill's abuse; she abets it. Of course she didn't create Bill's problem, but she sees from the outset how she can benefit from it. She needs Bill not as a husband but as a lifelong partner in crime. And Bill profits from the arrangement because Hillary has agreed to become his collaborator and cover-up artist. His addiction is safe with her.

So Bill has, over time, become dependent on Hillary. That's why he's still out there in his dotage, campaigning for her. Otherwise Bill would be long gone at this point. By making Bill reliant on her—emotionally and politically—Hillary has over decades secured a marriage that was never really a marriage. She got Bill for life in exchange for facilitating his behavior and, whenever it became necessary, going after the victims of that behavior.

This theory of Hillary's active enabling may strike some as outrageous, so let's test it by looking more closely at some of those sex crimes. I'll start with the ones that seem minor because they involve consensual sex, but they're not, because they all involve abuses of power. In this category I would list Bill's relationships with Gennifer Flowers, Sally Miller, Elizabeth Ward Gracen, and Monica Lewinsky. In every case Bill was the powerful political figure and these women were vulnerable to his power.

Lewinsky, in her early twenties, was the lowliest employee for the most powerful man in the world when he began his "relationship" with her—essentially a routine in which she was smuggled through White House security to give him oral sex and then exit without being observed. The consequence of Bill using his power over her in this way was to make Lewinsky, in her own words, "the most humiliated person in the world." That's a lot to endure in your early twenties.

Sure, women like Lewinsky went along; in this respect they consented. But this consent is similar to the young actress who submits to the producer's couch, or the student who succumbs to the lecherous teacher, or the twenty-something political aide who is fondled by her middle-aged congressman. There is, at the least, a seediness about this that should make everyone, most of all feminists, very uncomfortable.

In the private sector, such behavior gets one reprimanded or even fired. In academia, professors are absolutely forbidden from having even consensual relationships with students enrolled in their classes. Several Harvard professors, for instance, have been reprimanded, demoted, or fired because of sexual relationships with students.

I remember discussing the issue with Harvard's longtime dean Henry Rosovsky when he invited me to campus to guest-lecture in a class he taught. Rosovsky was dealing with one particular case at the time. Even though the professor insisted the student had consented, Rosovsky argued her consent was irrelevant. "My position," he told me "is that when power is so inequitably distributed between professor and student, consent is not a defense."

In the political realm, Republicans could never get away with what Bill Clinton did. South Carolina Governor Mark Sanford was widely castigated within his party for having a love affair with a woman from Argentina. Sanford, unlike Clinton, wasn't just exercising his sex organs; he was genuinely smitten by the woman. The affair was consensual, and the two of them got engaged, although they subsequently parted ways and never married. Republicans, however, promptly initiated impeachment proceedings against Sanford.

Contrast Republican intolerance for sexual harassment with Democratic approval for it. Democrats ferociously resisted Republican attempts to impeach Bill Clinton. Not only did Democrats pooh-pooh Bill's conduct but they even excused his lying under oath, insisting that lying about sex should not be counted in this category. Throughout Bill's career, Democrats have turned a blind eye to his history of sordid behavior toward women.

THEY ALL SAID NO

Consensual affairs, however distasteful, are one thing. But now I turn to the more serious of Bill's sex offenses. Carolyn Moffet, a legal secretary in Little Rock in 1979, said she met Governor Clinton at a political fundraiser. He asked her to his room. "When I went in," she said, "he was sitting on a couch, wearing only an undershirt. He pointed at his penis and told me to suck it." When Moffet refused, "he got mad, grabbed my head, and shoved it into his lap. I pulled away from him and ran out of the room."

Bill met Paula Jones, a low-level state employee, at an Arkansas trade convention. He summoned Jones to meet him at the Excelsior Hotel, where he was staying. There, according to Jones, he dropped his pants in front of her, and asked her to suck his penis. "And the next thing you know he pulls down his pants. He sat on the couch and he was fondling himself and he asked me to kiss it."

Jones said, "I jumped up and said, 'No, I'm not that kind of girl. And I need to be leaving immediately.' So of course he was embarrassed.

He turned red. He pulled his pants up. And I went up to the door and was trying to get out."

Then, Jones added, "He momentarily put his hand on the door so I couldn't completely get it opened. And he said, 'You're smart. Let's keep this between ourselves.'" Jones saw a state trooper with a smirk on his face as she dashed out of the room.[11]

A former flight attendant on Bill Clinton's campaign plane, Christy Zercher, said that Clinton harassed her on an overnight flight from New York to California in early 1992. According to Zercher, Clinton tried to pull her into the campaign jet bathroom while his pants were unzipped. Then he tried grabbing her breast from his seat, while Hillary slept nearby.[12]

On November 29, 1993, when Bill was president, Kathleen Willey came to him looking for a job. She was in a very awkward situation. Her husband Ed, a prominent lawyer and Democratic fundraiser, had stolen from his clients and was facing prosecution and financial ruin. Willey came seeking full-time employment to relieve her family's desperate plight.

According to Willey, Clinton said to her, "I've wanted to do this since the first time I laid eyes on you." Then, in her words, "President Clinton put my hand on his genitals, on his erect penis. He then proceeded to overpower me and rub his hands up my skirt, over my blouse and my breasts." Utterly shocked, Willey was trying to decide whether to slap him or yell for help.

Fortunately for her, at that moment there was a knock on the door. Clinton was late for a meeting with his economic advisors. "I made a dive for the door, yanked it open and burst into the Oval Office," Willey said.[13] Her family situation, however, only got worse. The very day that Clinton assaulted her, Willey found out that her husband went into the woods, inserted a gun into his mouth, and killed himself.

In 1999, Juanita Broaddrick told Lisa Myers of NBC *Dateline* that Bill raped her. The two had met at an industry convention in 1978. Bill proposed a business meeting, and when Broaddrick suggested they have coffee in the lobby of the Camelot hotel where she was staying, Bill said it was too noisy and insisted they meet instead in Broaddrick's room.

As Broaddrick tells it, Clinton grabbed her and tried to kiss her. She drew back. "Then he tries to kiss me again. And the second time he tries to kiss me he starts biting my lip. I tried to pull away from him. And then he forces me down on the bed. And I just was very frightened, and I tried to get away from him, and I told him, 'No,' that I didn't want this to happen. But he wouldn't listen to me.

"It was a real panicky, panicky situation. I was even to the point where I was getting very noisy, yelling to 'please stop.' When everything was over with, he got up and straightened himself, and I was crying at the moment, and he walks to the door and calmly puts on his sunglasses. And he turned and went out the door."[14]

So here we have five women, unconnected with each other, making these allegations. One of them, Jones, filed a sexual harassment lawsuit against Bill. None of these women have a political ax to grind. Moffet, Zercher, Jones, and Broaddrick were not, as far as we know, political people. Willey was a longtime Clinton supporter. All were in a vulnerable position, yet each came forward, taking a big risk in taking on the Clinton machine.

We can see, from the quotation at the beginning of this chapter, that Hillary has said women who allege sexual harassment have a right to be heard and believed. Hillary herself has articulated this position throughout her career. During the Anita Hill hearings, for instance, she insisted that Hill's allegations against Supreme Court nominee Clarence Thomas should be presumed true, even though Thomas vehemently denied them.

This is the orthodox feminist position. Obviously we can use it to expose Hillary's hypocrisy, and the hypocrisy of her feminist allies. But is the position valid? I don't think so. Women have a right to be heard, but not necessarily to be believed. Women sometimes have a motive to lie, and women sometimes do lie. We have to decide each case on its merits.

But look at the merits of the situation here. It's conceivable that one accuser may be lying, but all five? We know that Paula Jones was not lying. Initially Bill said she was, but we know Bill is a liar. (He lied on national TV about his affair with Gennifer Flowers and he lied under oath about his relationship with Monica Lewinsky. "I did not have sexual relations with that woman, Miss Lewinsky.")

In what will surely go down as one of the most bizarre footnotes in presidential history, Jones gave a description of what she termed a "distinguishing mark" on Bill's penis. Eventually Bill and Hillary gave up: they paid Jones an $850,000 settlement to go away. We can be sure they would not have paid her if they could have exposed her allegations in court as lies.

BLAMING THE VICTIMS

Hillary's role with each of these women—indeed with all Bill's women—has been to deride, discredit, and intimidate them. In the White House, Hillary led a kind of war-room strategy which has been described as, "Go after specific things about the story—dates and times. Attack the motives and details." This seems chillingly reminiscent of how Hillary got her rapist client exonerated on a technicality.

Hillary led the team to handle the Paula Jones case. Here the attack focused on attacking Jones's motives. Hillary and her team portrayed Jones as a low-class woman who would say anything to get money. The Clintons' flunky James Carville disparaged Jones. "Drag a $100 bill through a trailer park, you never know what you'll find." Another flunky, Betsey Wright, dismissed the allegations of women like Jones as "bimbo eruptions" on the part of "gold diggers."

After the Broaddrick incident, Hillary personally accosted Broaddrick and whispered in her ear, "I just want you to know how much Bill and I appreciate the things you do for him." Broaddrick recalls, "I just stood there. I was sort of you might say shell-shocked." Hillary repeated, "Do you understand. Everything you do." Broaddrick adds, "She tried to take a hold of my hand and I left."

Broaddrick said she was terrified because she knew the power of the Clintons. She interpreted Hillary's remarks to her as something between a plea and a threat. Hillary was saying, in effect, we expect you to keep quiet about this. And Broaddrick did, for many years, until she felt compelled to speak out.

According to Willey, "My children were threatened by detectives hired by Hillary. They took one of my cats and killed another. They left a skull on my porch. They told me I was in danger. They followed me. They vandalized my car. They hid under my deck in the middle of the night. They subjected me to a campaign of fear and intimidation, trying to silence me."[15]

Hillary has never directly addressed the accusations that Bill is a sex abuser and a rapist. She pretends she doesn't have to. She is supported in this by a compliant media which—with the exception of Lisa Myers of *Dateline*—has generally buried the accounts of these women.

Even in the Myers case, NBC deliberately sat on the interview until after Clinton survived the impeachment vote. Myers interviewed Broaddrick in mid-January 1999. Clinton's impeachment vote in the Senate was February 12. NBC ran the interview two weeks after Clinton was acquitted. Had the interview run earlier, who knows how it might have affected the outcome?

Progressive journalists have from the beginning tried to protect Bill Clinton from the women he exploits. After the Gennifer Flowers scandal threatened to derail Bill's presidential bid, CBS producer Don Hewitt of *60 Minutes* staged an appearance by the Clintons. Questions were fed to them in advance. The episode was carefully edited.

Hewitt admitted later that his goal was to save Bill Clinton's 1992 candidacy for president. He said the Clintons "came to us because they were in big trouble. They were about to lose right there and they needed some first aid. They needed some bandaging. What they needed was a paramedic. So they came to us and we did it."[16]

They did it by creating a false tableau of the Clinton marriage. They created a false picture of Bill as the flawed but repentant husband, Hillary as the wronged wife determined to save their relationship. The message was that this decent couple was working out its marital issues by themselves, and the American people should leave them alone.

ACCESSORIES OF ABUSE

The progressive media is in the same camp on this as the feminists. These people are utterly shameless. Listen to how feminists, the soi-disant allies of women, talk about Bill. Erica Jong says she wants a president who's "alive from the waist down." What are women complaining about? "Oh," says Jong, "Imagine swallowing the presidential come."[17] I apologize for quoting this type of language but this is how these feminists talk.

Tina Brown went to a White House dinner and found Bill the hottest man in the room. "Forget the dog-in-the-manger, down-in-the-mouth neo-puritanism of the oped tumbrel drivers," she wrote in the *New Yorker*, "and see him instead as his guests do: a man in a dinner jacket with more heat than any star in the room." If this is how Brown responds to a rapist, think of how orgasmic she'd feel if Bill had been a *serial* rapist.

Gloria Steinem suggests that women who have a problem with Bill's behavior and Hillary's covering for Bill are insecure about their own marriages. "I began to understand that Hillary represented the very public, in-your-face opposite of the precarious and unequal lives that some women were living."[18] In sum, women who criticize Hillary secretly wish that they had husbands who were more like Bill.

Hillary can count on these shameless people to protect her husband. They are, in a quite conscious sense, her criminal accessories. For these people, Hillary identified the real enemy, "this vast right-wing conspiracy that has been conspiring against my husband."[19] In this never-never land, the Clintons bear no responsibility; the real culprits are those who speak out against their abusive behavior and lies.

The response of the feminists and the media clearly show that they are willing to go along with this narrative, even when they know it is false. These are people who don't very much care whether Bill Clinton rapes his grandmother, as long as he's a political ally. Bill votes for feminist policy positions, and that's all that matters.

The worst example of this attitude comes from writer Nina Burleigh, who infamously said several years ago that she'd be happy to give Bill Clinton a blowjob herself in gratitude for his efforts to keep abortion legal.[20] Burleigh seems to think that for Clinton, abortion is a matter of high principle.

In reality, of course, sex abusers love abortion because it facilitates their abuse. Imagine if they had to contend with the risk of their victims having their babies! Poor, dumb Burleigh is willing to become a convenient sex object herself out of appreciation for Bill Clinton supporting measures to make all his victims into convenient sex objects.

At one time feminists like Steinem, Jong, and Burleigh held that "the personal is political." In other words, your personal behavior is indicative of your political commitment. Now that seems to have gone out the window. Today's feminists take the view that if you're on their team, they'll go to bat for you no matter what you do. No wonder that young women are staying away from this cynical, morally bankrupt ideology.

AN ACTIVE ENABLER

Hillary's behavior, however, is what we have to watch most closely. This is how we can discover if she's a passive or an active enabler. A passive enabler might accommodate her husband's behavior, but she would also do what she could to prevent it. Hillary, however, has never shown the slightest interest in thwarting the sexual schemes of Bill. On the contrary, she seems utterly indifferent to them.

The active enabler has no desire to stop the behavior, because she benefits from it. She knows, however, that other women may attempt to stop Bill—his victims may speak out against him. Thus the active enabler goes into assault mode against those victims. Her behavior is predictable; she has to uphold her part of the deal, which is to protect the criminal and vilify his targets. This Hillary has done with a vengeance.

She recruited Craig Livingston, a former barroom bouncer and Democratic operative, to get dirt on Bill's women. Livingston, who was accustomed to getting dirt on political candidates, proved outstanding at his job. He delivered files on women to Hillary and she assembled them into a database that could be used if any of the women became a political problem.

In 1981, Hillary hired Ivan Duda, an Arkansas detective, to produce a list of women Bill had slept with. Again, Hillary had no interest in preventing Bill's liaisons. Rather, her goal was to be prepared for any charges that might come up from any of these women during a political campaign. Duda's practice was to confront the women and warn them that if they spoke out against Bill they would be completely ruined. Most of them, consequently, did not.

In 1992, according to Dick Morris, Hillary had a team of detectives building dossiers on Bill's women. One of those detectives was Anthony Pellicano, a hard-nosed operative who was later convicted of illegal firearms possession, wiretapping, and racketeering. Pellicano, known for tactics such as placing a dead fish with a red rose in its mouth on the windshield of a targeted reporter's car, was specifically assigned to discredit and intimidate Gennifer Flowers.

The Clintons also hired Jack Palladino, who was paid around $100,000 for his services by the Clinton campaign. Palladino had previously represented a San Francisco developer accused of having sex with under-age prostitutes. According to the developer, "I needed somebody to go down and talk to the women who were the accusers. They were the kind of witnesses that if you talked to them long enough, they'd give four or five different accounts of what happened. It was important to gain their confidence, and Jack's operatives did that."[21]

What did Hillary's goons do for her? According to Sally Perdue, a former Miss Arkansas who had an affair with Bill Clinton, they fired a shotgun blast at her Jeep, shattering the rear windshield. Perdue was so freaked out by this that she left the country for a while.

Gennifer Flowers said they broke into her apartment seeking incriminating evidence of her affair with Bill. They were looking for tapes of their conversations, sex tapes, anything they could find. Flowers, however, had already removed tapes of her conversations with Bill. She came home to see her house ransacked, her mattress overturned, boxes on the floor, clothes tossed everywhere.

She realized then that they were not just searching for stuff; they were also sending her a message that they were deadly serious. This message was reinforced for Flowers when Palladino approached a former roommate of hers, Loren Kirk, and asked her, "Is Gennifer Flowers the sort of person who would commit suicide?" At this point Flowers—I think legitimately—came to believe her life might be in danger.

For a presidential candidate to use private investigators with this shady background to do surveillance and then seek to intimidate women who might come forward against him is unprecedented in American politics. Who can deny that it is a big story in itself? Yet with the exception of a single article in the *Washington Post*, it went unreported by the entire press contingent covering the Clinton campaign.

The media knew—but didn't report the fact—that Hillary was the self-appointed public prosecutor of other women. The White House team also recognized that the wife was in charge of the cover-up operation for the husband. It was, one might say, all in the family. Bill seems to have known throughout that he could count on Hillary because this is what her role was from the outset.

A VERY SICK ARRANGEMENT

Let's conclude this chapter by seeing how this bizarre, sick arrangement between Bill and Hillary might have developed in the first place. What follows is less a description than an interpretation. Some of what I say here is unverifiable, but I'm trying to make sense of the freakish relationship of these two, and this is my best effort to do so. You decide how congruent it is with the facts we do know.

Bill and Hillary came to Yale Law School burning with ambition. Bill wanted to be a major figure in Arkansas politics, setting him up to run for president. Hillary may not have known then she wanted to be president, but she too shared Bill's volcanic ambition. She too wanted influence and power.

Hillary, however, had a problem, which was that no one—male or female—liked her. They considered her ugly, petulant, and bitchy. This was not something she could change; this was her personality. In high school they called her "Sister Frigidaire"—the appellation under her

name in her yearbook[22]—and no one today can say that they are aston-
ished or that she has changed much since then. So how does a woman
like this make it to the zenith of power in the United States?

Hillary decided she needed to partner with a man who was ambitious, gregarious, and naturally likeable. Of course he might have no use
for her in the bedroom, but she didn't necessarily want him for that.
Rather, she wanted him to be her "pitch man." His job was to make her
attractive, not necessarily to him but to the people whom Hillary needed
to gain influence and power.

Of course she might initially have to subordinate her ambitions to
his. But only initially; later, she could make her move. At this point, she
would have to be sure she could rely on him. In other words, his dependence on her would have to be complete. From the outset, Hillary didn't
need a husband; she needed a partner-in-crime.

At Yale, Hillary met Bill and saw almost immediately that he was
a sex addict. She also saw that this was a proclivity that could easily cross
the line into sex abuse. This was exactly what seemed to have happened
in a case Hillary heard from friends about an incident involving Bill while
he was a Rhodes Scholar at Oxford.

There, Bill had sex with a nineteen-year-old coed named Eileen
Wellstone. Later Wellstone said she was sexually harassed. Bill insisted
that what happened was consensual. What exactly happened is not clear,
but Bill was asked to leave Oxford over the incident. Obviously, Bill was
treading a fine line. This, then, seemed to be Bill's problem, and here,
Hillary understood, was her opportunity.

Hillary knew that Bill's sex addiction would pose serious problems
for him politically. Arkansas voters don't want their top elected officials
to be philanderers, let alone sexual predators. Bill's abusive conduct—
witnessed and experienced by a long train of women—could prevent
him from his aspiration to be president someday. Bill understood this
as well as Hillary. So Bill had a problem and Hillary offered herself as
the solution.

Bill knew that in order for him to continue his sex abuse and yet
have a successful life in politics, he needed a special type of wife, one

who would accept and even embrace his sex addiction. Hillary offered to do this; even more, she offered to cover for him. No ordinary woman would do this. Very few women would have the skills to pull it off. None of the other women Bill knew would remotely qualify for the job.

Bill needed someone cynical, someone who would be as indifferent to his below-the-belt conduct as she would be ruthless in clearing up the debris. When Bill met sly, owlish Hillary, with her terrible clothes and her peering eyes, he saw she was exactly what he needed. And Hillary knew she needed him at least as much as he needed her. It was, one might say, a match made in hell.

Hillary, however, recognized that Bill's degeneracy could work to her advantage. She could become his cover-up artist and his blame-the-victim specialist. She could prosecute and go after Bill's women, discrediting their allegations if they ever surfaced and protecting Bill from the consequences of his actions. In this way Hillary would make herself indispensable to Bill, and Bill would become increasingly dependent on her.

Bill saw the benefits of this deal, and he went for it. Over time he developed a sense of immunity over his crimes, because he never seemed to be held accountable for any of them. No matter what he did, Hillary was there to clean up after him. And just as Hillary expected, Bill became fiercely attached—and hopelessly dependent—on his enabler-in-chief. It was an arrangement that worked.

Of course there were times when things got out of hand. Then Hillary screamed and shouted and threw stuff at Bill, "yellow legal pads, files, briefing books, car key, Styrofoam coffee cups," in one account. Kate Anderson Brower reports in *The Residence*, "The couple sometimes got into pitched battles, shocking the staff with their vicious cursing, and sometimes they went through periods of stony silence."[23]

These eruptions, dutifully reported to the media by White House staff and Secret Service agents, have been portrayed as evidence of how distraught Hillary must have been at Bill's shameful conduct. This portrait of the wronged wife has, as Democratic operative Harold Ickes pointed out to her, actually helped Hillary. The Monica Lewinsky scandal, for example, boosted Hillary's Senate campaign in New York because it converted this highly disliked woman into a victim.

But Hillary is no victim; she is actually his co-conspirator. Her rage at Bill has never been about what he did. She has known about that from the start. Hillary's disgust, rather, has to do with the fact that Bill is frequently so careless, he keeps getting busted, and once again Hillary has to put on a scene and drag out her goons to clean up the debris. This is what Hillary meant when, on more than one occasion, she slapped him and yelled, "How could you be so stupid?"[24]

THE BEST CONFIRMATION

The best confirmation of Hillary's role as an active enabler comes from Bill's female targets, who all seem to have figured out that Hillary had as much to do with their victimization as Bill did. "Women's rights? Ha! That's a joke!" Gennifer Flowers responds, when asked about Hillary's aspiration to be a spokesperson for American women. Flowers described Hillary as "an enabler that has encouraged him to go out and do whatever he does with women."[25]

Former Miss Arkansas Sally Miller says she's been stalked and spied on so much that she now sleeps with a loaded semi-automatic to protect herself against Hillary's goons. "There is a vengeful spiteful ugliness that some women have for other women," she says. "Hillary is just one of those women."[26]

Paula Jones is also on the warpath against Hillary. "She's such a liar. So two-faced. She don't care nothing about women. Hillary is only out for herself. Well, she stood by her man, alright. He helps her. She helps him. And they are the perfect pair for committing all of this stuff and lies and cheating people. It's a sickness, I think. On both parts."[27]

At first Juanita Broaddrick thought that Bill was solely responsible for raping her and then attempting to cover it up. But when Hillary came up and whispered in her ear, Broaddrick says, "What really went through my mind at that time is, 'She knows. She knew. She's covering it up and she expects me to do the very same thing.'"

Today Broaddrick continues to rail against Hillary with the fury of a woman who recognizes her real enemy—not just Bill, but also Hillary. "I think she has always known everything about him. I think they have this evil compact between the two of them that they each know what the other does and overlook it. And go right on. And cover one for the other."[28]

Willey writes of Hillary, "She has hurt so many people. She has disgraced so many women. She has demeaned us. She has terrorized us. What she has done is absolutely horrible. She has enabled her perverted husband to keep on doing it and that's because she doesn't care about women. She is the war on women." Willey has pledged to follow Hillary around on the campaign trail to expose her viciousness and hypocrisy.[29]

This eruption on the part of multiple women against the wife of the sex abuser is extremely rare. Victims typically only point the finger at the man who has violated them. In this case, however, the women all know that behind the man stands a woman who fully shares his culpability. I'm not even sure these women know the extent of Hillary's culpability. They are, however, quite right to point the finger at her as much as at Bill.

The relationship between Hillary and Bill is, in its sheer depravity and duplicity, uniquely odious in the annals of the presidency. Never before have two people with such low scruples ever reached the pinnacle of political power. Now Hillary the manipulator wants to abuse and victimize the country in the same way that she has been abusing and victimizing the women of Bill.

CHAPTER 9

PARTNERS IN CRIME
HOW THE CLINTONS WENT FROM DEAD BROKE TO FILTHY RICH

And the money kept rolling in from every side.
— Song from the musical *Evita*

The quotation above refers to the Juan and Evita Peron Foundation, established in 1948 by Evita Peron for the purpose of helping Argentina's poor. Evita professed to be a champion of the campesinos—the wretched workers who lived in shanties on the outskirts of Buenos Aires—and they trusted Evita. She had, after all, risen up herself from poverty and obscurity. Her fame was the result of her marriage to the general who became the military leader of the country, Juan Peron. Long before the Clintons, Argentina had its own power couple that claimed to do good and ended up doing very well for themselves.

There are, obviously, differences between the Clintons and the Perons. Despite her personal popularity, Evita remained an appendage of her husband, seeking but never obtaining political office. At one point, Evita had her eye on an official position, but the political establishment vigorously opposed her, and her husband never supported her in this effort. Hillary, by contrast, was elected senator and now, having deployed her husband on the campaign trail, seeks election to the nation's highest office previously held by him.

The Perons also had a foundation that took in millions of pesos—the equivalent of $200 million—from multiple foreign sources, Argentine businesses, as well as contributions from various individuals and civic groups. With its 14,000 employees, the foundation was better equipped and more influential than many agencies within the Argentinian government.

Evita and her cronies were experts at shaking down anyone who wanted something from the government; donations became a kind of tax that opened up access to the Peron administration. Trade unions sent large contributions because they saw Evita and her husband as champions of their cause. In 1950, the government arranged that a portion of all lottery, movie, and casino revenues should go to the foundation.

While the foundation made symbolic, highly publicized gestures of helping the poor, in reality only a fraction of the money went to the underprivileged. Most of it seems to have ended up in foreign bank accounts controlled by the Perons, who became hugely wealthy through their public office profiteering. When Evita died in 1954 and the foundation was shut down, Argentines discovered stashes of undistributed food and clothing. No one from the foundation had bothered to give it away, so it sat unused for years.

Helping the poor, after all, wasn't the real reason Evita set up her foundation. No, she had a different set of priorities. Like so many Third World potentates, the Perons used social justice and provision for the poor as a pretext to amass vast wealth for themselves. The Clintons have done the same thing in America; indeed, Hillary may be America's version of Evita Peron.

THE ULTIMATE PAYOFF

This chapter is about the ultimate payoff of progressive politics—the chance to get virtually unlimited wealth and power. This payoff is what really motivates progressives. The motive, as we have seen, is camouflaged, because progressive Democrats typically claim to be championing some higher cause. From Andrew Jackson to Hillary Clinton, Democrats have long played Evita's tune, insisting they are just looking out for the ordinary guy or the little guy. Somehow that little guy always remains where he is, however, while progressive elites advance to new heights of wealth and power.

How do we know the progressives' real motives? We know by checking out the bottom line. Bank accounts, in this respect, are quite revealing. As we saw with Jackson, his patriotism may not be in doubt, but when we examine his bank balance, we can be sure that he consistently looked after his own interests. Here we will see that, patriotism aside, Hillary Clinton is very much in the corrupt, self-serving Jackson tradition. She is also in the tradition of all the crooked Peronistas in the world who grow richer off their country's wealth while they make their countries poorer.

Once we understand Hillary as single-mindedly pursuing her own interest and financial gain, we can for the first time make sense of recent Clinton scandals. Consider the email scandal. What we know is that Hillary created and maintained an entirely private email server, insulated from her State Department requirements. This took great effort and required the collaboration of a whole team of aides as well as State Department bureaucrats.

Why did Hillary do this? Her official explanation is convenience. Hillary simply wanted to get things done, and she was a little careless about how she went about doing them. She claims she got into all this trouble because she didn't want to have to carry two phones.[1]

But setting up a parallel email system is actually very inconvenient. Far from being careless, Hillary was careful to do it in a manner that would allow her to carry on private communications that would not show up on an official network, rendering the Freedom of Information Act useless. By doing this, in essence she stole the people's property.

Sending classified and secret information through a private network is not merely harmful to the national security; it is also illegal. Former CIA director John Deutch, former National Security Adviser Sandy

Berger, and General David Petraeus were all punished for doing it. Their offenses pale before Hillary's.

Moreover, Hillary, in the middle of a government investigation, went through her private emails, deleting thousands of them that she didn't want the government or the public to see. Normal people who do such things end up in prison. Hillary, clearly, sees herself as politically protected by the Obama gang. She acts like she's above the law, and so far she has been proven correct.

As a seasoned public official—one who has been in public life for decades now—Hillary at every stage knew what she was doing. Her actions, far from revealing the clumsy conduct of an amateur, show the confidence of a career criminal who knows where all the alarms are and how to avoid prosecution.

Hillary had two purposes for foreign policy: to conduct the nation's business, as she and the Obama administration saw it, and this is what her State Department network was for; and to conduct her own private business, as she saw fit, and this is what her private email network was for. In the end, Hillary's interests seem consistently to have trumped the national interest.

The Benghazi scandal puzzled many Americans because so many warnings had been sent to the State Department about the danger to American lives in and around the American diplomatic compound in the Libyan port city. Following the Obama administration's acquiescence in the assassination of Qaddafi—an action cynically celebrated in Hillary's phrase, "We came, we saw, he died"[2]—Libya devolved into a country controlled by marauding militias. One militia controls the airport, another the municipal offices, a third the main route out of town. Americans in Benghazi, from Ambassador J. Christopher Stevens to the ordinary CIA contractor—always knew they were in someone's telescopic sights.

So Benghazi was known to be dangerous. But what was Hillary's real offense? Even critics of her action—or more precisely, inaction—in Benghazi fault her at most with shocking negligence. She seemed indifferent to the danger posed to American lives and insensitive when lives were actually lost. In classic Clinton fashion, she also tried to shift the blame from the terrorist perpetrators to an anti-Islamic video, which supposedly stirred up local sensibilities.

As the House Benghazi hearings made clear, Hillary knew better. The very day of the attack, Hillary emailed her daughter Chelsea informing her that Americans had been killed in Benghazi "by an al Qaeda-like group." She said the same thing that evening on the phone to Libyan President Mohamed Magariaf, and the following afternoon, in a phone call, she notified Egyptian Prime Minister Hesham Kandil, "We know that the attack in Libya had nothing to do with the film. It was a planned attack—not a protest."[3]

Yet if Hillary was lying to cover up an inconvenient situation, why did she find herself in an inconvenient situation to begin with? Why didn't she pay attention to incoming calls and cables warning of the danger to American lives in Benghazi? This is the part of the Benghazi scandal that has gone unexplored. Hillary's indifference is clear, but the motives for that indifference remain opaque.

An important clue comes from where Hillary got the idea for the bogus Internet video story. She got it from one of her longtime confidants, Sidney Blumenthal. A former journalist, Blumenthal is known in Washington to be one of the shadiest figures this side of the Nile. The Obama administration vetoed Hillary's petition to employ him at the State Department. So he went to work at the Clinton Foundation where he fed Hillary with "intelligence," some of it aimed at fending off critics, some of it aimed at business opportunities for the Clintons.

When Hillary received Blumenthal's "intelligence" about the Internet video, she seems to have immediately seen its promising potential to mislead the public. So she ran with it. But this wasn't Blumenthal's only contribution to the Libya campaign. We also learn from Hillary's secret emails—obtained from a Romanian hacker and published online—that Blumenthal was working to figure out how to obtain contracts for the rebuilding of Libya from the post-Qaddafi regime.

So the plot thickens. Blumenthal, we learn, was specifically looking into the creation of homes, schools, and "floating hospitals" to take care of the war wounded. He worked with other Clinton cronies on this. One of them, Democratic fundraiser Bill White, told the *New York Times*, "We were thinking, Ok, Qaddafi is dead, or about to be, and there's opportunities. We thought, let's try to see who we know there."[4] As we saw in an earlier chapter with Haiti, the Hillary gang knew there was money to be made in Libya.

Blumenthal's memo to Hillary concerning business opportunities in Libya also reminds me of Andrew Jackson's surveyor writing him about how much Jackson stood to benefit from the American Indian land that would become available once the Indians were evacuated. In much the same way, Blumenthal spotted a "silver lining" in Libya for the Hillary gang. Of course, the resettlement project would require the clearance of the U.S. government. Happily, the head of the agency in charge—the State Department—was Hillary herself.[5]

So now the smoke begins to clear and we can better understand Hillary's real objectives in Libya. She and her associates were busy with moneymaking schemes to profit from the chaos in Libya that Hillary had herself helped to create. This "commercial diplomacy," to use Hillary's own term, takes work, especially in treacherous territory like Libya. Hillary's full attention was devoted to this self-serving enterprise.

Making money in a war-torn country like Libya isn't easy; it takes concentration and dedicated effort. So when the warning cables came in, Hillary couldn't be bothered; all that, to her, was a nuisance. She wasn't going to let violence and the safety of her employees get in the way of extracting money from a country in a precarious position. Hillary has always been a woman who stays on task.

Hillary's famous eruption "What difference does it make?" reflects her unique take on Benghazi. Her point is that nothing that happened to Ambassador Stevens or anyone else there made any difference to what she was trying to accomplish in Libya. Here Hillary can be compared to the bank robber who is interrupted because someone in the bank requires medical attention; from the thief's point of view, this is a mere annoyance. What difference does it make? Can't you see we're trying to rob a bank here?

Even Hillary's fake "alibi" is revealing. Her bogus Internet video story wasn't merely an effort to protect the Obama administration; she wanted to deflect attention away from her own private activities in Libya—activities that help to explain why she persuaded the U.S. government to intervene in Libya in the first place.

Hillary's enthusiasm for invading Libya—and Obama's acquiescence in it—both remain questionable. Obama and Hillary insisted they had to prevent genocide in Libya, even though no genocide was taking place in Libya. There had been an uprising against Qaddafi, as part of the Arab Spring, which not surprisingly Qaddafi was trying to squash. A few hundred rebels and terrorists had been killed, but keeping this in context, the regime of Bashar al-Assad in Syria has killed tens of thousands to suppress armed resistance in that country. Yet Obama refuses to use the term genocide to describe Syrian atrocities and has not supported any efforts to kill Assad.

Assad, let's remember, is America's adversary. He is also closely allied with Iran, another hostile nation. After the civil war, Assad also teamed up with Russia. Qaddafi, by contrast, was a bad guy who had been behaving himself because past administrations had effectively neutered him. After America got his attention with the invasion of Iraq, Qaddafi recanted terrorism, paid reparations to terrorist victims, agreed not to harbor terrorists, and cooperated with America's campaign against Islamic militants. In addition, he exposed the sale of nuclear secrets by Pakistan's A. Q. Khan.

There was no rational reason for America to aid in the overthrow or assassination of Qaddafi. Yet Hillary pushed for it from the outset. The dictator himself could hardly believe that America would participate in a plot to get rid of him. Right until the end, his son Saif made frantic phone calls to the State Department offering peace and attempting to plead Qaddafi's case. Neither Hillary nor anyone else would take his calls.[6] It seems that she had her own reasons for wanting Qaddafi gone.

Hillary was not merely involved in amassing rebuilding contracts for her buddies, just as she had done in Haiti. She was also reportedly involved in orchestrating the sale of confiscated Libyan weapons to the

Syrian Free rebels who turned out to be terrorists in Syria. This occurred without the knowledge of Congress and at the very time Obama declared his public opposition to the U.S. arming the Syrian opposition. What Obama knew of Hillary's actions is unknown; what we do know is that whole stashes of high-grade weapons—including high-grade missiles— went missing in the aftermath of the Libya operation.[7]

This is how these weapons deals go down. Hillary knew that, under the shelter of clandestine U.S. operations, there would be little or no public scrutiny of where the weapons ended up. The topic couldn't be— and wasn't—even raised in the Benghazi public hearings. Hillary intended for herself and her pals to prosper during the rebuilding efforts.

There are some indications that the scheme went awry—the *New York Times* reported that Blumenthal's Libya scheme fell apart in the aftermath of the chaos there—but no one apart from the people directly involved really know. What we do know is that Hillary contributed to the destruction of a whole country and that her associates planned to make money on it. Then she deleted the evidence of her actions. This is the real story behind Benghazi and the private email server.

THE TAMMANY HALL DEMOCRATS

Corruption in American politics is hardly new, of course, but previously, for the most part, it was conducted mainly on the local level. It was also conducted by Democrats. There were exceptions, of course, especially during Reconstruction, and in the administration of President Grant, and in the Teapot Dome scandal of the Harding administration.

But generally, when we think of political corruption, we think of the Democratic Party machines in America's big cities, of the city "bosses" using the political system to rig votes, install cronies in office, extort favors from businesses, collect bribes for the assignment of city contracts, and generally rip off the local taxpayer and loot the treasury.

Just as slavery and white supremacy were the tools of Democratic exploitation in the South, the boss system was the party's tool of corruption and theft in cities throughout the country. The most famous

Democratic bosses were Edward Crump, mayor of Memphis from 1910 to 1916; Tom Pendergast, who ran the Jackson County Democratic Club and controlled local politics in Kansas City, Missouri, from 1911 until his conviction for tax fraud in 1939; Frank Hague, mayor of Jersey City from 1917 to 1947; and Richard Daley, who was mayor of Chicago from 1955 to 1976.

The boss system may seem a relic of the Democratic past, but it continued well into the twentieth century. Bosses are widely credited with securing Harry Truman's nomination for vice president at the 1944 Democratic convention. Chicago boss Richard Daley is said to have swung a very close election in JFK's favor through use of an old boss tactic: dead people's votes. Nixon honorably refused to contest the 1960 election even though he knew that the Illinois result had been rigged.

The boss system of the Democrats was a racket to take advantage of new immigrants who came to this country in waves starting in the late nineteenth century and continuing through the twentieth. Many immigrants came with nothing, speaking little or no English, and had no easy way to establish themselves in this country. Just as progressive Democrats found a way to control poor blacks under the guise of helping and providing for them, they also found a way to control poor immigrants under the same pretext.

Democratic bosses built their power by making themselves indispensable to these northern immigrants. At first the immigrants didn't need the Democratic Party. They relied on private fraternal organizations that provided food to the destitute, instruction in speaking English, civic lessons to help immigrants assimilate, and also information about employment and sometimes training skills for construction and manufacturing jobs.

It wasn't long, however, before Democratic Party bosses saw immigrant groups as sources of political power, whose votes could be acquired through patronage—that is, through tapping the city treasury. Dressed up as aid for the disadvantaged, or as social justice, such looting schemes were a way to gain votes, maintain power, and profit off the public purse.

Democrats, in other words, found a way to do what Democrats have always done, namely, steal for their own benefit.

Once in power, Democratic bosses offered lucrative no-bid contracts to businesses in exchange for large contributions to the Democratic machines. They also handed out service contracts to their own cronies, padding the bill so that projects that should have cost a few thousand dollars ended up costing tens, even hundreds of thousands, of dollars by the time the bosses received their take.

In exchange, the immigrant had to agree to vote early and vote often. This is not a joke; Democrats perfected "repeater" techniques in which the same guy voted more than once. Even dead people showed up at the polls, judging by the resemblance of voter identification with the gravestones in local cemeteries.

How ironic that a party named "Democrat" would specialize in such perversions of the democratic process. Even today the party supports same-day voter registration and opposes voter identification requirements. These positions are intended to clear the way for illegals to vote. So the vote-rigging scam continues in a modified form.

The most famous—or infamous—of the Democratic bosses was Boss Tweed who ran the Tammany Hall racket in New York City. Few progressives today defend the Tweed ring. But Terry Golway in his book *Machine Made* makes the case that Tweed "helped create modern government and urban politics."[8] Golway means that Democratic dominance of cities today is largely maintained through Tweed-style operations. He's right. My only disagreement with him is that he thinks that's a good thing, and I think it's a very bad thing.

Golway doesn't sugarcoat Tweed, a former bookkeeper who built his early following by starting a local gang devoted to bribes and street-corner protection rackets. Eventually Tweed established a powerful fraternal group, the Society of St. Tammany. His title was Grand Sachem of the society. The name of the group alone is interesting because curiously Tammany's name does not appear in the Catholic Church's recognized roster of saints.

Tweed did not seek high public office for himself. He didn't have to. He was much more powerful operating as a shadow government, appointing and controlling others who held the official positions. For twelve years, Tweed basically ran New York City. He established a one-party system; Republicans had no say. From his unassuming post as deputy street commissioner, Tweed appointed his proteges to important positions, such as city alderman and state Supreme Court justice.

Tweed built close ties to the Catholic Church, doling out small favors in exchange for the church's blessing. This was important to Tweed because most of his supporters were Catholic immigrants fiercely loyal to the church. Tweed also built close ties to unions that were only too happy to cooperate in his system of shakedowns, kickbacks, and payouts. These unions remained corrupt long after the Tweed era, and well into the twentieth century.

In the middle of the century, for example, many unions were controlled or influenced by New York's five mafia syndicates: the Gambino, Lucchese, Genovese, Colombo, and Bonnano families. Mob-controlled union bosses prospered through kickbacks and payoffs while ordinary workers got nothing. Union members who protested against corruption were regularly threatened and in some cases killed. This ugly history of American unions is generally downplayed in progressive historiography.

Many poor Irishmen loved Tweed, because of his highly publicized distribution of turkeys during Thanksgiving and other symbolic acts of charity. In reality, Tweed made sure the big bucks always flowed back in his own direction. He regularly raked in huge kickbacks from city contracts. Typical of the Tweed racket is the way he bilked New York taxpayers for the construction of the city courthouse.

The courthouse had been budgeted to cost $250,000. But Tweed paid a carpenter $350,000 for a month's work that should have cost a few thousand dollars. He charged the city nearly $3 million for furniture and half a million for carpet. Hundreds of thousands were paid in "repairs" and "alterations" to a firm with close ties to Tweed. In the end, this single project ended up costing taxpayers $14 million.

Eventually the *New York Times* published a series of articles exposing the Tweed racket. Cartoonist Thomas Nast of *Harper's* launched a
one-man crusade against Tammany Hall, caricaturing the Tweed group
as rapacious pigs with their snouts in the trough and Tweed supporters
as ignorant, drunken Irishmen. Tweed disputed the charges with Hillary-
style resolve, but over time the criticism took its toll.

Samuel Tilden, who was the chairman of the New York Democratic
Party, was finally pressured to take action. Tilden knew that the corrup-
tion was not unique to Tweed; it ran deep within the ranks of the party.
Tilden also knew that Tweed had gone too far, and Tweed's identification
with the Democratic Party could end up severely damaging the party.
Tweed, therefore, would have to go.

So Tilden gathered evidence against Tweed. He took his time, however. Tilden's inquiry lasted almost ten years. Historians have subsequently wondered why it took so long. The reason is that Tilden wanted
to protect the Democratic Party that was vulnerable to being taken down
with Tweed. Tilden wanted to take down Tweed but to protect the party.
Indeed, he had an idea of how the Democrats could, over time, make
Tweed's type of racket legal.

Eventually Tweed was indicted on 120 charges ranging from forg-
ery to grand larceny. He was found guilty and sentenced to twelve years
in prison. Accompanied by several henchmen, Tweed fled to California
and then to Spain. But someone recognized him there from one of
Nast's cartoons, and he was extradited to New York. He died in prison
in 1878.

In bringing down Tweed, Tilden is credited with being one of the
first "reform" Democrats. This "reform" tradition is closely associated
with progressivism. Some historians gullibly assume that the progressives
were all about ending Democratic corruption. In reality they were all
about streamlining it, legalizing it, and making it part of the Democratic
way of doing business.

A Tammany Hall flunky, George Plunkett, whose sayings were collected and memorialized by writer William Riordan in a book titled
Plunkett of Tammany Hall, candidly laid out the formula. Here we find

Plunkett dispensing telling advice to his fellow Democrats. "Politicians do not have to steal to make a living because a politician can become a millionaire through honest graft."[9] I'm quite sure that Harry Reid has a copy of this book by his bedside, and three generations of Democrats have become rich following Plunkett's advice.

Although Tweed's reign lasted for just over a decade, the Tammany Hall domination of New York politics continued from the 1860s through the 1930s. It only ended with the Great Depression. The reason it ended is that it was incorporated into a bigger scheme. FDR in a sense took over the Tammany scheme and made it national. FDR's famous tirades against the boss system in New York were not because he opposed the system in principle. He didn't like local bosses because he wanted himself to become the big national boss.

FDR, however, didn't completely end the boss system in American cities. He merely federalized its principles for the benefit of the national Democratic Party. FDR, it's important to note, was already wealthy when he came to the White House; his goal in taking the boss racket to a national level was power, not personal enrichment.

The criminal genius of the Clintons is that they have taken the urban racket to national, even international, heights for personal gain, selling the prestige of the presidency during Bill's tenure and selling American foreign policy itself during Hillary's tenure as secretary of state. In this respect, the Clintons are in a corrupt league of their own.

Hillary famously claimed she and Bill were "dead broke" when they left the White House. Admittedly the Clintons had accumulated substantial legal bills because of their various scandals, from Whitewater to the Paula Jones sexual harassment case to the Monica Lewinsky investigation. Undoubtedly, their net worth took a hit when Bill had to pay Paula Jones $850,000 to go away—this one Hillary couldn't make disappear without a settlement.

Yet Hillary had, prior to their departure, negotiated a $6 million book contract. Bill had already declared his intention to hit the speaker circuit for fees estimated in the $50,000 to 100,000 range. Hillary's statement about being broke was derided, and rightly so.

Since they left the White House, however, the Clintons have increased their wealth at warp speed. They have gone from zero to $200 million in just a few years. Their foundation—which is basically an extension of the Clintons—has accumulated much more much faster.

How did the Clintons get all this money? They didn't invent anything or start any businesses. They've been in politics all their lives, and government salaries aren't that lucrative. Book contracts and speaking fees can hardly account for this kind of wealth. So where did it come from?

AN EARLY START

It came from cronyism, corruption, and theft, something the Clintons have practiced, with greater or lesser success, over the entirety of their political lives. The stakes may have been less in Arkansas, but that's where they polished their skills, honing them even further at the White House. Let's briefly review some of the early Clinton cons before focusing on their more recent corruption schemes at the Clinton Foundation.

Remember how Hillary invested $1,000 in 1979 in cattle futures and promptly netted $100,000? That's a 10,000 percent profit in nine months! Hillary had no experience investing in commodities. Most people who make such investments lose money. Hillary explains her extraordinary success by saying "she followed the markets closely" and "did my best to educate myself about cattle futures and margin calls."[10]

But in fact she didn't make any margin calls. Rather, Robert "Red Bone," a Chicago-based broker who previously worked for—and was closely connected to—Tyson Foods, handled her brokerage account. Red Bone was a slippery character; just a year earlier, he had had his brokerage license pulled for a year by the Chicago Mercantile Exchange for allocating trades to investors after determining the winners and losers, a corrupt practice known as "straddling."

This is how Red Bone seems to have orchestrated Hillary's big score. Moreover, there was something very odd about Hillary's mode of investing with Red Bone. Normally investors are required to keep a minimum amount of cash in their accounts so that they can cover declines in the prices of the commodities futures they own. Hillary's $1,000 investment was well below the $12,000 deposit required by the Chicago Mercantile Exchange. In effect, Red Bone was covering for her so Hillary made money while taking no risk.

With the Clintons, there's always a payback. Here the payback went to Red Bone's former employer, "Big Daddy" Don Tyson, the chicken mogul of Arkansas. Tyson is the one who connected Red Bone and Hillary. And Tyson had important business before her husband, who had just been elected governor. During Clinton's gubernatorial tenure Tyson benefited from millions of dollars in tax breaks, state loans, and the relaxation of environmental regulations.

In short, the $100,000 payoff to the Clintons was a bribe. Tyson wanted something from Bill, so they figured out a way to get money to Hillary. Now $100,000 may not seem like a very big payoff, but it was a handsome sum for the Clintons, representing more than their joint income for that year. So Tyson made off like a bandit, and the Clintons got their first taste of how to profit handsomely from their political influence.[11]

Once the Clintons got to the White House, they put up just about everything in there for sale. Want a job? How much will you give us for it? Want to jump up and down on the bed in the Lincoln Bedroom? Here's our price. If you're willing to fork over an appropriate sum, you can sit at the president's table at the next state dinner or go jogging with him. Want a presidential pardon for your drug conviction or tax evasion? How much are you willing to pay?

Throughout the Clinton presidency, donors to the Clinton campaigns, the Clinton Foundation, or the Democratic Party were offered such perks as: two seats on Air Force One; six seats at private White House dinners; seats to White House events and ceremonies; spots on official delegations abroad; appointments to boards and commissions; dinners in the White House mess; and overnight stays in the Lincoln Bedroom. People who had never previously met Bill could, for an appropriate sum, dine at his table or go running with him.

Now it is customary for presidents to invite friends and donors to the White House. The Clintons, however, took this practice way beyond acceptable boundaries. Commerce Secretary Ron Brown frequently complained that he had become "a m*th*rf*ck*ng tour guide for Hillary" because foreign trade missions had become nothing more than payback trips for Clinton donors. The Clintons arranged for one fat-cat donor without any war experience to be buried at Arlington National Cemetery.[12]

They essentially converted White House hospitality into a product that was for sale. They had unofficial tags on each perk, and essentially donors could decide how much to give by perusing the Clinton price list. In a revealing statement, Bill Clinton said on March 7, 1997, "I don't believe you can find any evidence of the fact that I changed government policy *solely* because of a contribution."[13] Here we see the business ethic of the man; he seems to think it perfectly acceptable to change policy as long as it is only *partly* because of a contribution.

Remember Travelgate? In May 1993, the entire Travel Office of the White House was fired. The move came as a surprise because these people had been handling travel matters for a long time. The official word was that they were incompetent. But a General Accounting Office inquiry showed that the Clintons wanted to turn over the travel business to her friends the Thomasons.

Once the scandal erupted, Hillary, in typical Clinton evasive style, claimed to know nothing about it. She said she had "no role in the decision to terminate the employments," that she "did not know of the origin of the decision," and that she did not "direct that any action be taken by anyone with regard to the travel office."

But then a memo surfaced that showed Hillary was telling her usual lies. Written by Clinton aide David Watkins to chief of staff Mack McClarty, the memo noted that five days before the firings, Hillary had told Watkins, "We need those people out—we need our people in—we need the slots." Watkins wrote that everyone knew "there would be hell to pay" if they failed to take "swift and decisive action in conformity with the First Lady's wishes."[14]

Independent counsel Richard Ray concluded after his investigation that Hillary had provided "factually false" testimony to the GAO, the Independent Counsel, and Congress. He decided, however, not to prosecute her. This would be the first, but not the last, time Hillary's crimes would go unchecked by the long arm of the law. Just as Bill kept up his predatory behavior toward women because he was never arrested for it, Hillary kept up her moneymaking crime schemes because she was never indicted for any of them. In essence, the Clintons' behavior was encouraged by lack of accountability.

THE GREAT PARDON SALE

In the waning days of the Clinton administration, Bill pardoned a long list of drug traffickers, fugitives, tax cheats, relatives, and friends who had fallen afoul of the law. The details can be found in Barbara Olson's *The Final* Days. As Olson documents, some of these crooks were longtime Clinton and Democratic Party donors. Others became new donors—following their exoneration, they turned around and dispatched large sums of cash to the Clintons, the Clinton Library, or other Clinton causes.

The Clintons, for example, pardoned drug kingpin Carlos Vignali and also Almon Glenn Braswell, an herbal remedy magnate convicted of mail fraud and perjury. Braswell was a millionaire who supported Democratic Party projects, and Vignali's family had funneled large amounts of money to the Democratic Party since Carlos's imprisonment in 1994. Moreover, Hillary's brother Hugh Rodham pressed for the pardons and received $400,000 in fees for helping to secure them. Hillary said she had no idea that Hugh stood to gain from the deal. She called on him to return the money, but Hugh didn't think that was a good idea.

The Gregory brothers, Edgar and Vonna Jo, from Brentwood, Tennessee, owned United Shows of America. They were convicted in 1982 on charges of bank fraud. Upon their release, they became buddies of the Clintons, spending time with them at Camp David. They even organized White House parties in 1998 and 2000. Longtime contributors to the Clintons—including to Hillary's Senate campaign in 2000—the Gregorys also gave $35,000 to the Democratic National Committee in 1998, and $50,000 in 2000. Of course, Clinton pardoned them.

Once again, a Hillary relative was involved. Hillary's other brother Tony Rodham had struck a deal with the Gregorys, as they later confessed. The two brothers admitted approaching Tony Rodham to help them, and confessed to paying him while declining to specify how much. The Gregorys issued a statement that said, "We have a business contract with Tony Rodham. The compensation definitely fits the work he's done. He has not been overpaid."

Joseph Hendrick, a North Carolina automobile dealer, was convicted of mail fraud in a racket involving millions in cash and jewels that he gave to executives at Honda Motor Company in exchange for favorable treatment from those executives. Hendrick is a close friend and former business associate of Hugh McColl, chairman of Bank of America. Two weeks before he got his pardon from the Clintons, the Bank of America's charitable foundation pledged $50,000 to the Clinton Library. Of course the Bank denied any connection between the gift and the pardon, but as the Greek saying goes, *res ipsa loquitur*, which means "the thing speaks for itself."

In the late 1990s Clinton's agriculture secretary Mike Espy was accused of illegally accepting gifts from major food corporations, notably from Clinton's old buddy John Tyson. Tyson got immunity for cooperating with the investigation. Espy was acquitted, but two Tyson Foods employees were sentenced to prison. The Clintons pardoned them, no doubt continuing the favor swapping with the Tyson group.

Longtime Clinton pal Jesse Jackson—who was summoned to advise Clinton in the wake of the Lewinsky scandal, even though he was carrying on his own affair with an aide at the time—successfully sought a pardon for his buddy, former congressman Mel Reynolds, who along with two aides had been sentenced to prison for bank and wire fraud. Reynolds had also served a two-year term for having sex with a teenager. One can see how Bill might identify with both Jackson and Reynolds.

Jackson also prevailed on the Clintons to pardon Dorothy Rivers, a former top official at Jackson's Rainbow-PUSH Coalition. In 1997, Rivers pleaded guilty to stealing $1.2 million in federal grants following her indictment for fraud, theft, tax evasion, obstruction of justice, and making false statements. She took money intended for the homeless to buy a fur coat, a Mercedes for her son, and clothes and gifts for her live-in boyfriend. Clinton pardoned her as well.

Clinton advisors William Kennedy III, David Dreyer, and James Hamilton got clemency for various cocaine traffickers, money launderers, and tax cheats who happened to be Clinton supporters and Democratic donors. Clinton also pardoned his former Housing Secretary Henry Cisneros, who made secret payments to his mistress Linda Jones and then misled the FBI about them. The Clintons pardoned both Cisneros and his mistress.

Harry Thomason convinced Clinton to grant pardons to two Arkansas tax evaders, and DNC Chairman Terry McAuliffe successfully pressed Clinton to pardon lobbyist James Lake, convicted of masterminding an unlawful campaign contribution scheme.

Are we done yet? Actually, no. The Clintons pardoned Christopher Wade, a real estate agent involved in Whitewater who concealed his assets in a bankruptcy case and pleaded guilty to fraud charges. President Clinton also pardoned Art and Doug Borel, a couple of Arkansas crooks who were caught rolling back the odometers on used cars.

The Clintons' most notorious pardon involved Marc Rich, a wealthy financier and oil trader whose customers included Fidel Castro, Muammar Qaddafi and Ayatollah Khomeini. Rich faced life in prison for illegally trading with the government of Iran and for evading $48 million in taxes. These crimes got him on the FBI Most Wanted List. Rich fled to Switzerland with his ex-wife Denise and his business partner.

Denise pressed the Clintons for a pardon. Bill said he was having difficulties even though he was "doing all possible to turn around" the White House counsel who objected to the idea. Eventually Rich got his pardon, but only after Denise Rich gave $100,000 to Hillary Clinton's 2000 New York Senate campaign, $450,000 to the Clinton Library, and more than $1 million to the Democratic Party. She also gave the Clintons several items of furniture for their post–White House digs and in November 2000 presented Bill with a gold saxophone.

At the time, the pardons stirred outrage. Even the *Washington Post*—usually friendly to the Clintons—said the "defining characteristic" of the Clintons was that "they have no capacity for embarrassment." In a rare break with party unity, Democrats condemned the Clintons' behavior. Former president Jimmy Carter said it was "disgraceful." Congressman Barney Frank called it "contemptuous" and "unjustified" and a "real betrayal" by the Clintons.

Given the heat the Clintons took over Marc Rich, one might expect them to feel a bit remorseful, if not out of conscience—this may be expecting too much—then at least out of the tactical realization that this one backfired on them. The Clintons, however, have never backed down. Bill even wrote a disingenuous self-defense in the *New York Times* falsely claiming that respected attorneys Leonard Garment, William Bradford Reynolds, and Lewis Libby had approved the Rich pardon. As the *Times* subsequently wrote in an editorial disclaimer, this was not true.[15]

How can we explain the Clintons' unyielding obstinacy in the Rich case? Peter Schweizer seems to have figured it out. Schweizer recently revealed that in the years since Rich's pardon, millions more have flowed from Rich and his associates to the Clintons and the Clinton Foundation. Russian investor Sergei Kurzin—who worked for Rich in the 1990s looking for investment opportunities in the former Soviet Union—donated $1 million to the Clinton Foundation. Other Rich cronies gave smaller amounts.

The big payoff, however, came from Rich's close friend and business associate Gilbert Chagoury. Chagoury was convicted in Geneva of money laundering and aiding criminal organizations in connection with billions stolen from Nigeria during the reign of dictator Sani Abacha. As a result of a plea deal, however, Chagoury got his conviction expunged from the record. Chagoury paid Bill Clinton $100,000 to speak in 2003, donated millions to the Clinton Foundation, and in 2009 pledged a whopping $1 billion to the Clinton Global Initiative.[16]

In retrospect, the Rich pardon was the Clintons' most lucrative pardon sale and the initial contributions from Denise Rich to the Clintons and the Democrats were merely a down payment.

The Clintons' last act before leaving the White House was to take stuff that didn't belong to them. The Clintons took china, furniture, electronics, and art worth around $360,000. Hillary literally went through the rooms of the White House with an aide, pointing to things that she wanted taken down from shelves or out of cabinets or off the wall. By Clinton theft standards $360,000 is not a big sum, but it certainly underlines the couple's insatiable greed—these people are not bound by conventional limits of propriety or decency.

When the House Government Reform and Oversight Committee blew the whistle on this misappropriation, the Clintons first claimed that the stuff was given to them as gifts. Unfortunately for Hillary, gifts given to a president belong to the White House—they are not supposed to be spirited away by the first lady. The Clintons finally agreed to return $28,000 worth of gifts and reimburse the government $95,000, representing a fraction of the value of what they took.

One valuable piece of art the Clintons attempted to steal was a Norman Rockwell painting showing the flame from Lady Liberty's torch. Hillary had the painting taken from the Oval Office to the Clinton home in Chappaqua, but the Secret Service got wind of it and sent a car to Chappaqua to get it back. Hillary was outraged. Even here, though, the Clintons got the last laugh: they persuaded the Obama administration to let the Clinton Library have the painting, and there it hangs today.

In *Living History,* Hillary put on a straight face and dismissed media reports about the topic. "The culture of investigation," she wrote, "followed us out the door of the White House when clerical errors in the recording of gifts mushroomed into a full-blown flap, generating hundreds of news stories over several months."[17]

THE CLINTON FOUNDATION RACKET

Just two months after leaving the White House, Clinton sat down with progressive writer Taylor Branch to offer some White House recollections. In the course of the discussion, Clinton relaxed and said what was really on his mind. What was really on his mind was money. Clinton knew there was a lot of money to be made. "I know where to find this money," he said. "I think I can find it so that's what I want to do."[18]

And that's what the Clintons did, together. They figured out a charity racket and decided to name it the Clinton Foundation. It gives only 10 percent of its income to charity and actually serves as a war chest for the Clinton machine and Hillary's presidential campaign. To date the Clinton Foundation has raised more than $3 billion in contributions. How the Clintons got that money is the theme of Peter Schweizer's *Clinton Cash*. Other publications have supplemented Schweizer's reporting with their own investigations. Here, from these sources, are a few choice details.[19]

A substantial portion of the money donated to the Clinton Foundation came from foreign governments. Some sixteen nations together gave $130 million. Among those are the countries of Algeria, Saudi Arabia, United Arab Emirates, Oman, and Qatar. Most of this money was donated while Hillary was secretary of state.

It just so happened that, during this very time, Hillary's State Department approved more than $150 billion in arms sales to the very nations whose governments were donating to the Clinton Foundation. Many of these deals involved countries whose human rights records were suspect. Yet somehow they all got clearance from Hillary's team to buy American-made weapons.

Wow, you might say, what world-class thieves the Clintons are. But a world-class thief knows that there is more money to be made on these same transactions. At the same time the Clinton Foundation was raking it in from foreign governments, it was also taking money from defense contractors who had lucrative deals with the U.S. government to make the weapons. Lockheed Martin gave $250,000; Hawker Beechcraft, $500,000; General Electric, $1 million; and Boeing, $5 million.

The Foundation, though ostensibly a charitable enterprise, gives only one dollar out of ten to charity. The Clintons have developed a penchant for traveling in high style, and use a substantial amount of donation money on private planes and penthouse suites. Clearly they are their own favorite charity. The rest of the foundation's loot seems to have been accumulated into a war chest that is at the behest of the Clintons and the Hillary presidential campaign.

Here's an example of how the Clintons work through the Foundation to collect money in exchange for favors. Frank Giustra is a Canadian billionaire who had his eye on the uranium wealth of the tiny country of Kazakhstan. He donated $31 million to the Clinton Foundation. His business partner Ian Telfer directed another $2.3 million to the foundation.

Following these donations, things began to happen. The Clintons took Giustra to Kazakhstan to meet the dictator there, Nursultan Nazarbayev. Hillary gives a benign account of her Kazakhstan trip in *Living History*. She writes, "I visited a small women's wellness center funded through U.S. foreign aid."[20] And that's it. No mention of the real purpose of the trip.

Mukhtar Dzhakishev, who oversees Kazakh mining, revealed the real purpose. Dzhakishev reports that Hillary Clinton pressured Kazakh officials to sell uranium assets to Giustra's firm and said that Hillary refused to meet with him until he agreed to approve Giustra's deal. He did so.

After a series of mergers, Giustra's firm was acquired by a Russian conglomerate that built the Bushehr nuclear reactor in Iran. This conglomerate applied to the Committee on Foreign Investment in the United States to buy a controlling interest in U.S. uranium mines. This committee, made up of high-ranking officials, counted among its number one Hillary Clinton.

In the midst of this transaction requiring cabinet-level clearance, a Canadian company named Salida Capital made a $780,000 donation to the Clinton Foundation. This was a down-payment; between 2010 and 2012, Salida would give more than $2.6 million. The group also sponsored a talk by Bill in Calgary. Peter Schweizer discovered that the 2011 report of the Russian state nuclear agency Rosatom identifies Salida Capital as a wholly owned subsidiary.

Once again, the bribe seems to have worked. Despite obvious national security concerns, the committee approved the Russian take-over. No surprise, Hillary was in favor. Giustra and his partners got more than a lucrative Kazakh deal; they also got control of one-fifth of the entire U.S. uranium production capacity. Bill and Hillary got rich off this deal, and so did Frank Giustra and his partners. The Russians got what they wanted. Everyone benefited—except the United States of America.[21]

Along the same lines, mining tycoon Stephen Dattels in 2009 donated two million shares of stock in his company to the Clinton Foundation. Two months later, with the support of the U.S. government, including one Hillary Clinton, the U.S. ambassador to Bangladesh pressured that nation to reauthorize a mining permit that benefited Dattel's company. The Clinton Foundation never disclosed Dattel's donation.

In 2008, the Swedish telecom company Ericsson found itself under investigation by the U.S. State Department for selling telecom equipment to the regimes of Iran, Sudan, and Syria—all considered state sponsors of terrorism. In 2011, a State Department report proposed putting restrictions on telecom companies like Ericsson that worked with terrorist-supporting regimes.

That year, Ericsson sponsored a speech by Bill Clinton and paid him a whopping $750,000, around three times Clinton's fee at the time. Ericsson had never previously sponsored a Clinton speech. Ericsson's timing could not have been more fortuitous. Later that year, the State Department unveiled its new sanctions list; telecom companies were given a pass.

Douglas Becker is CEO of Laureate Education, a for-profit educational firm that provides online instruction to students in several foreign countries, including Brazil, China, and Saudi Arabia. Laureate named Bill Clinton an "honorary chancellor" and paid him to speak several times a year, netting him around $1 million in speech income from Laureate alone. Altogether Bill has received more than $16 million from

Laureate. But on the required disclosure forms, Bill merely says he was paid "more than $1,000" by Laureate.

Becker also runs a nonprofit group called International Youth Foundation (IYF). Once Bill got on the Becker payroll and Hillary became secretary of state, U.S. government funds through USAID to IYF increased dramatically. From 2010 to 2012, IYF received annual grants exceeding $20 million, for a total of nearly $65 million.

In addition, the International Finance Corporation, a division of the World Bank—headed by Clinton pal Jim Yong Kim—made a $150 million equity investment in Laureate. Once again, the Clintons' good fortune corresponded with good fortune for a large contributor.

"CASH HAS NO PROOF"

Sant Chatwal got into trouble in 1997 with the Federal Deposit Insurance Corporation. According to the *Washington Post*, the FDIC sued Chatwal "over his role as a director and guarantor of unpaid loans at the failed First New York Bank for Business." Chatwal owed a cool $12 million. He claimed he couldn't pay, even though he lived in a multi-million-dollar penthouse in New York, besides maintaining other residences.

So Chatwal decided to improve his prospects for favorable treatment on the part of the government by raising money for Hillary Clinton. In the fall of 2000, he held a fundraiser for Hillary's Senate campaign, raising $500,000. That same December, while the Clintons were still in the White House, the FDIC "abruptly settled" the case, in the *Washington Post*'s words, allowing Chatwal to pay just $125,000 and be done with it.

While Hillary was in the Senate, Chatwal also connected the Clintons to various wealthy Indians, who funneled millions of dollars into the Clinton Foundation. Those donations continued when Obama appointed Hillary as secretary of state. Again, Chatwal and his pals had an ulterior motive. They wanted Hillary to back a U.S.-India nuclear deal that Hillary had previously opposed. Sure enough, Hillary's position "evolved" in the direction of the incoming cash. Chatwal knew the score. "In politics," he boasted, "Nothing comes free. You have to write checks. I know the system. So I did as much as I could."

Chatwal knew that Hillary could be bought. This is exactly what the campaign finance laws were passed to prevent, the buying and selling of influence. While Hillary has dodged every prosecution, however, Chatwal, like me, got into trouble with the government for exceeding those laws. (Chatwal is Asian Indian; we Asian Indians appear to specialize in campaign finance violations.)

Except in my case I gave $20,000 over the limit to a college friend without expectation of any return. Chatwal was charged in 2014 with using straw donors as fronts to give more than $180,000 above the limit to Hillary Clinton and a whole group of Democratic candidates. In addition, Chatwal was convicted of witness-tampering; the FBI recorded him trying to get witnesses to lie in court. "Never, never" admit to reimbursements, Chatwal said on tape. "Cash has no proof."

While my case involved no corruption whatever, I got an eight-month confinement sentence, narrowly escaping the Obama administration's attempt to send me to federal prison. Chatwal got no prison, no confinement.[22] There's progressive "justice" for you. What these two cases prove is that if you're going to be a crook, it helps to be a crook working on behalf of the Democratic Party. That's where the big crooks like Hillary operate without accountability and even the small crooks like Chatwal get all the breaks.

Hillary's entire tenure at the State Department seems to have been devoted to exchanging cash for favors. Microsoft gave her $1.3 million and, in exchange, she lobbied the Chinese on software piracy. Hillary convinced Russia to buy fifty Boeing 737s for $3.7 billion, and two months later Boeing gave $900,000 to the Clinton Foundation. In appreciation for Hillary lobbying India to remove restrictions on large retail stores like Walmart, Walmart gave $1.2 million to the Clinton Foundation and has paid an additional $370,000 in membership fees.[23]

Jeffrey Epstein gave $3.5 million to the Clinton Foundation in 2006, shortly after the FBI began investigating him for participating in the exploitation of teenage girls as sex slaves. Epstein's standard practice was to fly celebrities on his plane to a private island near the U.S. Virgin Islands. The plane was nicknamed the Lolita Express and the island Orgy Island because both were venues for older men to have sex with under-age girls.

The case came to public light when one of the girls, Virginia Roberts—now thirty-two, but pimped out by Epstein starting at the age of fifteen—spoke out about Epstein's sex trafficking operation. Roberts named Bill Clinton as one of the regular travelers on the Lolita Express. Flight records show that Bill made twenty-six trips on Epstein's jet—on at least five occasions ditching his Secret Service detail in order to avoid a record of his travel on the Secret Service logs.

Epstein faced a long prison sentence, but somehow the investigation was concluded in 2008 with a secret settlement. Epstein pleaded guilty to one count of soliciting underage girls, for which he served a year in prison. All other charges were dropped, and all the records in the case were sealed. Only Swiss bank records leaked by a whistle-blower brought the secret settlement to public light. So far Hillary has not said a word about the case, even though she undoubtedly knows about it.[24]

This is the level of sordid depravity that we can expect if Hillary is reelected and the Clintons are returned to the White House. Are we not done with this larcenous duo? Their criminal schemes were bad enough in Arkansas and during Bill Clinton's two terms as president. They escalated during Hillary's tenure as secretary of state. How much these partners in crime have already stolen! Yet, from their perspective, there is a lot more to take, if only they get the opportunity to return to the White House.

CHAPTER 10

REPUBLICANS TO THE RESCUE

STOPPING HILLARY'S AMERICA

If not now, when? If not us, who?
—Progressive slogan from the 1960s

This is not an election about Donald Trump; it is an election about Hillary Clinton. The big question goes beyond the two candidates. It is: which gang are we going to put in power, the Republican gang or the Democratic gang? I believe I have shown that there is only one answer: the Republican gang.

Why? It's not because the Republicans necessarily deserve to rule. It's not because they always know how to rule. The GOP can be exasperating. There's a reason some people call it the Stupid Party. Even so, I'm a proud member of the Stupid Party because the alternative is the Evil Party.

Politics is not an individual endeavor; it is a team activity. The Democrats led by Hillary are trying to steal America, and Republicans led by Trump are trying to stop this from happening. That's the basis for my conclusion that every Republican—no matter who he is—is preferable to every Democrat.

Look at who the Democrats are. For more than a century, this party focused its oppression on blacks and American Indians. The venue of this oppression was the slave plantation and the Indian reservation. The Democrats stole the land from the Indians, and the labor and lives of the blacks. In this era, one may say that the Democrats took everything from some people.

Since the rise of progressivism in the 1930s, the Democrats shifted to a new strategy. As blacks moved to cities, Democrats re-created the plantation there. These urban plantations were built to accommodate not blacks but also poor immigrants. To the plantation, one might say, the Democrats added the immigrant ghetto and barrio. In all these places, poor people were kept from rising beyond a minimal level, and minority suffering was used to justify the expanding and increasingly confiscatory progressive state. So in this era, Democrats went from taking everything from some people to taking something from everyone.

But now we are in a new era. The Hillary Democrats want to complete the stealing of America that has already come a long way in the Obama years. Progress toward the goal of complete seizure and complete control—this is what Democrats mean when they use the word "progressive." These thugs have gone from taking everything from some people to taking something from everyone to—their final goal—taking everything from everyone.

Once this happens, we have lost America, or to put it differently, we will all be serfs in Hillary's America. The medieval serf typically turned over half his produce to the lord he served. Serfdom, in this sense, represents the midway point between freedom and slavery, because slavery means we have no claim whatever on what we produce.

For Hillary, serfdom is not enough. The Hillary Democrats would not be satisfied with a marginal tax rate that topped out at 50 percent. They want full control over the wealth and productivity of America, which means full control over your wealth and the fruit of your labor. Essentially Hillary wants to take the historic Democratic rip-off scheme to its final limit. She wants to turn all of America into a plantation.

How to stop Hillary's America? There is only one way. To see why, let's consider how previous incarnations of subjugation, exploitation, and theft have been stopped in this country. The British, of course, were the original culprits, ruling America from afar and slowly but systematically stealing wealth from this country. It took the American Founders—led by George Washington—to stop them.

There was no Republican Party in 1776, but the Republican Party has, from its founding in 1854, been the custodian of the principles of the American Revolution. In fact, this is what it means to be a conservative in America today; we are conserving the ideals of the nation's founding. So conservatives and Republicans are the inheritors of the founding legacy.

A REVOLUTIONARY TRADITION

There is, admittedly, an irony in this; American conservatism is distinct in that it protects not the *ancien régime* or tradition per se. Rather, it protects a revolutionary tradition. Moreover, this revolutionary tradition is the tradition of classical liberalism and involves three types of freedom: political freedom, economic freedom, and freedom of thought and religion.

The Founders didn't just care about freedom; they also cared about justice. For them, justice had two main components, the justice of economic allocation and the justice of rights. The justice of economic allocation is the justice of free market capitalism: the basic idea is that people should keep the fruits of their labor. The other main form of justice was equality of rights under the law. The Founders knew this second type of justice was betrayed by slavery; that's why they set up institutions designed over time to get rid of that form of systematic theft.

The contradiction between the principles of the Founders and the practice of American slavery came to a head two generations later, in the Civil War. In 1860, once again America's core principles, and indeed America's survival as a nation, were threatened. The threat came not from "the South." The idea that the South is wholly to blame is a progressive canard. What the canard leaves out is what caused southern secession in the first place.

Why does this matter? After all, it was the South, not the Democrats, who seceded. But the South seceded because its party, the Democratic Party, lost the election. Had the Democrats won, slavery would have been safe and the South would have remained within the union. The defeat of the pro-slavery party in 1860 caused the Civil War.

Once the Civil War started, northern Democrats like Stephen Douglas panicked. They had coddled slavery but they had not expected to carve the nation itself in two. So the northern Democrats condemned secession and pledged fealty to Lincoln. But it was a false fealty; a powerful faction of Copperhead Democrats worked overtime to undermine Republican prospects for winning the war.

The truth is that the Copperhead Democrats wanted Lincoln to lose the war. They wanted to make peace with the South so that slavery, if not extended, could at least be retained. The slogan of the Democratic Party in 1864 was to keep things just as they were before the war. In other words, restore the union but let the South have slavery.

These grim facts make it clear that it was Lincoln's reelection, and the success of Lincoln's armies, that ultimately sealed the fate of slavery. So slavery was not ended by "the North" because the North was divided between Lincoln loyalists and Copperhead Democrats. Slavery was actually ended by the Republican Party.

After losing the war, the Democrats could not restore slavery so they switched to enslavement. They carried out this enslavement through a series of horrific schemes aimed at blacks: the Black Codes, segregation, Jim Crow, and the domestic terrorism of the Ku Klux Klan.

Republicans again fought back with Reconstruction, going to the extent of having military governors throughout the South to thwart the Democratic effort to suppress, disenfranchise, and murder blacks. The GOP measures were heavy-handed at times but a certain amount of heavy-handedness was necessary to deal with Democratic thuggery and exploitation.

Republicans didn't always win. They could not overturn segregation laws that were passed by Democratic legislatures, signed by Democratic governors, and enforced by Democratic sheriffs and other government officials. Republican anti-lynching bills were thwarted by one progressive Democrat, Woodrow Wilson, and then by another progressive Democrat Franklin Roosevelt. Both were allied with some of the worst racists in America.

Although GOP anti-lynching measures were defeated, the party did stop the Klan just a few years after its founding, at least until it was revived again by Democrats in the early twentieth century. Republicans also led the first civil rights revolution, which resulted in the passage of the Civil Rights Act of 1866, as well as the three Civil War amendments: the Thirteenth, Fourteenth, and Fifteenth amendments.

The Democrats *de facto* nullified these amendments, turning them into dead letters in the South and preventing blacks and other minorities from enjoying their rights for another three quarters of a century. But the GOP won in the end, even though it took a second civil rights revolution, almost a century later, to actually enforce the Civil War amendments.

Ironically it was a Democratic president, Lyndon Johnson, who introduced the Civil Rights Act, but he did so out of low political motives. The main opposition came from his own party, not from the GOP. Indeed, without Republican pressure, and without Republican votes, LBJ would not have been able to sign, and likely would not have wanted to sign, the Civil Rights Act of 1964, the Voting Rights Act, and the Fair Housing Bill.

Contrary to progressive propaganda, the Democrats have, almost without interruption, proven to be the party of bigotry while the Republicans have a consistent record of opposition to bigotry. The Democrats are the party of subjugation and oppression while the Republicans are the party of equal rights and the level playing field. From slavery through modern progressivism, Democrats have always stolen the fruits of people's labor while Republicans stood for letting people keep what they produce and earn.

WHAT WENT WRONG?

Why, then, has the GOP proven largely ineffective in the age of Obama and why does it seem to be in such trouble at the presidential level in 2016? What has happened to the party of Lincoln and Reagan? After eight disastrous, dispiriting years of Obama, the GOP should be the runaway favorite in November; yet this is not the case. I count three serious disadvantages facing the GOP in this election.

First, the Democrats are highly motivated. This by the way is not unusual. All criminals are highly motivated. "Stealing is hard work," one convict told me in the confinement center. The progressive Democrats know this. Stealing is how they make a living. So it's a mistake to consider the progressives to be an indolent, do-nothing group. They are very industrious in conniving and carrying out designs on your wealth and your life.

By contrast, the Republicans seem relatively listless. Even politically active Republicans appear to engage around election time, only to return to "normal life" when the votes are counted. I sometimes hear it's because Republicans have jobs and because they don't have as much at stake as the Democrats, many of whom depend on federal programs for their livelihood. But in reality Republicans have even more to lose than Democrats, because Republicans who lose elections become easy prey for the progressive Democratic state to go after their income and their wealth.

Make no mistake, the progressives aren't just about raising the top income tax rate a few percentage points. They want to return to the halcyon days in America where marginal tax rates topped out at 80 to 90 percent. That was the wartime rate under FDR during World War II. Moreover, Democrats want to take your wealth by establishing increasing state control over all you own and what you do. If this isn't enough to motivate you, I'm not sure what is.

The disproportion between Democratic and Republican seriousness and effort can be seen in the Supreme Court, which is also at stake in the 2016 election. Although the majority of court nominees are Republicans, the Supreme Court has been precariously balanced for a decade. Neither side has enjoyed a clear advantage.

Why? Because Democrats can with almost Euclidean certitude count on their votes, while Republicans must keep their fingers crossed about more than one of their nominees. "Hope we get Kennedy this time! Whew, we got Kennedy. Oops, we lost Roberts." This is the pathetic Republican predicament.

Democrats are never in this predicament. Democratic justices on the court act like good Democrats and vote the party line, while Republicans seem to decide each case on its merits. While Republicans come to the court to perform constitutional rumination, Democrats come to the court to advance Democratic Party objectives.

This disproportion of conviction and application leads me to the second advantage the progressive Democrats enjoy. Over the past generation, they have one by one taken over the most influential institutions of our culture. Here I am referring to Hollywood, Broadway, the music industry, the world of comedy, the mainstream media—both TV and print—higher education, and increasingly also elementary and secondary education.

I call these the megaphones of our culture, because these are the ways that information is transmitted to the American people. Young people get their knowledge mainly from what they learn in school and college. Many of them today get their political information from comedians like Bill Maher, Stephen Colbert, and Jon Stewart. All Americans are shaped by the music they listen to and by what their see on TV and in the movies.

While conservative Republicans have been fighting in one corner of the battlefield—can we take the House and Senate? Will we win the presidency this time?—the Democrats have been occupying the high ground of the culture. Incredibly the Right has let this happen. To take one depressing example, in the sphere of comedy, they have Maher, Colbert, and Stewart and we have nobody, nobody, and nobody.

Long-term, the GOP cannot win if it doesn't take some of this ground back. This requires a serious commitment of funds and effort. This is not philanthropy or political contributions; this is survival money. Just as people who moved west and built homesteads had to invest in fences and gunslingers to protect them from hoodlums, conservatives and Republicans must recognize that not just America's wealth is at stake here; their own livelihood is too.

In the long run, it's not enough to send speakers like me to college campuses or even to establish alternative educational institutions like Hillsdale College. I speak on a campus Monday and am gone by Tuesday, while the progressive faculty is there day after day, drumming their propaganda into the students. Conservative colleges like Hillsdale are islands of liberty in a sea of repression, but they offer no chance to alter the general landscape of higher education.

Thirty years ago, the situation seemed hopeless. Then it seemed that conservatives would have to build three hundred new campuses to rival the ones that have been taken over by the progressives. Today, thanks to technology, we don't have to do that. We do, however, have to build the academic iPhone. If we can figure out how to supply high-quality college education at a fraction of the cost, we can threaten—if not wipe out—the whole progressive infrastructure.

Similarly, conservatives have to invest heavily in media and movies. This is why I shifted my career and went from being a writer, speaker, and think-tank guy to also making documentary films. I got the idea from Michael Moore, who made *Fahrenheit 911* and dropped it in the middle of the 2004 election. I said, "If that guy can do it, how hard can it be?"

Even so, I have no illusion that documentary films carry much weight in Hollywood. The big guy in Hollywood isn't Michael Moore, it's Steven Spielberg. The progressives in Hollywood convey their political messages not just through documentaries but also through romantic comedies, thrillers, horror films, and animated family films. Long term, we have to challenge their supremacy in these areas too.

But in the short term, we have an election to win. How to win it? Here, I'm afraid, some Republicans have gone off track. They don't seem to have learned the lessons of the past—the lessons of successful Republicans like Lincoln and Reagan. Lincoln was the most successful GOP leader of the nineteenth century, and Reagan of the twentieth. We shouldn't blindly copy them, but we should learn from them.

There is a reason why those men achieved so much and yet retained the allegiance of a majority of Americans while others—from Herbert Hoover to the two Bushes—bungled their chances, discredited the Republican brand, and aroused a popular reaction that elected FDR, Bill Clinton, and Obama.

PRINCIPLE AND PRAGMATISM

What Lincoln can teach us is that principles and pragmatism are not enemies—they actually go together. Principles reflect the goal we are aiming at, and pragmatism reflects the means to get there. To win an election and retain a majority, we need both. Lincoln was anti-slavery on principle but his election platform was based on the pragmatic policy of stopping the extension of slavery.

Today some conservatives might accuse Lincoln of "selling out." Could Lincoln be a RINO? Perish the thought. Lincoln understood that the best way to get rid of slavery was to win the 1860 election—that was the first step. If Lincoln lost, slavery would surely have had a longer life. So Lincoln was actually following the best anti-slavery option available at the time. Pragmatism is a step by step means for realizing goals that cannot be achieved all at once.

To stand on principle and reject the pragmatic option is both short-sighted and foolish. Of course the abolitionists were this way, and they felt really good about themselves. But left to themselves the abolitionists would have lost the 1860 election. They would have remained politically marginalized.

Fortunately, they were integrated into a broader anti-slavery coalition led by Lincoln. Lincoln never called himself an abolitionist—he resisted the label—but in the end it was Lincoln, and the Republican Party he led, who achieved the abolitionist goal of ending slavery through a pragmatic political platform that won electoral victory. That's an important lesson.

We can also learn from Reagan, chiefly how he took ideas and employed them to achieve his principal goals. This is not merely "waiting for Reagan" or mechanically applying Reagan's solutions to today's issues. Reagan's world was very different from ours. He was dealing with runaway inflation, high interest rates, a Soviet bear on the prowl. His remedies were designed for those problems. We need remedies that deal with our problems.

Still, there's a lot we can learn from Reaganism, which was based on three broad ideas. In foreign policy, Reagan held that the world is a dangerous place and there are bad guys around who couldn't just be talked out of being bad guys. No amount of UN resolutions or lengthy conversations would do the trick. Thus regrettably but inevitably, force is a necessary ingredient of American foreign policy.

The Reagan Doctrine was a middle position between isolation-ism—staying out of world affairs—and interventionism—as reflected in the Bush Doctrine of preemptive invasion. Reagan began with the prem-ise that American troops should not be deployed to secure other people's freedom. They should be willing to fight for it themselves. If they proved willing to do that, then America would help.

In Afghanistan, for instance, America didn't send troops to repel the Soviet invasion there. Rather, the Afghans—aided by Muslims from other countries—did the fighting, and America helped equip them with military hardware and strategic advice. In Nicaragua too, Reagan helped to arm the resistance which held the Marxist Sandinistas at bay until the Sandinistas were ultimately ousted from power in a free election.

We can learn from Reagan in recognizing that in foreign policy, Americans simply want two things: don't bomb us, and trade with us. Trade on the basis of mutual advantage is the general basis for our deal-ings with other countries. But we recognize that there are people in the world who wish to terrorize us and blow us up.

America's message to those people is: We are not against your reli-gion and we have no intention of ruling or occupying your countries. So if that's your concern, we can work with you to allay it. But if you try and bomb us—take note, Islamic radicals—then we are going to anni-hilate you. How we do it is a matter of debate, but that we will do it, you can be sure. So if you want to get to heaven really fast, we can help you with that.

In domestic policy, Reagan began with the premise that the entrepreneur, not the bureaucrat, is the creator of wealth and jobs. The free market—technological capitalism—is the best way to generate mass prosperity and rising standards of living. To this end Reagan supported tax cuts, reducing the top marginal rate from nearly 70 percent to 28 percent; privatization—dispatching tasks previously done by government to the private sector—and deregulation, making it easier for companies and workers to get things done.

The GOP today should draw on Reaganite principles to affirm the idea that technology, not government, is responsible for materially improving people's lives, not just in America but around the world. Government policy should support technological capitalism—not crony capitalism but genuine capitalism.

Government should confine itself to its proper domain—doing just the things that are enumerated in the Constitution—and not be a general scheme for taking from people the fruits of their labor. This means that taxes should be as low as possible and proportional. Proportional, not progressive taxation—everyone doesn't pay the same amount of taxes, but everyone pays taxes at the same rate.

Personally, I would set that rate at around 15 percent. But what I think doesn't matter: the rate can be set democratically. If the government needs more money due to a national security threat or some other legitimate reason, people can vote to raise the rate. But here's the rub: in raising the rate they would also be raising their own rate. We have to get away from the idea that people can simply vote to raise other people's taxes while not affecting what they pay.

Finally, in social policy Reagan affirmed that a good society isn't just based on individualism; it is also based on family, on church, on community, and on patriotism. These are what Burke called the "little platoons" of human happiness. Reagan sought to make the GOP a party of inclusion, civic order, and social decency.

Today this means a generous, reformed immigration policy that, while opposing illegal immigration, offers legal, vetted immigrants the opportunity to bring their skills, talents, and work ethic to our country and our economy; it is immigration that's in the national interest. Once here, we should expect those immigrants to assimilate to the American way of life; that, after all, is what drew them to come here in the first place.

In the tradition of Reagan, we should be a pro-life and pro-family party, but this requires prudence and pragmatism in how we go about reducing the number of abortions and rebuilding respect for traditional family values. I don't favor gay marriage but the heterosexual family— the family that is the cradle for the overwhelming majority of Americans—has plenty of challenges of its own and we should deal first with those, getting our own house in order.

Reagan preached a broad vision of America and didn't believe he needed to make a special appeal to women, to blacks, to Hispanics, and to other minorities. But the GOP has lost ground with these groups even since the Bush years. Bush, for example, got 40 percent of the Hispanic vote while Romney four years later got only 23 percent. So this year I believe a direct appeal to minorities is a good idea and could bring huge dividends.

The Republican message to women and minorities is this: Don't fall for the progressive Democratic con. The Republicans have from the beginning been the party of women's rights and minority rights. We have stood by you in the past, and today the principles of the GOP are the best way for women and minorities to advance on your merits and claim your share of the American dream.

To women we say: This is not about electing the "first woman president" and why in any case would you want to elect the scariest member of your sex? As collaborative sex abusers, the Clintons are no solution to the war on women; they are the war on women. We tried the "first" black thing with Obama; look how that worked out. Instead of pushing for another "first" who will come back to haunt us, let's concentrate on how we can give equal rights under the law—a Republican idea—to all Americans, male and female.

To Hispanics we say: We're not against immigrants; we want immigrants who believe in the American dream and want to assimilate to the American way of life. Ever wonder when you have fully "become American"? We believe it is when you become a Republican! So come aboard, and join the party of economic opportunity, upward mobility, and self-reliance. In short, get out of the Democratic barrio where they'll keep you poor, miserable, and dependent.

To blacks we say: You've been voting Democratic for seventy-five years, and look where it's gotten you? You have been in America longer than most of the other ethnic groups and yet in a short time they have surpassed you. Don't fall for the same old captivity song of the Democrats; don't let them use you anymore. It's time to try something different. It's time to leave the plantation.

Reagan was the outsider when he ran for president in 1980. The Republican establishment opposed him and derided him. Yet Reagan never railed against them. He fought them privately, sure, but he maintained a cordial public demeanor. He abided by his famous eleventh commandment of not speaking ill of other Republicans. With victory, the establishment became his. But after Reagan, the doofuses went back to their old ways.

Today Reagan would be appalled at the self-serving careerism and petty infighting within the GOP, where the establishment serves itself rather than its members, where consultants rake in huge bucks while losing one election after another, and where even Republican electoral victory doesn't seem to advance conservative policy goals.

Reagan would also be appalled by narrow-minded Republicans who act as if they're more interested in defeating fellow Republicans—as too moderate or too conservative—than in beating the Democrats. That's one big reason why the GOP—the the party with the best ideas—is the "minority party" in America and has been for the past seventy-five years.

We need to win this election in the short term and, in the long, to make the GOP the majority party in America for the next fifty years. That's how we undo what Obama has done, that's how we fumigate the country and get rid of the bad influence and the residual bad odor of the

Democrats, that's how we begin the work of rebuilding and restoring America. This is not the work of a single election; it's the work of a generation.

So listen up, libertarians—you are not going to get a libertarian candidate, so be content with one who is generally free market. Listen up, social conservatives—there is no prospect of ending abortion or gay marriage now, so let's support a candidate who will make pro-life and pro-family Supreme Court appointments. Listen up, GOP establishment types—you are not going to run the show the way you used to, so get behind the candidates that Republican voters actually choose.

NEVER HILLARY

In the end, of course, this election is not about Trump. It is about Hillary. Worse than Obama, she is the frightening culmination of all that is twisted and wrong about American politics. All the #NeverTrump nonsense collapses when we realize that this has always been a Hillary up or down election. My position is #NeverHillary.

Moreover, the Republicans are the good guys and the Democrats the bad guys. Not everyone on our team is a good guy but the team that jointly works to prevent stealing and exploitation is always an improvement on the team that carries out the stealing and exploitation. Or, as I have been trying to convey throughout this book, the party that takes down the plantation is better than the party that builds the plantation.

How to beat Hillary and her gang? I offer two specific ways. First, please help me get the word out about this book and the accompanying movie to everyone you know. Books operate on the mind; they provide intellectual ammunition. Movies operate on the mind too but they mostly appeal to the senses and the emotions. We should not deride these; they are also involved in the art of persuasion.

To win the election, we must rally the base and also reach moderate Democrats and independents. Most of the people who read this book or see the accompanying film will be conservatives and Republicans. That's fine; it's been a rough campaign. The book and the film lay out what we're up against; they should help our team to unify and get mobilized.

But we also need to reach beyond the base. Here's how you can help. Get together with your friends or social group and go see the film opening weekend. It's a Hollywood secret that the opening weekend is critical for a movie. If a film is in 1,500 theaters opening weekend and does well, it will be in more theaters the next week. If we do poorly that weekend, we will be in fewer theaters. So this is how you put fuel in our rocket; this is how you can help the film get shown everywhere in the country and reach more people.

If you're actively involved in a Republican or conservative group, you can also organize your own campaign to reach independent voters. How? The names and addresses of these voters is known. The RNC and various political PACs and groups have their contact information. So get it and provide the information that will help these voters make an intelligent choice.

Where will that information come from? You can generate your own, but for my part, I am putting my best "messaging" at your disposal. The Hillary movie accompanying this book will come out in DVD/Home Box Office a month before the election. That is a critical time. Your group can purchase DVDs at a reasonable price and drop them into the mailboxes of independent voters in Florida, Ohio, Colorado, and the other swing states that will very likely decide this election.

This is called using your influence. It is a creative, targeted, and lethal way to make a difference. This is how you become a Very Dangerous American. It doesn't cost a lot of money, because books and DVDs just cost a few bucks apiece. Of course there may be other ways to strike, but here I am giving you the one that brings our forces together.

You have more influence than you realize. Today with Facebook and Twitter and even email, we can reach large numbers of people for free. We can build networks and disseminate information as if each of us was an individual publisher. Even if you're technologically challenged, the new technology is actually no more difficult than turning on the TV and using the microwave oven, once you get used to it. So get used to it, and expand your influence.

Lincoln once said that America is ruled by public opinion. He did not mean by this that America is ruled by the opinions of the public. The ordinary American doesn't care very much about politics. He or she votes every two or four years, typically if it isn't raining. This voter is "undecided," not because of a divided mind, but because he doesn't know what's going on.

What shapes the mind of these voters is the creativity and enthusiasm and involvement of the people who do know what's going on. That's you. If you're a party delegate, or a blogger, or actively involved in a political group, you are part of the smaller subset of hands-on Americans who actually shape the course of events. I estimate that group to be two to five million people, far fewer than the hundred million who will vote in November. You should be one of those people.

Through your active involvement—not just in the election but also after—you can set the goal posts for American politics. This is how, in Lincoln's sense, you become one of the rulers of America. Democratic self-government is achieved by the citizens who choose to participate on a regular basis in the formation of the rules that shape our society.

Don't be discouraged; we have far more power than we realize. Years ago a professor of mine told me the story about the lion tamer and the lion. So there's the lion, and there's the lion tamer, a little guy with a stick. Yet every time the lion tamer gesticulates, the lion responds. The lion is following the dictates of the lion tamer.

But here my professor raised a provocative question: Who's more powerful, the lion tamer or the lion? Obviously it is the lion. Now, however, we have a puzzle. If the lion is more powerful, why does the lion so obediently and sycophantically obey the instructions of the lion tamer? The answer, of course, is that the lion doesn't know its own power. The lion thinks the lion tamer is more powerful.

In the same way, we sometimes feel hopeless because we are just citizens and the people in Washington—or in the White House—have all the power. But in reality it is not so. In democratic politics, at least at election time, we are the ones who have the power. Their scams cannot go through without our consent. So let's remember that we are the lion, and if only we recognize our power, and use it, we can help, in this desperate time, to put the Democratic lion tamers out of business.

ACKNOWLEDGMENTS

I want to thank Kimberly Dvorak for her research support and editorial suggestions. She's thorough, reliable, and a joy to work with. Aaron and Sonia Brubaker are always there for me, getting it done, in some cases even before I realize it needs to be done. I want to thank our entire film team, especially producer Jerry Molen, whose life and character are a reminder of what we're fighting for. My longtime editor Harry Crocker helped shape this project and kept my arguments on course, even though some of them initially confounded him. My friend and co-conspirator Bruce Schooley provided indispensable counsel, both for this book and the accompanying film, which reflect his influence at every stage. Danielle, my daughter, is a constant inspiration and perennial sounding board; soon she'll be out of college and giving me a run for my money. And to my wife Debbie—thanks, honey, for all your help, encouragement, and love. You are my highly competent "happiness manager," and have brought so much joy into my life.

NOTES

CHAPTER 1

1. John Milton, *Paradise Lost*, Book 2, literaturepage.com.
2. Markos Moulitsas, "Hillary Clinton: Too Much of a Clinton Democrat?," *Washington Post*, May 7, 2006.
3. William Safire, "Blizzard of Lies," *New York Times*, January 8, 1996; Maureen Dowd, "Obama's Big Screen Test," *New York Times*, February 21, 2007.
4. Cited by David Brock, *The Seduction of Hillary Rodham* (New York: Free Press, 1996), 24.
5. Hamilton Jordan, "The First Grifters," *Wall Street Journal*, February 20, 2001.
6. James Grimaldi and Rebecca Ballhaus, "Hillary Clinton's Complex Corporate Ties," *Wall Street Journal*, February 19, 2015.
7. Sophie Tatum, "Elizabeth Warren: Donald Trump 'Built His Campaign on Racism,'" CNN, May 4, 2016; Robert Reich, "Trump: The American Fascist," billmoyers.com, March 11, 2016.
8. Paul Bedard, "DNC Raises Confederate Flag, Civil War, to Slam Trump," *Washington Examiner*, February 20, 2016.
9. Walter Russell Mead, "Andrew Jackson, Revenant," *American Interest*, January 17, 2016.

10.   Abraham Lincoln, First Inaugural Address, March 4, 1861, abrahamlincolnonline. org.

11.   David Catron, "Republicans and Women's Rights," *American Spectator*, April 30, 2012,

12.   Jo Freeman, "How 'Sex' Got Into Title VII," first published in *Law and Inequality*, Vol. 9, No. 2, March 1991, uic.edu.

13.   See e.g. Matthew Yglesias, "Wrong or Race?," *Atlantic*, December 24, 2007.

14.   Eugene Rivers, "On the Responsibility of Intellectuals in the Age of Crack," *Boston Review*, February 1, 1992.

15.   Michael Omi and Howard Winant, *Racial Formation in the United States* (New York: Routledge & Kegan Paul, 1986), 262.

16.   Steve Guest, "Bill Clinton's Alleged Former Mistress: 'Hillary Is A Lesbian,'" *Daily Caller*, February 16, 2016; Gennifer Flowers, *Passion and Betrayal* (Del Mar, CA: Emery Dalton, 1995), 41–42.

17.   Maureen Callahan, "Bill's Libido Threatens to Derail Hillary—Again," *New York Post*, February 14, 2015.

18.   Brock, *The Seduction of Hillary Rodham*, 291.

19.   Peter Schweizer, *Clinton Cash* (New York: HarperCollins, 2015), 5.

CHAPTER 2

1.   Cited by Steve Inskeep, *Jacksonland* (New York: Penguin Press, 2015), 45.

2.   "Haitians Protest Outside Hillary Clinton's Office Over 'Billions Stolen' by Clinton Foundation," Washington Free Beacon, March 20, 2015; "Clinton Foundation HQ Protested for 'Missing Money' in Haiti Recovery," Washington Free Beacon, January 12, 2015.

3.   Peter Schweizer, *Clinton Cash* (New York: HarperCollins, 2015), 159.

4.   Alana Goodman, "Haiti Fraudster Had Line to Clinton at State Department," September 2, 2015.

5.   Deborah Sontag, "An Award for Bill Clinton Came with $500,000 for His Foundation," *New York Times*, May 29, 2015.

6.   Mary Anastasia O'Grady, "The Clinton Foundation and Haiti Contracts," *Wall Street Journal*, March 8, 2015.

7.   Sarah Westwood, "Clinton Foundation Travels to Haiti Amid Criticisms," *Washington Examiner*, July 30, 2015.

8.   Kevin Sullivan and Rosalind Helderman, "How the Clintons' Haiti Development Plans Succeed—and Disappoint," *Washington Post*, March 20, 2015.

9.   Steve Eder, "Tony Rodham's Ties Invite Scrutiny for Hillary and Bill Clinton," *New York Times*, May 10, 2015.

10.   Schweizer, *Clinton Cash*, 189.

11.   PBS, "The Democratic Party," pbs.org.

12.   Dinitia Smith and Nicholas Wade, "DNA Test Finds Evidence of Jefferson Child by Slave," *New York Times*, November 1, 1998.

13.   Robert Turner, "The Myth of Thomas Jefferson and Sally Hemings," *Wall Street Journal*, July 11, 2012.

14.   Lucia Stanton, "Sally Hemings," Thomas Jefferson Foundation, monticello. org; Annette Gordon-Reed, *Thomas Jefferson and Sally Hemings: An American Controversy* (Charlottesville: University of Virginia Press, 1998);

Annette Gordon-Reed, *The Hemingses of Monticello* (New York: W.W. Norton, 2008); Eric Foner, "The Master and the Mistress," *New York Times Book Review*, October 3, 2008.

15. Joyce Milton, *The First Partner* (New York: William Morrow, 1999), 94.
16. Inskeep, *Jacksonland*, 92, 104.
17. William McNeill, *Plagues and Peoples* (New York: Anchor Books, 1976).
18. Thomas Jefferson, *Notes on the State of Virginia*, xroads.virginia.edu.
19. Ralph Lerner, *The Thinking Revolutionary* (Ithaca: Cornell University Press, 1987), 163.
20. Joseph Ellis, *American Creation* (New York: Vintage Books, 2008), 139.
21. Thomas Jefferson, message on Indian trade, January 18, 1803; Thomas Jefferson, letter to William Henry Harrison, February 27, 1803.
22. Sean Wilentz, *Andrew Jackson* (New York: Times Books, 2005), 6.
23. David Crockett, *Narrative of the Life of David Crockett, by Himself* (Lincoln: University of Nebraska Press, 1987), 89–90.
24. Letter from Andrew Jackson to Rachel, March 28, 1814, in Harriet Owsley et al., *The Papers of Andrew Jackson* (Knoxville: University of Tennessee Press, 1980), vol. 3, 54; Timothy Horton Ball and Henry Sale Halbert, *The Creek War of 1813 and 1814* (Montgomery: White, Woodruff & Fowler, 1895), 276–77.
25. Jackson to the Creek Indians, March 23, 1829, in Owsley et al., *The Papers of Andrew Jackson*, vol. 7, 112–13.
26. Jon Meacham, *American Lion* (New York: Random House, 2009), xvii.
27. Inskeep, *Jacksonland*, 205.
28. Arthur Peronneau Hayne to Jackson, August 5, 1817; in Owsley et al., *The Papers of Andrew Jackson*, vol. 4, 130–31.
29. Inskeep, *Jacksonland*, 88–89.
30. Ibid., 91.
31. Ibid., 99.
32. Ibid., 104.
33. Washington County Court, November 17, 1788; Robert Remini, *Andrew Jackson and the Course of American Empire, 1767–1821* (New York: Harper & Row, 1977), vol. I, 15.
34. Meacham, *American Lion*, 303.
35. Lewis Cass, "Removal of the Indians," *North American Review*, January 1830, vol. 30, 75.
36. Crockett, *Narrative of the Life of David Crockett, by Himself*, 205–6.
37. *Worcester v. Georgia*, 31 U.S. 515 (1832).
38. Inskeep, *Jacksonland*, 294–95.
39. Manning Marable, "Clarence Thomas and the Crisis of Black Political Culture," in Toni Morrison, ed., *Race-ing Justice, En-gendering Power* (New York: Pantheon Books, 1992), 82; "Backlash against Sowell," *Business Week*, November 30, 1981, 119; "Final Cut: Spike Lee and Henry Louis Gates, Jr. Rap on Race, Politics and Black Cinema," *Transition*, Issue 52 (1991), 185.
40. Inskeep, *Jacksonland*, 323.

CHAPTER 3

1. Abraham Lincoln, "Fragment on Labor, 1847, in Mario Cuomo and Harold Holzer, eds., *Lincoln on Democracy* (New York: HarperCollins, 1990), 32.

2. Michael Warren, "Hotel Denies Hillary's Claim of Employing Illegal Immigrants," Weekly Standard, November 25, 2014.

3. Ta-Nehisi Coates, "What This Cruel War Was Over," *Atlantic*, June 22, 2015.

4. Cited by Manisha Sinha, *The Counterrevolution of Slavery* (Chapel Hill: University of North Carolina Press, 2000), 191.

5. John Hope Franklin, "The Moral Legacy of the Founding Fathers," *University of Chicago Magazine*, Summer 1975, 10–13; Dennis Farney, "As America Triumphs, Americans Are Awash in Doubt," *Wall Street Journal*, July 27, 1992, A-1; Bill Bradley, statement before the town hall of Los Angeles on March 23, 1992, reprinted in "The Real Lesson of L.A.," *Harper's*, July 1992, 10; Thurgood Marshall, address to the San Francisco Patent and Trademark Law Association, May 6, 1987.

6. Thomas Jefferson, *Notes on the State of Virginia*, xroads.virginia.edu.

7. Jon Meacham, *American Lion* (New York: Random House, 2009), 305.

8. Thomas Jefferson, letter to Henri Gregoire, February 25, 1809.

9. Frederick Douglass, "Address for the Promotion of Colored Enlistments," July 6, 1863.

10. Mary Boykin Chesnut, *Diary from Dixie* (Boston: Houghton Mifflin, 1949), 172, 184, 244.

11. Cited by James McPherson, *Battle Cry of Freedom* (New York: Oxford University Press, 2003), 196; Drew Gilpin Faust, *James Henry Hammond and the Old South* (Baton Rouge: Louisiana State University, 1982), 176.

12. McPherson, *Battle Cry of Freedom*, 56.

13. Ibid., 196.

14. Clyde Wilson, ed., *The Essential Calhoun* (New Brunswick: Transaction Publishers, 1992), xxi, xxv, 396, 404; see also Paul Finkelman, *Defending Slavery* (New York: St Martin's Press, 2003), 54–60; Jerry Tarver, "John C. Calhoun's Rhetorical Method in Defense of Slavery," in Waldo Braden, ed., *Oratory in the Old South* (Baton Rouge: Louisiana State University Press, 1970), 169–89.

15. Eugene Genovese, *The World the Slaveholders Made* (Middletown, Connecticut: Wesleyan University Press, 1988), 131.

16. *Dred Scott v. Sandford*, 60 U.S. 393 (1857).

17. McPherson, *Battle Cry of Freedom*, 19.

18. Harold Holzer, ed., *The Lincoln-Douglas Debates* (New York: HarperCollins, 1993), 151–52.

19. Harry Jaffa, *Crisis of the House Divided* (Chicago: University of Chicago Press, 1982).

20. Cuomo and Holzer, eds., *Lincoln on Democracy*, 3, 90, 120, 129, 131, 136, 207, 151, 316, 328.

21. William Gienapp, "The Crime against Sumner," *Civil War History*, September 1979, 218–45.

22. Cited by Sinha, *The Counterrevolution of Slavery*, 229.

CHAPTER 4

1. Melissah Yang, "Hillary Clinton's Graduation Speech at Wellesley College Was Inspiring in 1969 & Her Words Still Hold True Now," Bustle.com, April 14, 2015; Emma Roller, "What's Changed Since Hillary Clinton's 1960 Graduation Speech—and What Hasn't," *National Journal*, April 21, 2014.
2. Frederick Douglass, "The Destiny of Colored Americans," *North Star*, November 16, 1849.
3. Eric Foner, *Reconstruction: America's Unfinished Revolution, 1863–1877* (New York: Harper & Row, 1988), 26.
4. Cited by Bruce Bartlett, "Whitewash," *Wall Street Journal*, December 24, 2007.
5. George Fredrickson, *White Supremacy* (New York: Oxford University Press, 1981), 278.
6. John Townsend, Address to the Edisto Island Vigilant Association, October 29, 1860, civilwarcauses.org.
7. George Orwell, *Burmese Days* (New York: Harcourt, Brace, Jovanovich, 1934), 39.
8. Kenneth Stampp, *The Era of Reconstruction* (New York: Vintage Books, 1965), 50–51.
9. Andrew Johnson, "Third Annual Message to Congress," December 3, 1867, presidency.ucsb.edu.
10. Charles Carroll, *The Negro a Beast* (St. Louis: American Book and Bible House, 1900); Charles McCord, *The American Negro as a Dependent, Defective and Delinquent* (Nashville: Benton Printing, 1914); Robert Shufeldt, *The Negro, a Menace to American Civilization* (Philadelphia: F. A. Davis, 1914); Robert Shufeldt, *America's Greatest Problem: The Negro* (Philadelphia: F. A. Davis, 1915).
11. Cited by John Hope Franklin, *From Slavery to Freedom* (New York: Alfred A. Knopf, 1967), 341.
12. Cited by A. Leon Higginbotham, Introduction, Genna Rae McNeil, *Groundwork: Charles Hamilton and the Struggle for Civil Rights* (Philadelphia: University of Pennsylvania Press, 1983), xvi.
13. *Plessy v. Ferguson*, 163 U.S. 537 (1896).
14. Dinesh D'Souza, *The End of Racism* (New York: Free Press, 1995), 176.

CHAPTER 5

1. Margaret Sanger, *The Pivot of Civilization* (New York: Dodo Press, 2007), 56.
2. Kevin Vance, "Sec. Clinton Stands By Her Praise of Eugenicist Margaret Sanger," *Weekly Standard*, April 15, 2009; Mona Charen, "Mrs. Clinton Can't Defend Patron Saint of Planned Parenthood," *National Review*, April 24, 2009.
3. Margaret Sanger, letter to Clarence Gamble, October 19, 1939, Sanger manuscripts, Smith College.
4. AP, "Truman's Racist Talk Cited by Historian," *Seattle Times*, November 3, 1991; William Lee Miller, *Two Americans: Truman, Eisenhower, and a Dangerous World* (New York; Vintage Books, 2012), 353.

5. Mike Riggs, "Sen. Robert Byrd Not Only Was a KKK Member but Led His Local Klan Chapter," Daily Caller, June 28, 2010; David Love, "The Evolution of Robert Byrd's Racial Politics," TheGrio.com, June 28, 2010.

6. Reid Pillifant, "Hillary Clinton Remembers 'Friend and Mentor' Robert Byrd," *Observer*, June 28, 2010; Ann Gerhart and Anne Kornblut, "At Memorial Service, West Virginia Says Farewell to Big Daddy Robert C. Byrd," *Washington Post*, July 3, 2010; Eric Zimmerman, "Clinton Says Byrd Joined KKK to Help Him Get Elected," Hill, July 2, 2010.

7. Mary Boykin Chesnut, *Mary Chesnut's Diary* (New York: Penguin Books, 2011), 81–82.

8. Frederick Douglass, "What the Black Man Wants," address to the annual meeting of the Massachusetts Anti-Slavery Society, Boston, April 1865, lib. rochester.edu.

9. Margaret Sanger, *Women and the New Race*, pamphlet from the Eugenics Publication Company, 1923.

10. Margaret Sanger, *The Autobiography of Margaret Sanger* (Mineola, NY: Dover Publications, 2004), 374–75.

11. *Buck v. Bell*, 274 U.S. 200 (1927).

12. Ira Katznelson, *Fear Itself* (New York: Liveright Publishing, 2013), 145.

13. Woodrow Wilson, "The Author and Signers of the Declaration," September 1907, teachingamericanhistory.org.

14. Katznelson, *Fear Itself*, p. 167–68.

15. Cited in ibid., 89.

16. Roger Newman, *Hugo Black* (New York: Pantheon, 1994), 98.

17. Howard Ball, *Hugo L. Black* (New York: Oxford University Press, 1996), 98–99.

18. Cited by Katznelson, *Fear Itself*, 253.

19. Ronald Kessler, *Inside the White House* (New York: Simon & Schuster, 1995).

20. Ronald Kessler, *The First Family Detail* (New York: Crown Forum, 2014), 32.

21. Byron Shafer and Richard Johnston, *The End of Southern Exceptionalism* (Cambridge: Harvard University Press, 2006).

22. Kevin Phillips, *The Emerging Republican Majority*, (New York: Arlington House, 1969).

CHAPTER 6

1. Cited by John Diggins, *Mussolini and Fascism* (Princeton, NJ: Princeton University Press, 1972), 279.

2. Steve Bennen, "Under My Plan, Tuition Will Be Affordable for Every Family," MSNBC, August 11, 2015.

3. Laura Meckler and Josh Mitchell, "Hillary Clinton Proposes Debt-Free Tuition at Public Colleges," *Wall Street Journal*, August 10, 2015.

4. Jonah Goldberg, *Liberal Fascism* (New York: Doubleday, 2007), 260.

5. Michael Mullins, "JFK in Diary Admired Nazi Germany and Hitler, Book Claims," *Newsmax*, May 24, 2013; Allan Hall, "How JFK Secretly Admired Hitler," *Daily Mail*, May 23, 2013.

6. Cited by Wolfgang Schivelbusch, *Three New Deals* (New York: Metropolitan Books, 2006), 19.
7. Isaac Chotiner, "Is Donald Trump a Fascist?" *Slate*, February 10, 2016.
8. *Birth Control Review*, May 1919.
9. *Birth Control Review*, April 1933.
10. Cited by Goldberg, *Liberal Fascism*, 260.
11. Lothrop Stoddard, *The Rising Tide of Color Against White World Supremacy* (New York: Charles Scribner Sons, 1926), 303, 306.
12. Madison Grant, *The Passing of the Great Race* (New York: Charles Scribner, 1926), xxviii–xxxi, 77, 167.
13. Margaret Sanger, "My Way to Peace," speech to the New History Society on January 17, 1932, nyu.edu.
14. Harry Laughlin, *Immigration and Conquest* (New York: Chamber of Commerce, 1939).
15. Richard Hofstadter, *Social Darwinism in America* (Boston: Beacon Press, 1944); Thomas C. Leonard, "Origins of the Myth of Social Darwinism: The Ambiguous Legacy of Richard Hofstadter's *Social Darwinism in American Thought*," *Journal of Economic Behavior & Organization* 71 (2009), 37–51, Elsevier.com.
16. Ed Blewitt, "Marx and Engels on The Origin of Species," worldsocialism.org, February 2009.
17. Cited by Goldberg, *Liberal Fascism*, 135.
18. Schivelbusch, *Three New Deals*.
19. Goldberg, *Liberal Fascism*, 14, 23.
20. Schivelbusch, *Three New Deals*, 15.
21. Patricia Vardin and Ilene N. Brody, ed., *Children's Rights: Contemporary Perspectives* (New York: Teachers College Press, 1979).
22. Kenneth Keniston and the Carnegie Council on Children, *All My Children* (New York: Houghton Mifflin, 1978).
23. Rahm Emanuel, statement to *Wall Street Journal* conference of corporate CEOs, November 19, 2008.

CHAPTER 7

1. Saul Alinsky, *Rules for Radicals* (New York: Vintage Books, 1989), xxi.
2. Rebecca Kaplan, "Obama's Post-Presidential Life Begins to Take Shape," CBS, May 13, 2015.
3. Cited by David Brock, *The Seduction of Hillary Rodham* (New York: Free Press, 1996), 14.
4. Sanford Horwitt, *Let Them Call Me Rebel* (New York: Vintage Books, 1992).
5. "The Professional Radical: Conversations with Saul Alinsky," *Harper's*, June 1965; "A Professional Radical Moves in on Rochester: Conversations with Saul Alinsky, Part II," *Harper's*, July 1965; "Interview: Saul Alinsky," *Playboy*, March 1972. The subsequent quotations from Alinsky are, unless otherwise indicated, from these interviews.
6. Mario Puzo, *The Godfather* (New York: Signet Books, 1978), 192–97.
7. Alinsky, *Rules for Radicals* (New York: Vintage Books, 1989), 30–31, 36.

8.   Saul Alinsky, *Reveille for Radicals* (New York: Vintage Books, 1974), 224.

9.   Alinsky, *Rules for Radicals*, 24–25.

10. Horwitt, *Let Them Call Me Rebel*, xv–xvi.

11. Hillary Clinton, *There Is Only the Fight: An Analysis of the Alinsky Model*, Wellesley College, 1969, economicpolicyjournal.com.

12. Ibid.

13. Ibid.

14. Horwitt, *Let Them Call Me Rebel*, 539.

15. Hillary Clinton, *Living History* (New York: Scribner, 2004), 38.

16. Michael Tomasky, *Hillary's Turn* (New York: Free Press, 2001), 9.

CHAPTER 8

1.   Hillary Clinton, tweet from @hillaryclinton, November 23, 2015. A few weeks earlier, on September 14, 2015, Hillary tweeted, "To every survivor of sexual assault…You have the right to be heard. You have the right to be believed. We're with you."

2.   Andrew Kaczynski, "Watch This Rare, Long-Forgotten Interview with Young Hillary Clinton," BuzzFeed, May 12, 2015.

3.   Tim Murphy, "How Bernie Sanders Learned to Be a Real Politician," *Mother Jones*, May 26, 2015.

4.   Steven Nelson, "Biden Swims Naked, Upsetting Female Secret Service Agents," usnews.com, August 1, 2014.

5.   Ronald Kessler, *The First Family Detail* (New York: Crown Forum, 2014), 29–32; Robert Dallek, "Three New Revelations about LBJ," *Atlantic*, April 1998.

6.   Hillary Clinton, *Living History* (New York: Scribner, 2004), 466.

7.   Eric Foner, "The Master and the Mistress," *New York Times Book Review*, October 2, 2008.

8.   Drew Gilpin Faust, *James Henry Hammond and the Old South* (Baton Rouge: Louisiana State University Press, 1982), 86–87.

9.   Zach Noble, "Listen to Hillary Clinton Laugh while Talking about Getting a Suspected Child Rapist Off the Hook," Blaze, June 16, 2014; Daniel Greenfield, "Former 12-Year-Old Rape Victim: 'Hillary Clinton Took Me through Hell,'" frontpagemag.com, June 20, 2014.

10. Sally Bedell Smith, "Hillary's Humiliation," *Daily Mail*, January 14, 1998.

11. 11 , "Exclusive—Paula Jones: Hillary Clinton 'Two Faced,' 'Liar,' "Cares Nothing About Women At All," Breitbart, January 3, 2016.

12. "This Time, A Stewardess Says Bill Groped Her in '92 Aboard His Campaign Plane," *New York Daily News*, March 28, 1998, articles.philly.com.

13. Kathleen Willey, Foreword, Roger Stone and Robert Morrow, *The Clintons' War on Women* (New York: Skyhorse Publishing, 2015), 11.

14. "Exclusive: Juanita Broaddrick Says Bill Clinton Called Her Repeatedly after Alleged Rape," Breitbart, January 17, 2016.

15. Kathleen Willey, Foreword, 12.

16. Cited by Joyce Milton, *The First Partner* (New York: HarperPerennial, 1994), 223.

17. Marjorie Williams, "Clinton and Women," *Vanity Fair*, May 1998.

18. Michelle Goldberg, "Gloria Steinem Has a Theory about Why Women Don't like Hillary Clinton," *Slate*, October 20, 2015.
19. David Maraniss, "First Lady Launches Counterattack," *Washington Post*, January 28, 1998.
20. Cited by Paul Bedard, "Mainstream Media Scream: Newsweek Scribe's Sex-Slam over Indiana Religion Law," *Washington Examiner*, April 6, 2015.
21. Cited by David Brock, *The Seduction of Hillary Rodham* (New York: Free Press, 1996), 274.
22. Milton, *The First Partner*, 18.
23. Kate Anderson Brower, *The Residence* (New York: HarperCollins, 2015), 96.
24. Christopher Anderson, *American Evita* (New York: William Morrow, 2004), 167.
25. "Hillary Nightmare: Gennifer's Back," *World Net Daily*, October 11, 2015.
26. Steve Guest, "Bill Clinton's Alleged Former Mistress: 'Hillary is a Lesbian,'" Daily Caller, February 16, 2016.
27. "Exclusive—Paula Jones," Breitbart.
28. "Broaddrick Says Bill Clinton Called Her Repeatedly after Alleged Rape," Breitbart, January 17, 2016.
29. "Kathleen Willey Vows to Haunt Hillary Throughout Campaign," *World Net Daily*, October 5, 2015.

CHAPTER 9

1. Lucy Nicholson, "Clinton to Be Interrogated by FBI Over Email Scandal," RT.com, May 6, 2016.
2. Corbett Daly, "Clinton on Qaddafi: 'We Came, We Saw, He Died,'" CBS News, October 20, 2011.
3. Kimberley Strassel, "She Knew All Along," *Wall Street Journal*, October 23, 2015.
4. Nicholas Confessore and Michael Schmidt, "Clinton Friend's Memos on Libya Draw Scrutiny to Politics and Business," *New York Times*, May 18, 2015.
5. Ben Mathis-Lilley, "Off-Books Clinton Libya Adviser Had Business Interest in Libyan Regime Change," *Slate*, May 18, 2015.
6. Pamela Brown, Catherine Herridge, "Emails Show Qaddafi Son Offered Talks—But Clinton Ordered Top General To 'Not Take the Call,' Source Says," Fox News, October 7, 2015.
7. Sharyl Attkisson, "Thousands of Libyan Missiles from Qaddafi Era Missing in Action," CBS News, March 25, 2013.
8. Terry Golway, *Machine Made* (New York: Liveright Publishing, 2014), xxiv.
9. William Riordan, *Plunkett of Tammany Hall* (New York: E. P. Dutton, 1963), 261.
10. Hillary Clinton, *Living History* (New York: Scribner, 2004), 87.
11. Marc Joffe, "The Clinton Scandal That Still Matters Is Not the One You Think," *Fiscal Times*, February 2, 2016.
12. Barbara Olson, *Hell to Pay* (Washington, D.C.: Regnery, 2001), 287–88.
13. Cited by Ann Coulter, *High Crimes and Misdemeanors* (Washington, D.C.: Regnery, 1998), 223.

14. "Memo Places Hillary Clinton at Core of Travel Office Case," *New York Times*, January 5, 1996; see also David Brock, *The Seduction of Hillary Rodham* (New York: Free Press, 1996), 381, 408.

15. Bill Clinton, "My Reasons for the Pardons," *New York Times*, February 18, 2001; Editor's Note, *New York Times*, February 19, 2001.

16. Peter Schweizer, "Bill Clinton's Pardon of Fugitive Marc Rich Continues to Pay Big," *New York Post*, January 17, 2016.

17. Judi McLeod, "Clintons' Looting Worse than Tacky Taste," Canada Free Press, April 6, 2006; Dick Morris, *Rewriting History* (New York: Regan Books, 2004), 181; Clinton, *Living History*, 431.

18. Alana Goodman, "Bill Clinton in 2001: 'I've Never Had More Money in My Life,'" freebeacon.com, October 13, 2015.

19. Peter Schweizer, *Clinton Cash* (New York: HarperCollins, 2015), 64, 73–78, 101–4, 128–30, 133–34.

20. Clinton, *Living History*, 431.

21. Jo Becker and Mike McIntire, "Cash Flowed to Clinton Foundation Amid Russian Uranium Deal," *New York Times*, April 23, 2015.

22. Stephanie Clifford, "Hotelier Avoids Prison for Violating Campaign Finance Laws," *New York Times*, December 18, 2014.

23. James Grimaldi and Rebecca Ballhaus, "Hillary Clinton's Complex Corporate Ties," *Wall Street Journal*, February 19, 2015.

24. Malia Zimmerman, "Flight Logs Show Bill Clinton Flew on Sex Offender's Jet Much More than Previously Known," Fox News, May 13, 2016.

INDEX